# Online Journalism

## a basic text

## Tapas Ray

FOUNDATION®
BOOKS

DELHI • BANGALORE • MUMBAI • KOLKATA • CHENNAI • HYDERABAD

Published by
**Foundation Books Pvt. Ltd.**
CAMBRIDGE HOUSE
4381/4, Ansari Road, Daryaganj
New Delhi - 110002

C-22, C-Block, Brigade M.M., K.R. Road, Jayanagar, **Bangalore** 560 070
Plot No. 80, Service Industries, Shirvane, Sector-1, Nerul, **Navi Mumbai** 400 706
60, Dr. Sundari Mohan Avenue, 1ˢᵗ Floor, **Kolkata** 700 014
21/1 (New No. 49), 1ˢᵗ Floor, Model School Road, Thousand Lights, **Chennai** 600 006
House No. 3-5-874/6/4, (Near Apollo Hospital), Hyderguda, **Hyderabad** 500 029

© Foundation Books Pvt. Ltd.
First published 2006

ISBN 81-7596-333-6

Typeset by Techastra Solutions Pvt. Ltd., Hyderabad

Published by Manas Saikia for Foundation Books Pvt. Ltd.
Printed & bound at Raj Press, R-3 Inderpuri, New Delhi-110 012.

To my Father,

Lakshminarayan Ray
(L.N. Ray to his friends and acquaintances)
without whose support I might not have survived
the dark days of my life to write this book.

# CONTENTS

# PREFACE

In the summer of 2003, I was asked to teach a course in online journalism for Jadavpur University's postgraduate diploma programme in mass communication. Since this was the first time it was being offered, I was given a free hand in designing the curriculum.

When I began to prepare teaching material after chalking out the syllabus, I failed to locate a single book my students might find useful. One or two titles were available in libraries, but it was clear that these had been written with a Western audience in mind. Moreover, these passed over topics like the history of the internet, with which I wanted my students to be familiar. The only option then was to develop my own material, an experience I thoroughly enjoyed in spite of the extremely limited access to relevant books and journals in Kolkata.

When classes got underway, I found that most students were quite enthusiastic. This was natural – by then, the internet had penetrated sizeable sections of Indian society as a recreational tool if not as a medium of communication, serving a variety of functions related to study and work. This was particularly true of the urban middle- and upper-class students who came to my class.

Prof. Samar Bhattacharya, a member of the University's engineering faculty, had been asked to help launch the course. At some point along the way, he had suggested that I should write a textbook for my students. I thought this over and decided not only to take up the project but also to broaden its scope. I decided to include topics that might not be of immediate interest to students of professional courses, but would be useful to those who wished to find a starting point for the academic study of the internet in India as a new medium of mass communication.

This is how the idea of this book was born, and I am grateful to Prof. Bhattacharya for providing the first spark in my mind. I hope it will be useful to the readers I had in mind while conceiving it, and perhaps also to others. I am grateful to Foundation Books for their infinite patience with my slow progress.

*Tapas Ray*

Who needs a book on online or electronic journalism[*] in India when millions still do not have basic telephone services in this and other parts of the world? Indeed, who needs online journalism itself, or journalism of any kind, in a country where millions of people are illiterate to this day? I refer here to written forms of journalism, since illiteracy by definition is not a hindrance to accessing broadcast journalism, at least at a certain level.

The answer to these questions is probably obvious to many of us. To those who share the common, somewhat uncritical type of liberal democratic thinking, journalism's raison d'être is to keep citizens informed about important issues, enabling them to make informed decisions about public affairs and exercise control over the powers that be. The traditional Marxist view, on the other hand, is that in class-divided society, journalism's function is to earn profits and shore up the ideological superstructure that favours and naturalises exploitation. A more sophisticated Marxism-influenced view is that the media are a tool of hegemony. Yet another view, which sounds much like the naïve democratic one but in fact is more nuanced, is that the mass media are – or should be – an important component of the public sphere. The public sphere, in the words of Habermas, is "a realm of our social life in which something approaching public opinion can be formed".[†]

All these may contain elements of truth, but their merits are not at issue here. What is important is that all four, as also other theories, recognise that journalism affects the *whole* of society. Since the poor and the illiterate are as much part of society as are the rich and the

---

[*] 'Online journalism', 'electronic journalism' or 'e-journalism' are terms that will be used somewhat interchangeably in this book. Strictly speaking, however, e-journalism can be said to consist of both online journalism and computer assisted reporting (CAR).

[†] Habermas, Jürgen, *New German Critique*, tr. Sara and Frank Lennox, Fall 1974, issue no. 3, pp 49–55. Retrieved on 6 June 2004 from http://search.epnet.com/direct.asp?an=5316891&db=aph (Academic Search Premier database). Originally published as an encyclopedia article in Fischer Lexicon, *Staat und Politik*, new edition (Frankfurt am Main, 1964), pp. 220–226.

educated, the lives of the former cannot but be affected by the media, whether they can access these or not. In fact, one may even argue that the poor and the illiterate need journalism – including those types, which they cannot access or comprehend – more than their more fortunate countrymen and women, because the issues that are discussed in the media or are expected to be discussed according to Habermas' idea of a sphere of 'rational-critical debate', are also the ones that can lift them out of their poverty and illiteracy or push them deeper into misery.

Of course, this precludes the spectacularisation of politics and the tabloidisation of news, which characterise large segments of the media today and are sought to be justified in the name of 'bottom-line pressures'. Because of the nature of internet technology and its affordances, and the fact that publishing online does not call for investment on a scale comparable to the print and broadcast media, online journalism has the ability to go against this current, and, therefore, can be particularly valuable to the poor and the illiterate, even though they cannot access it themselves as consumers, let alone as producers.

While India has come to the internet late, the use of this medium here has been growing rapidly over the last few years. From an exotic technology used only by scientists a few years ago, it has become an important and near-ubiquitous medium of communication. It may not yet be as common as the telephone, but a large number of households are already 'wired', and for those who do not have a connection at home, every street corner in the cities and larger towns has its cybercafe. The use of email has become widespread, and the state and central governments, many NGOs and educational institutions, and all major corporate bodies and news organizations have their own websites.

When a technology reaches such a stage in the life of society, people tend to take it for granted. As it passes from the domain of innovation and innovators to the domain of mainstream commercial use, people easily lose their initial awe at its novelty and may even slip into a state of disinterest. This is when its real potential gets short shrift. It then develops along a limited number of paths determined by commercial considerations, and time eventually wipes out all traces of the many other trajectories it could have traversed but did not because of their real or perceived lack of commercial potential. For society as a whole this implies a sad and unnecessary loss of opportunities.

I would argue that this fate is likely to befall online journalism in India if it confines itself *exclusively* to recycling the content of print and broadcast media and selling merchandise, and makes no effort to utilise the internet's characteristics so as to help journalism become an ideal medium of rational-critical debate, which is crucial for the health of our democracy and hence for the well-being of our people. Innovative forms like open-source and citizen journalism, which are being developed in countries such as South Korea and the USA and are being tried in Japan, can be adopted in India, too (and adapted to local conditions, if necessary), and further innovations can be carried out. After all, journalism itself was an imported cultural form in India at one time.

Since online journalism is at a relatively early stage of development in this country in spite of the internet's rapid spread, it still has an opportunity to choose this democratic path. Whether it will utilise this opportunity or not, only time will tell.

In this book I discuss, among other things, what news organisations are doing in practice as against the things that can be accomplished with the internet. This is a time of hope for those, like me, who would like to see a vibrant media culture based on the net, since this medium has unique characteristics that take it beyond the print and broadcast media in certain ways.

A common view is that journalism on the web is the same as print journalism, differing from the latter only in the minor detail that matter is presented on the computer screen instead of paper. Those who think in these terms cannot be blamed, for perceiving the internet's potential, let alone realising these in practice, requires an insight into the nature of the medium that cannot be gained by simply reading news items or features on news sites, any more than a real insight into the nature of television as a medium can be gained by simply watching TV. The objective of this book is to impart some of these insights to the reader.

Apart from being a medium of communication, the internet is also a vast and continuously growing storehouse of information, which journalists can use to very good effect. But this requires certain skills, and one of the objectives of this book is to equip the reader with these skills.

There are 12 chapters, with the twin objectives of giving the reader an insight into the unique nature of the medium and e-journalism as a mode of cultural production in the broad social context, and to impart some knowledge of the practical aspects of computer assisted journalism and online journalism.

The more theoretical aspect is usually considered the province of academic courses, but it is in fact no less important for students of professional courses. Learning to use email and preparing news packages for the web without understanding the way these connect with the larger scheme of things will produce journalists with a severely limited vision of their own profession. However, discussion of the practical aspects is more pronounced than that of theoretical considerations in some chapters and vice versa, and it is up to the teacher to selectively prescribe chapters or sections of chapters in her curriculum to suit the specific objectives of her course. The material includes a large number of references, mostly online, to enable the interested reader to pursue the subject further along various lines of inquiry. The chapters are followed by a glossary.

The first chapter is intended to help readers conceptualise the internet as a multilevel environment for the practice of journalism. Technical features of the net, such as TCP/IP, email, listservs, telnet, FTP and the world wide web, have been introduced here.

Chapter two contains a brief history of the internet and the web, including their development in India. Figures have been provided to give readers a sense of the speed at which the net and the web have been growing, and their present size. In response to eager questions from my students, I have included in this chapter a discussion of the prospects of online journalism in India with reference to trends in internet use, online advertising, etc.

Chapter three discusses in detail the unique characteristics of online journalism, namely, hypertextuality, interactivity and multimediality.

New types of journalism brought into being by the web, namely annotative reporting and open-source journalism, are discussed along with their implications in chapter four. The concept of hyperadaptivity is mentioned.

Chapter five discusses computer assisted journalism or reporting (CAJ or CAR), its advantages and pitfalls. Strategies to be employed in CAJ/CAR – using search engines (including methods of evaluating search results), email and discussion groups – are discussed.

Chapter six presents an online journalism tool kit, in which the reader will find rules of best practice for preparing online news packages for various types of topics, and includes a discussion of news-editing practices.

Chapter seven is on web authoring and publishing. It discusses how web pages are made, how they can be put online and what should be done to ensure their visibility to users. Among other things, HTML and other languages and metalanguages are discussed.

Chapter eight discusses revenue generation through subscription and advertising, the ethics of online journalism and cyberlaw.

Chapter nine addresses points of continuity and change in the roles of journalists, their professional values, et cetera, between print and the internet. The changes are discussed with reference to such sociological concepts as gatekeeping and agenda-setting.

Chapter ten contains a brief introduction to the ongoing debate between utopian and dystopian views on the internet. This covers the debate on multiple levels, over claims of the net as a perfect marketplace and as a realm of freedom from existing power relations, state control, territoriality, rootedness, etc. It also covers the following topics, centred mainly on questions of access and barrier: the digital divide, language barriers (predominance of English), censorship and control, surveillance, and governance of the internet.

Chapter eleven discusses two major trends in technology, business and media practice, namely, convergence and broadband.

Chapter twelve introduces the reader to the exploration of interactions between the internet, on the one hand, and the individual and society on the other. This includes discussions on the experience of subjectivity, space and time on the net.

Although I have tried to present the material in a logical order so as to make it easy to assimilate, it may be necessary to 'rewind' or 'fast-forward' at some points. I hope the book will serve as a basic text for professional courses, as a starting point for students interested in continuing their studies along academic lines, and as a guide for beginners in the fields of media and advertising.

# 1.
# Internet and Journalism: An Introduction

It is more than likely that the reader of this book has used the internet (the 'net' in short) at least occasionally, and has a fair idea as to what it is, but a definition is still necessary for the sake of clarity. According to the *Concise Oxford English Dictionary*, 11th Edition (2004), it is a "global computer network providing a variety of information and communication facilities, consisting of interconnected networks using standardized communication protocols."

We should note that while the physical infrastructure is owned by companies, governments and individuals (as in the case of subscribers' computers), the network as a whole is not owned by any individual or organization. It is organized on a cooperative principle. It functions through the cooperation of various national governments, global and multinational organizations, corporate and non-corporate bodies, and individuals. The question of governance is of fundamental importance in understanding the internet and its place in human society. It will be discussed in greater detail in chapter two.

An online tutorial of the University of California in Berkeley defines the internet* as "a network of networks, linking computers to computers sharing the TCP/IP protocols." It is enough to note that the net is a worldwide network of computers, which are able to communicate with one another, that is, exchange information in digital form. The TCP/IP protocols are rules implemented by computer programs that allow different kinds of computers to 'understand' one another.

The Berkeley tutorial goes on to explain that the net can be seen as a vehicle for transporting information stored in 'files' or documents on one computer to another computer. However, as we will see later in this chapter, the net is much more than a vehicle for transporting data – it includes the data itself, and the 'platforms' on which it is stored.

## Net as a Medium of Communication

Most of us have grown up in a culture that largely relies upon books, films, and the print and broadcast media to reproduce itself. As a result, these appear to us as part of the natural order of things. The internet, on the other hand, seems to be an enigma. Therefore, it is necessary to spend a little time to understand its nature as a medium of communication that grew out of the older media, but is also different from it.

Marshall McLuhan (1911–1980) wrote in *Understanding Media: The Extensions of Man* (1964) that the crucial points to note about any medium of communication are that (1) it extends one or more of our senses, and (2) what he called its 'subliminal charge'. By 'subliminal charge' he meant the fact that its effect on society arises first and foremost from the change it brings about in our 'patterns of perception'[1] rather than from the messages it is used to convey. This is the concept he sums up in his famous aphorism, "The medium is the message."

---

\* The tutorial, as well as many other writers, spell 'Internet' with a capital 'I', but I have used the small 'i' in this book in keeping with another current trend, which seems more logical because the internet has become such a common technology that spelling it with a capital 'I' would be like spelling 'Telephone' with a capital 'T'. For the same reason, I have spelt the 'world wide web' and its short form, the 'web' with the lower-case 'w'.

To understand how a new media technology changes our patterns of perception, it is necessary to identify the older technologies from which it evolved, since "no medium has its meaning or existence alone, but only in constant interplay with other media".[2] Moreover, the 'content' of any medium, according to McLuhan, is always another medium. "The content of writing is speech, just as written word is the content of print, and print is the content of the telegraph."[3] Similarly, the content of a film is a novel or a play or an opera.[4]

Had McLuhan been alive today, no doubt he would have noted that print (that is, text as it appears in newspapers, magazines and books) and broadcast (audio and video as in radio and television) are the contents of the internet. But the net, as a new medium in its own right, is obviously more than the sum of its contents. I shall make an attempt here to explore the way in which it changes our patterns of perception. It should be noted that McLuhan's writing is not expository but notoriously aphoristic and collage-like. Hence, applying his concepts to the net, a medium that did not exist as we know it today during his lifetime, has its risks.

In *The Gutenberg Galaxy* (1962), McLuhan gives an example of the way different media technologies lead to cultural change. He says the phonetic alphabet shifted the focus from the aural world to the visual, and this meant a shift away from the holistic, mythic consciousness of tribal society to the consciousness of linearity and fragmentation that marked later Western society. But there are also differences between media that register on the same sense. In *Understanding Media*, he says the radio (an aural medium) is a 'hot' medium. Since it is rich in information, it demands a low level of activity or involvement from the audience. Whereas the telephone (also aural) is a 'cold' medium that conveys much less information and therefore demands a higher level of involvement from the user. By the 'information content' of a medium, McLuhan presumably refers to its bandwidth. Bandwidth can be described as the range of sound pitch that a medium can carry in the form of fluctuating electric currents or electromagnetic waves. This range is much broader for the radio than it is for the telephone. As for visual information, McLuhan says cinema is 'hot' while television is 'cold', clearly because images in cinema have much greater resolution than images on television.

We need to note that the internet offers not only written text but also still photographs, pictures, sketches, animation, audio files and video files.[†] The availability of sound in net telephony and streamed web radio means the net performs the function of both the telephone and the radio, that is, extends our sense of hearing to every corner of the earth, and whether it is 'hot' or 'cold' in audio terms depends on the particular service it is used for. It does the same for video, especially webcams (web-enabled video cameras) and web TV. It extends our sight to every point on the globe. If we consider pictures of the earth taken by artificial satellites and posted on the net, we can also say that the net extends our vision to outer space, resulting in a radical shift in our point of view – from our bodies looking *outward* to the satellite looking *inward*.

The manner in which written text appears on the computer screen has some similarities with newspapers, magazines and books. The internet maintains the linearity and sequential nature of thought which are marks of modernity. But through the instantaneous nature of audio and video transmission (with electromagnetic waves travelling at the speed of light across the globe) it turns our consciousness into that of villagers in McLuhan's 'global village'. This is a term McLuhan used to describe the effects of electric media, mainly television, which creates the impression of a tightly interrelated world that resembles in some ways pre-modern society with an integral consciousness.

Thus, we can see that the net is a complicated pastiche for the senses, and implicit in this is a tension between the tribal/mythic and modern/linear types of consciousness in the same subject (the user). This may seem to be a matter merely of academic interest, but it does have important implications for the student of electronic journalism. The journalist's consciousness has a synergic relationship with the culture in which she is situated, and the prevailing forms of journalism are an important component of this culture. To be aware of the tension and to recognize its source is to take a step towards either its resolution or a new type of tension, both of which imply a step towards a newer, more evolved form of journalism. Needless to say, this movement belongs to a domain that is very different from that of writing and other technical skills, on which education in journalism usually focuses its attention.

---

[†]  One hears of experiments to convey smells and the sense of touch through the net, but the practical use of these technologies being unknown as yet, their implications will not be discussed here.

# Features of the Net

We have seen that at the level of sense perception, the internet is a far more complex medium than its individual predecessors and constituents, that is, print, broadcast and cinema, and in fact more complex than all of these put together.[‡] However, the focus of this book is not the internet itself but the phenomenon of e-journalism, that is, the special type of journalism that utilises the internet as its tool, as well as its medium. This requires us to move on now to a different perspective, which can be gained from a point of view located outside and above the audience or the users of the internet, while the mode of perception had to be explored from the user's point of view. This will help us to conceptualise the net as an environment with specific characteristics in which journalism is practised.

This new vantage point allows us to view the net as a conjunction of three different spaces, as Luciano Floridi has noted[5]:

1. the infrastructure, which constitutes its physical dimension;
2. the memory platform, which is the digital dimension; and
3. the semantic space, which is the cyberspace dimension.

## The Infrastructure

The network of computer networks which comprises the physical infrastructure of the internet is an open one and its constituent networks are autonomous – any individual or organization can join it or leave it at any time, as long as their computers have proper connectivity and share the TCP/IP protocols. Computers connected through telecommunication links occupy various nodes of the network, some of which are more important than others. The telecommunication links are of several types – ordinary telephone wires, coaxial cables, fibre-optic cables, wireless local-access links (in wireless 'hotspots' for instance), terrestrial microwave links and satellite microwave links.

---

[‡] It is important to keep this in mind while studying the net at the level of textual content, which has to be the level for this book, because journalism is about texts and a text can have meaning to 'readers' or the 'audience', by definition, only through the senses.

## The Memory Platform

The physical infrastructure brings into existence a global memory platform, which is the aggregate of all the (electronic) memories available on all the computers connected to the internet. Since the network itself is open and constantly expanding but has a finite extension at any given moment, the global memory platform is constantly increasing in size (as more and more computers get connected to the net across the globe) but is finite at any given moment. The platform is continuous and seamless, i.e., there cannot be any blank space of zero memory within its domain. It hosts enormous amounts of digital data in various forms – software, applications, interfaces, and various types of documents in digital form, such as text, graphics, animation, audio and video.

## The Cyberspace

The process of signification[§], hence journalism, takes place in the cyberspace which derives from the memory space or platform described above. "The totality of all documents, services and resources", Floridi writes, "constitutes a semantic or conceptual space commonly called *cyberspace*." The characteristic features of cyberspace are:

1. It is seamless, because the memory platform is seamless.
2. It is semi-ubiquitous, that is, any digital document Y on the net can be accessed from any other document X on the net without passing through a third document Z. In other words, any two distinct and separate documents X and Y are always proximate, irrespective of their physical distance.
3. It is saturated, that is, like the global memory platform that underlies it, cyberspace, too, cannot contain any blank spot.

Floridi writes that the second and third properties make it possible for interactive communication to take place in cyberspace, unlike in broadcast.

---

[§] The term has come down to us from the work of the Swiss linguist Ferdinand de Saussure (1857–1913), who analysed the relationship between objects and their representation through sign systems, such as languages. Since journalism is a process of describing reality through language, it involves signification.

However, it should be noted that the second feature or semi-ubiquity is not a necessary condition for interactive communication. There is, logically, nothing to prevent interactive communication from taking place between documents X and Y via Z, which now assumes a mediating role vis-a-vis X and Y. Indeed, the TCP/IP protocols, which are a necessary condition for any computer to exist on the internet, can be said to have precisely this mediating role and in that sense, they can be viewed as document Z.

The real implication of semi-ubiquity lies in the practical domain. As we will see in a brief history of the net provided in the next chapter, it is the result of a particular feature, which the internet's original designers had incorporated with certain goals related to the security of the USA. Furthermore, the effect of semi-ubiquity (the fact that any document, stored on any server anywhere, is accessible to any user almost as if it were stored on his/her own computer) is diminished by the anisotropic nature of the net, that is, by the fact that the density of information flow in relation to capacity (bandwidth) is not uniform throughout cyberspace, and there are congestions around sites or documents that happen to be in high demand. The pattern of this anisotropy is dynamic, as Floridi points out, it changes with time as the demand for sites or documents fluctuates.

## The World Wide Web and other Services

Now that we have gained some understanding of the nature of the internet as a medium of communication, we will look at the different modes in which users interact with it. We will limit ourselves to those modes which are relevant to the net as a journalistic tool and a mass medium. The following modes are the different services available on the internet, not necessarily all at the same time to every individual user.

- The first and the most popular of these is electronic mail (email). It enables users to exchange messages on a one-to-one basis and also on a one-to-many basis through discussion groups, also called listservers (listservs).
- The telnet facility permits an individual using one computer terminal to log onto another computer and use it as if she were present at the second (remote) terminal.

- FTP (file transfer protocol) is used for error-free copying of complex files from a remote computer to the user's computer.

- Gopher is a text-only method for accessing internet documents, used in the early years of the net before the graphic web browsers became popular.

We have now reached the richest feature of the internet, which is also the most important one in the context of e-journalism. The world wide web (www or the web) not only incorporates all of the services mentioned above, it actually consists of a much wider array of features. The web, which is a part of the internet, can also be visualized as the net's graphic interface.

The computer programs that mediate this interface (the web) for the user are called browsers. Browsers are stored on computers connected to the internet, and their task is to enable users to access and open web documents, taking advantage of text formatting, hypertext links, images, sound, motion and other features. Internet Explorer is currently the most popular browser, followed by Mozilla Firefox, Netscape, Opera, Neoplanet, etc. Browsers rely on plug-ins, which are smaller pieces of software (programs) that can be attached to them, to handle the less common types of files found on the web.

To access the internet, a computer needs to be connected to telecommunications links through a device called the modem, and then to the server. The server is a particular type of computer equipped with a particular type of software designed to 'serve' users' computers. The server belongs to an ISP (internet service provider), which is a company or some other entity that provides internet connection to its customers/clients, such as VSNL, BSNL and Satyam in India, AOL, MSN and Mindspring in the USA, and Lineone in the UK.

The following is a rudimentary list of the net's main sections, followed by a simplified diagram (Figure 1.1) that shows their interconnections.

- The user's computer: This is usually a multimedia PC or notebook or laptop. The term 'multimedia' refers to the ability to play audio and video files in addition to displaying all types of text and graphics. A PC is a personal computer, which is a desktop machine. Notebooks and laptops are much smaller, portable machines.

- User communication equipment: This is usually a modem, either internal, that is, installed inside the computer's processing unit as one of its cards, or external, that is, a small box outside the processing unit, connected to it through a cable. Its function is to connect the user's computer to the local loop, that is, that part of the telecommunication network, which lies between the user's computer and the ISP's server.

- Local Loop Carrier: This connects the user location to the ISP's Point of Presence (POP) server.

- ISP's POP: Connections from the user are accepted and authenticated here.

- User Services: These are meant for the user's access purposes, such as DNS (domain name server), email, etc.

- ISP Backbone: That part of the telecommunication network, which interconnects the ISP's POPs, as well as different ISPs

- Hosts: These are computers, connected to the internet, which host the websites that users interact with.

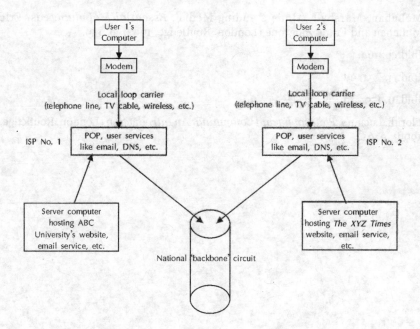

FIGURE 1.1 Main sections of the internet

## Exercises

1. Do you agree with Marshall McLuhan's manner of dividing the media into 'hot' and 'cold', and his characterisation of the telephone, radio, television and films? Explain.

2. Do you agree with Marshall McLuhan that the 'cold' media demand greater audience involvement than the 'hot'media? What may be the implications for the net if this hypothesis is true? What are the implications for web journalism?

3. What would be the implications for web journalism if cyberspace had discontinuities or blank spots?

## References

1   McLuhan, Marshall, 'Understanding Media', *Essential McLuhan,* eds. Eric McLuhan and Frank Zingrone (London, Routledge, 1997), p. 159.

2   Ibid., p. 164.

3   Ibid., p. 151, etc.

4   Ibid. p. 159.

5   Floridi, Luciano, *Philosophy and Computing: An Introduction* (London, Routledge, 1999), p. 61.

# 2.
# The History and Evolution of the Internet

The history of the internet and the world wide web has been comprehensively documented, appropriately enough, on a number of websites. Richard Griffiths writes that the origin of the internet can be traced to 1957. It had been designated as the International Geophysical Year dedicated to the collection of data on the upper atmosphere during a period of intense solar activity. In 1955, President Dwight D. Eisenhower of the USA had announced that his country wished to launch an earth-orbiting satellite as part of these activities.

With competition between the two superpowers (USA and USSR) for technological supremacy in the prevailing Cold War atmosphere, the USSR announced that it, too, hoped to launch a satellite. The Soviet Union won the race by launching Sputnik, the world's first artificial satellite on 4 October 1957. Clearly, American power was not necessarily supreme any longer.

The USA responded to this challenge by setting up the Advanced Research Projects Agency (ARPA) within its defence establishment. ARPA's mission was to adapt the latest technologies to military applications in order to regain and maintain American technological lead over the USSR. It was also given control of the US satellite programme until the creation of NASA in October 1958. The initial focus of ARPA's activities was therefore space, ballistic missiles and nuclear test monitoring. Another important priority was communication between its operational base and its sub-contractors through linked computers.

## Creation of ARPAnet

The two most important governing principles of the internet, namely, the galactic network and packet switching, took shape in 1961–1962, and were brought together in an ARPA programme started in 1962. John Licklider, a scientist of the Massachusetts Institute of Technology (MIT), who had been working on the first concept, was the leader of this programme. He had visualised a computer network in which every node would be accessible to everyone at every other node. Leonard Kleinrock of MIT is generally considered the pioneer in packet switching, on which he published the first paper in July 1961.[1]

According to some sources[2], however, packet switching was invented in 1962 by Paul Baran at RAND, the Pentagon think tank. This technology breaks up every message into 'packages', puts these into 'envelopes' bearing the address of their common destination computer, sends the 'envelopes' separately through the transmission network, so that they find their own individual and possibly separate paths according to network traffic conditions, and reassembles the 'packages' into the original message at the receiver's end.

The implementation of this system meant that unlike conventional links (such as a pair of wires between two telephones) the transformation of information would not depend on a single route. This had two security-related advantages: (1) even if a part of the network were destroyed, say by a Soviet missile, transmitted information would still reach its destination, since the packets would find other paths, and (2) it would be more difficult for enemies to eavesdrop on the messages being exchanged, since at no point on the network other than its terminal points (sender's end and receiver's end) would all the data packets be available together.

Teams of scientists at MIT, RAND and the National Physics Laboratory (UK) had all been working on networks for computers dispersed over large geographical areas, without any knowledge of one another's efforts. Their ideas, as well as a protocol to enable the computers to send and receive messages and data to other computers, were brought together in October 1969 to successfully link computers at the University of California in Los Angeles and Stanford University in such a way that users at one location could access files stored on the computer at another location.

This was the birth of the first of those networks, which would later coalesce into the internet. Named ARPAnet, it grew to include 23 computers by December 1971. Other networks also began to be set up and important technological advances followed, one of these being the development of email by 1972. The first international connection on ARPAnet was established in 1973 for the University College of London.

One of the most important milestones reached around this time was the development of TCP/IP jointly by scientists of ARPA and Stanford in 1974. TCP/IP enabled different networks to communicate with one another and made possible the open architecture which the net has today, making it the galactic network of Licklider's vision. The year 1974 also marked the opening of the first public data network called Telenet owned by Stanford University.

Important developments that would make the net what it is today were taking place in the sphere of hardware as well. Till the mid-1970s, networked computers were all large mainframes belonging to big corporations, government institutions and universities. But small microcomputers and versions of TCP/IP suitable for these were also being developed. These microcomputers were the predecessors of the personal computer (PC) used today and by extension of the notebook or laptop.

## Usenet

One factor that influenced the philosophy of the internet, in which mailing lists (email discussion groups) have an important place, was the birth of Usenet in 1979.[3] In the USA, postgraduate students at Duke University and the University of North Carolina created a network linking computers at these two institutions as a 'poor man's ARPAnet', as access to the latter was thought to be extremely expensive, and to require political connections.

A problem with ARPAnet was that there were both technical and procedural restrictions on its mailing lists. It was so because the main functions of the network were to serve as a vehicle for carrying out research on computer networking and as a means of long-distance collaboration among ARPA contractors. Moreover, each ARPAnet mailing list had a central control that could determine what material could be posted on it, and who received the posts.

Usenet's main function, on the other hand, was to host discussion groups and unlike ARPAnet, receivers on Usenet groups controlled what they received. These features, as well as its accessibility to those who were outside ARPAnet's ambit, made Usenet popular in academic circles, and it was linked with ARPAnet soon.

## Extending the Net

Even as networks continued to expand and proliferate in the USA through the 1970s and the early 1980s, the trend was also evident in Europe. Eunet was set up in 1982, linking networks in the UK, Scandinavia and the Netherlands. Another network, called EARN (European Academic and Research Network), was set up in 1984. Griffiths locates the birth of the internet in the year 1982, as that was the year in which TCP/IP was adopted as the protocol for all networks. Until then, there had been little standardization, which meant there were serious difficulties in the way of realizing an open, galactic network. The 1980s saw an expansion of the net across the world and in 1988, Canada, Denmark, Finland, France, Iceland, Norway, and Sweden joined the US National Science Foundation's NSFnet, which had been created in 1986 and had become one of the networks connected to the internet. This expansion continued through the following years and India joined the NSFnet in 1990.

# Domain Name System

Domain name system (DNS) is an important innovation related to TCP/IP which has made the internet easy to work with, even for non-specialists. It has simplified the addresses of hosts (computers on the internet) – which are a series of numbers separated by dots, such as 135.234.0.87 – through an easy-to-remember system of tree-like hierarchy. It is used for sending information from one computer to another under the TCP/IP protocols.[4]

Since the internet started as a network confined within the USA's national border, the first domains did not have any provision for naming host computers located in other countries. Domains were the broad categories into which various organisations were classified according to the nature of their activities and their computers named accordingly. The first American domains were .com for commercial organizations, .edu for educational institutions, .gov for non-military government organizations, .mil for the military, .net for network resources, such as ISPs, and .org for other organizations. These are called generic top-level domains (gTLDs).

When the net spread beyond the USA, country-specific names were added to this list. Some examples are: .in for India, .au for Australia, .jp for Japan, .cn for China, .de for Germany (Deutschland), .fr for France, .ca for Canada, and .uk for the UK. Today, most countries have their own domain names called country code top-level domains (ccTLDs). Each TLD includes second-level domains, such as 'yahoo' in www.yahoo.com or 'un' in www.un.org.

The above examples refer to web addresses. But the same principle also holds for the rest of the internet and can be demonstrated with an example. (Though the terms 'web' and 'internet' are used interchangeably, these are not identical, and an explanation of their difference is given later.) In the email address 'tray@cal2.vsnl.net.in.', 'in' is the top-level country-specific domain (ccTLD). The second-level domain is 'net', since the address is within the systems of one of the network providers. The third-level domain is 'vsnl', since the address is located within that particular network which is maintained by VSNL. The fourth-level domain is 'cal2', since the address is in that particular server in VSNL's network, which has the name 'cal2'.

## Origins of the Web

Several factors such as smaller and cheaper computers and the widespread availability of connectivity through advanced, high-capacity telecommunications links like fibre-optic cables have contributed much to make the internet as widespread as it is today. But perhaps the single most important development that has turned it into a part of the daily life of large numbers of non-specialists across the world is the creation of the world wide web as a part of cyberspace. Tables 2.1, 2.2 and 2.3 [5] show that the net did not just multiply in size after the web was created in 1991; it expanded every year by orders of magnitude. In time, the web has proved itself as the most dynamic and powerful part of the net. On 11 November 2004, Google put the number of web pages it was searching at 8,058,044,651. Therefore, on that day, there were at least this many pages on the web, and possibly more. In any case, the number is increasing even as we speak.

In 1991, the scientist Tim Berners-Lee, working at the CERN (Conseil Européen pour la Recherche Nucléaire – European Council for Nuclear Research), Geneva released to the public, free of charge, a graphic browser calling it the World Wide Web. Thus, the web as we understand it today, derives its name from Lee's browser. In 1989, Lee had designed a network of sites (that is, a sub-space within cyberspace) that would contain not only text documents but also graphics and other types of files. The following year, he developed the WWW browser as an easy way of searching this 'web' space and retrieving documents from it.

Another searchable subspace of the net called gopher and designed by the University of Minnesota, USA, had come into being in 1991. This, too, was user-friendly and gained some initial popularity. But its appeal was limited, as it was a purely text-based system. Lee's web, on the other hand, was able to catch people's imagination, because it was graphic and could contain all types of files.

In fact, the web as we know it today, is a network of sites that contain various types of documents, including but not limited to text, forms, graphics, animation, audio and video (all of which need not be present simultaneously on the same site). It uses a protocol known as the Hypertext Transfer Protocol (HTTP) which has simplified the internet addresses of host computers.

When an address is specified, the protocol automatically searches the net for the corresponding site and calls up various types of documents contained in it for actions to be performed by the user, such as viewing (as in text, graphics, animation and video), listening (as in audio), and interaction (as in forms, buttons, etc.).

Meanwhile, new browsers which utilise various versions of the Hypertext Markup Language (HTML), a computer language, were being developed. Mark Andreesen of the US NCSA (National Center for Supercomputing Applications) launched Mosaic X in 1993. It was user-friendly and had vastly improved graphic capabilities, as well as other features that have become standard now. Later, Andreesen set up a company and commercially launched the Mosaic-based browser Netscape through it.

Netscape enjoyed high popularity for some years, but now has been overtaken by Microsoft's Internet Explorer. Several other browsers are also available on the web, some free of cost.

**Table 2.1 Growth of Internet Hosts**

| Month and year | Number of hosts |
|---|---|
| December 1969 | 4 |
| October 1984 | 1,024 |
| July 1989 | 130,000 |
| October 1990 | 313,000 |
| October 1992 | 1,136,000 |
| October 1993 | 2,056,000 |
| January 1995 | 5,846,000 |
| January 1998 | 29,670,000 |
| January 2003 | 171,638,297 |
| January 2004 | 233,101,481[*] |
| July 2004 | 285,139,107[*] |

(Source: Zakon.org)

**Table 2.2 Growth of Internet Domains**

| Month and year | Number of domains |
|---|---|
| July 1989 | 0 |
| July 1995 | Less than 200,000 |
| July 1996 | Nearing 500,000 |
| July 1997 | Over 1,400,000 |
| October 2003 | 31,041,287[†] |

(Source: Zakon.org)

---

[*] Source: Network Wizards, accessed 17 November 2004 on http://www.isc.org/index.pl?/ops/ds/

[†] Source: Netfactual.com, accessed 11 November 2004 on http://www.netfactual.com/

Table 2.3 Growth of the Web

| Month and year | Number of websites |
|---|---|
| December 1990 | 1 |
| December 1991 | 10 |
| June 1993 | 130 |
| June 1994 | 2,738 |
| December 1994 | 10,022 |
| January 1996 | 100,000 |
| April 1997 | 1,002,612 |
| April 1999 | 5,040,663 |
| February 2000 | 11,161,811 |
| February 2002 | 38,444,856 |
| January 2004 | 46,067,743 |

(Source: Zakon.org)

## Internet Governance

At the beginning of chapter one it was mentioned that the net is run on a cooperative basis and is neither owned nor controlled by any government, corporate or non-corporate body, or individual. This is the classic libertarian view of the net's ideal state, but it is no more than a rough approximation of current reality. Hence, a basic understanding of the issue calls for a little more detail. One can start by looking at the analytical frameworks suggested in the chairman's report [6] of a workshop on internet governance, organized by the International Telecommunication Union (ITU) in February 2004. The issue is still fundamentally problematic, as there is no agreement even on the way in which governance should be defined in relation to the internet.

The report notes that there could be two definitions – a broad one, which would include policy issues, and a narrow one, which would be confined to technical issues only. It also mentions another approach, in which governance is viewed both as a limited agenda of standards and resource management, and as a process that includes legal and social aspects.

While these differences existed, the report notes, there were also convergences. The delegates largely felt that doubts about the feasibility and desirability of governance had become irrelevant, and some form of regulation was needed, especially in areas such as spam, spyware, security and cybercrime, including content-related crime. However, the Danish delegation challenged the very competence of ITU to address such issues. It recorded the view that the ITU was exceeding its brief, since defining net governance was rightfully the responsibility of a working group to be set up by the UN Secretary General according to the recommendations of the World Summit on the Information Society (WSIS) held in December 2003.

Thus, the issue of governance is still in a fluid state. For the moment, we shall confine our discussion to a brief introduction of the international organisations that regulate issues of a generally technical nature. The three most prominent ones are the ICANN, ISOC and IETF.

The ICANN (Internet Corporation for Assigned Names and Numbers) is an international non-profit organization responsible for managing the internet's domain name system (DNS). Since the internet was created in the USA, DNS management was originally in the hands of the government of USA. As it spread beyond the borders of the US, it was felt that an international body should take over this responsibility. The management was transferred to ICANN through a memorandum of understanding with the US Department of Commerce. Participation in ICANN is open to anyone interested in global internet policy within ICANN's area of technical coordination.

The ISOC (Internet Society) is an international professional society with more than 150 organizations and 16,000 individuals as its members in over 180 countries. Its membership is open to any interested person. ISOC ensures global cooperation and coordination for the internet, and the technologies and applications that are used for connecting the net's constituent networks.

As such, ISOC serves as an apex body for groups that are responsible for laying down standards for the internet's infrastructure, such as the IETF (Internet Engineering Task Force) and the IAB (Internet Architecture Board). The IETF is an international community of network designers, operators, vendors, and researchers concerned with the evolution of the internet architecture and the smooth operation of the net. It is open to any interested individual.

# History of the Net in India

India, being a developing country, found place on the internet map some years after the advanced industrial countries did. In 1987 ERNET (Education and Research Network), India's first internet service, was launched[7] as a collaborative project of the Department of Electronics, Government of India, and the United Nations Development Programme (UNDP). Ordinary people had no access to the net at that stage, as ERNET was confined to educational and research institutions.

Commercial net access was introduced in 1995 in a bid, apparently, to boost the export-oriented software industry. Videsh Sanchar Nigam Limited (VSNL), which was then entirely in the public sector and had grown out of the government's erstwhile Overseas Communication Service (OCS) as the national carrier for international trunk telephony, launched the Gateway Internet Access Service (GIAS) on a commercial basis on 15 August 1995.

The liberalization of the government's ISP policy on 6 November 1998, led to a proliferation of private sector service providers; according to the Telecom Regulatory Authority of India (TRAI), 189 providers existed at the end of June 2004.[8] The resulting competition led to cheaper services and thereby a rapid growth in the number of internet connections. The explosive nature of this growth is evident in Table 2.4. However, the most interesting point to note here is that this growth has taken place *in spite of* the 'bubble-burst' phenomenon, which hit the Indian internet economy in 2001 just as it hit the industrialised countries. As Figure 2.1 shows, the only indication that something might be amiss in the internet economy, was a fall in the annual growth rate of the number of net users from 96.43 per cent in 1999–2000 to 27.27 per cent in 2000–2001. But this rate picked up during the following year, reaching 137.14 per cent. While the figures for 2003 and 2004 were not available at the time of writing, an estimate for January 2004 could be made by correlating the number of net users in Table 2.4 with the number of internet subscribers in Figure 2.1. For 2002, this correlation was about 5.2 users per subscriber, and this yields about 21.32 million users for January 2004, when the projected number of subscribers was 4.1 million. According to TRAI, there were 49,26,318 subscribers on June 30, 2004, hence 24,040,432 or over 24 million users on that day. Since the estimated population was 1,065,070,607,[9] only about 2.26 per cent of the population was using the net at the end of June this year.

Table 2.4 Growth of Internet Users in India

| Year | No. of internet users | Number of internet users per 100 population[‡] |
|------|------------------------|------------------------------------------------|
| 1992 | 1,000 | 0.00 |
| 1993 | 2,000 | 0.00 |
| 1994 | 10,000 | 0.00 |
| 1995 | 250,000 | 0.03 |
| 1996 | 450,000 | 0.05 |
| 1997 | 700,000 | 0.07 |
| 1998 | 1,400,000 | 0.14 |
| 1999 | 2,800,000 | 0.28 |
| 2000 | 5,500,000 | 0.54 |
| 2001 | 7,000,000 | 0.68 |
| 2002 | 16,600,000[§] | |
| 2004 (Jan) | 21,320,000 | |

(Source: United Nations[10] except for the years 2002 and 2004)

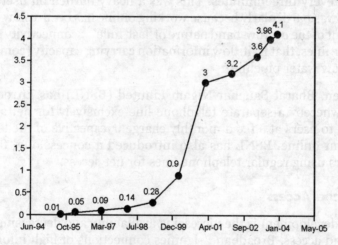

FIGURE 2.1 Internet subscribers in India (in millions)

(Source: International Telecommunication Union, UNO, quoting the Internet Service Providers Association of India)

---

[‡] This has been shown as nil (0.00) where the values were clearly negligible.

[§] Source: World Bank, accessed 11 November 2004 on http://devdata.worldbank.org/external/CPProfile.asp? SelectedCountry=IND&CCODE=IND&CNAME=India&PTYPE=CP

This is a very small percentage compared to countries like Malaysia, not to speak of the advanced capitalist countries. India ranks a miserable 119th among 178 countries.[11] However, the absolute numbers are impressive and it can be assumed that these have continued to grow at a reasonable rate, especially because certain positive developments have taken place during this period. By the end of 2005, India's population of net users is expected to be second only to China's in the Asia-Pacific region, excluding Japan,[12] and the government expects this population to reach 40 million by the end of 2010.[13]

## India: Factors behind Growth

### Cost of Connectivity

One of the factors driving the use of the internet is the falling cost of connectivity. Until a few months ago, anyone using a dialup modem had to pay, in addition to the ISP charge, telephone charges at the rate of one local call every three minutes. This was a heavy burden on users of the net. This was particularly because working online has been a slow process on account of the narrow-band nature of 'last-mile'[**] connectivity through telephone lines, that is, its low information carrying capacity (comparable to a narrow water pipeline).

Since then, Bharat Sanchar Nigam Limited (BSNL) has introduced a scheme whereby a separate telephone line exclusively for net access is provided to users at a fixed monthly charge irrespective of the length of time spent online. BSNL has also introduced a concessional tariff for customers using regular telephone lines for net access.

### Broadband Access

Another development is the increasing availability and decreasing cost of broadband access. Broadband signifies connections of high information carrying capacity (comparable to a large-diameter water pipeline), which do away with the frustrating slowness of online work using narrowband telephone lines and dialup modems. Broadband access is being provided through normal telephone lines (ADSL limited broadband), the coaxial

---

[**] The local loop between the subscriber's computer and the telephone exchange

lines of cable TV service providers, and dedicated lines. In Kolkata, broadband is available from BSNL, VSNL, Satyam and RPG Netcom, the last being the city's largest apex-level cable TV provider. BSNL cut the base monthly tariff of its ADSL broadband from Rs 500 to Rs 250 in the fourth quarter of 2005. This is actually substantially cheaper than narrowband access charges, because it does not have separate telephone and ISP components.

All over India, the number of households subscribing to cable TV is likely to increase to 70 million by 2004–2005 from 37.5 million in 2001–2002. About 10 per cent of all these households are also expected to subscribe to the internet through this service enthused by the lower prices of cable modems and lower access charges. This means that as many as seven million new subscribers may be added through this route alone. Internet connections are sometimes shared by a large number of people, such as in offices and cybercafes, and a smaller number of people in homes. So for every subscriber on an average there may be over 11 net users.[14] Therefore, seven million new subscribers implies a huge increase in the number of users. However, there may be certain technical hurdles on the cable road to growth. As the TRAI points out,[15] a large portion of the country's cable TV network is of poor quality and unsuitable for bi-directional communication. Also, internet connectivity through television cables may be a mixed bag, as we will see in chapter ten.

## Mobile Computing

Yet another likely route to rapid growth of the subscriber base is mobile phones. The number of users of mobile phones grew from 5.8 million in 2002 to 81.1 million by the end of January 2006 according to the *Broadband in India: India Broadband and Telecom Blog*. NASSCOM (the National Association of Software & Service Companies) is quoted as saying that about 25 per cent of all mobile phone users are likely to access the net through these devices in order to avail of m-commerce (mobile-commerce) facilities like banking, online trading and ticketing.

## Hardware Prices

Two major factors that are driving the growth in the use of internet are the falling prices and increasing power of personal computers and accessories. The following example will demonstrate the magnitude of this process. In Kolkata, a package consisting of an 'assembled' (that is, non-branded) multimedia PC with an Intel Celeron 400 processor, 64 MB RAM and 4 GB hard drive, a 28 KBPS external modem and a branded low-end colour inkjet printer, cost Rs 45,000 (about $1000 at the current rate of exchange) or more in late 1999.

Five years later in October 2004, 400 MHz processors and 4 GB hard drives were no longer available. Processors with speeds in excess of 2 GHz (1 GHz = 1000 MHz) and hard drives of 40 GB capacity had become standard equipment. An assembled multimedia computer with a 2.6 GHz AMD processor, 256 MB RAM, 80 GB hard drive and internal modem, along with a branded low-end colour inkjet printer, was sold for less than Rs 30,000 (about $667).

## Other Growth Trends

One must remember that India today is an emerging economic power with a huge middle class, spread throughout the country. This class represents a potential internet user base that is far from being properly tapped. This is partly because a section of the middle class resides in remote areas that are yet to be penetrated by the net. As the telecommunication infrastructure develops in size and quality, fast and reliable net connectivity will reach this section of the population, contributing to a surge in the number of users.

But a sharp increase in the number of users is not the net's only remarkable feature. According to IDC India, a market research company quoted by exchange4media.com, the internet touch-point ratio, that is, the number of locations (home, office, colleges, etc.) at which an average Indian user accesses the net is likely to increase substantially in 2004 and 2005 (Figure 2.2). Clearly, this is a boon to advertisers.

While the trends mentioned above are encouraging, these should not cause euphoria. The internet scene also has certain sobering aspects, which the TRAI has pointed out. While the number of internet subscribers has continued to grow, the rate of growth, according to TRAI, has already fallen and settled at a low level.[16] It was very high, about 200 per cent in 2000–2001, in the first two or three years after the government allowed the private sector and other organisations to enter the ISP business under its new ISP policy of November 1998. The new ISPs introduced lucrative packages, including free connections, such as in the case of Caltiger's non-premium internet accounts. An increase in PC penetration and teledensity (number of telephone connections per 100 population) had also helped the net's growth in those years. However, the rate of growth has dipped since then, even reaching negative levels at times, as indicated in Figure 2.3.

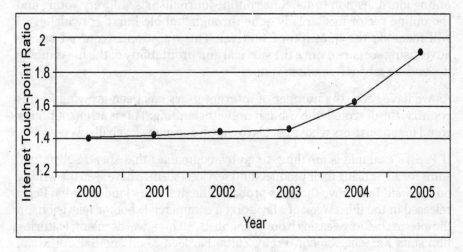

**FIGURE 2.2**   Indian internet user: internet touch-point ratio, 2000–2005

(Source: exchange4media.com)

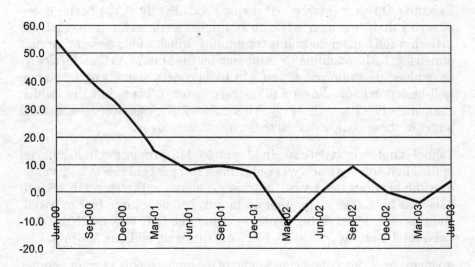

**FIGURE 2.3** Growth rate of internet subscribers in India

(Source: Telecom Regulatory Authority of India)

## Commercial Prospects of Online Journalism in India

We are now in a position to attempt an assessment of the prospects of online journalism in India. Since online journalism is still very young and the online sector has already gone through 'bubble-burst' convulsions, I will focus on the question of survival. This question is centred on the advertising scenario, since the survival and profitability of the mass media depend on advertisement revenue.

As we have seen, the number of internet users has been growing in this country, the dotcom bubble-burst notwithstanding. This is an encouraging trend for advertisers whose goal is to capture as many 'eyeballs' as possible.

If Pepsi's example is anything to go by, companies that spend substantial sums for advertising their products and services, seem to have seen the writing on the wall. In a move that was probably the first of its kind in India, Pepsi released in the third week of May 2003 a commercial shot for television, on the internet before releasing it on TV channels.[17] This advertisement, featuring film stars Kareena Kapoor, Preity Zinta, Fardeen Khan and Saif Ali Khan, was streamed on Yahoo!'s India portal at Yahoo.co.in.

The comment of a Pepsi executive on this development points to an important feature of the online advertising scene. Shashi Kalathil, Executive Director (Marketing), Pepsi Foods Pvt. Ltd., has been quoted as saying that "(the internet) is an additional medium for us to reach out to the hip and happening online community, which adds a new and vibrant dimension to the mainline TV campaign for the brand." As Kalathil clearly recognises, the online community in India consists largely of the young, well-heeled Indians who form the target consumers of products into which companies like Pepsi fit nicely. This community, therefore, is a natural target of these companies' advertisement campaigns.

Yahoo! is not an isolated case. In May 2003, MSN India, the Indian portal of the Microsoft Network, was reporting a 100 per cent rise in its revenue over the previous two years.[18] Shriram Adukoorie, Director, MSN South Asia, was quoted as saying that 60 brands had advertised on the portal, and this included such big names as Britannia, ING Vysya, ICICI, Coca-Cola, Intel, Seagram's, Cherry Blossom, Citibank, and Cox & Kings.

An increasingly important component of the online media's revenue comes from e-commerce. According to the Internet and Online Association

(IOA)[19], the market for B2C (business to consumer) e-commerce, which consists of retail purchases made through the internet, has almost doubled in India from Rs. 130 crore (about $29 million) in 2002–2003 to Rs. 255 crore (over $57 million) in 2003–2004. This is expected to climb to Rs 430 crore (about $96 million) during 2004–2005.

IOA president Preeti Desai has been quoted as saying that this can be attributed mainly to increasing online trade in travel-related services (including ticket purchases), electronic gadgets, household appliances and gifts. Desai also cites increased consumer confidence in the e-commerce concept. (Many people have had reservations about giving their credit card numbers online or ordering articles they have not actually seen physically.) According to IOA, the travel and ticketing sector contributed the largest share of e-commerce, at 56 per cent, in 2003–2004. This is likely to increase to 63 per cent in 2004–2005.

These considerations have made the online sector optimistic about advertisement revenues. IDC India expects advertising on the internet to sharply increase during the years 2004 and 2005.[20] According to MSN's Adukoorie, the total Indian advertising market was worth about $2 billion (over Rs 9000 crore at exchange rates prevailing on 11 November 2004), and the internet advertising market worth only $10 million (Rs 45 crore), that is, a mere 5 per cent of the total. But he expected this to grow to $100 million (Rs 450 crore) in five years.

No less important than this tenfold increase in the absolute value is the fact that the share of online advertisements as a percentage of India's total advertising expenditure is also increasing rapidly. In other words, the online medium is becoming an increasingly important channel relative to the other media, such as print, TV and hoardings, in the eyes of advertisers. Thus, online journalism in India is acquiring the financial underpinnings necessary for standing on its own feet.

## Prospects of Print in the Internet Age

So far, we have been discussing the prospects of the online media. When news sites began to appear in the USA, however, the discussion was largely centred on the future of the print media. There were fears that the net would sound the death knell for newspapers and magazines. This has not happened, as we know, although there are signs that online readership has made some gains at the expense of print readership in the advanced industrial societies.

Some observers believe that the new media may be a blessing in disguise for the old media. Writing in 2000, Boynton felt that online newspapers, webzines (online magazines) and e-books (books put online in digital downloadable format) could "preserve and extend the best aspects of the print culture while augmenting it with their various technological advantages." [21] A quick survey of the online scene today tells us that this optimism was not misplaced.

Boynton sites *The New York Times* as a print newspaper that has used the internet to its advantage. By April 2000, the paper's website had attracted 11.4 million registered non-paying readers (an increase of 61.9 per cent from the previous year). Since almost half of these individuals had never purchased a print copy of the *Times* (by their own admission), it was clear that the online version was "introducing the (*The New York Times*) brand to an entirely new group." The paper actually gained about 12,000 new subscribers through its website in the first half of 1999.

There have also been some instances of online publications giving rise to print versions. An example is *Nerve*, a US-based webzine specialising in erotica. It proved so popular that it was published in a print version. The obvious example in India is that of *Tehelka*, whose prominence following the defence deals exposé prompted the launch of a print version.

Boynton states that compared to newspapers, magazines in the US were slow to publish online versions, and this gave an early advantage to webzines. But there were exceptions – *Smart Money*, jointly produced by the Dow Jones news agency and the Hearst media chain, had a rich and active financial site. *The Atlantic Monthly*, a highly esteemed literary magazine, created *Atlantic Unbound*, a webzine that included not only the contents of the print version but also substantial extra material.

As for advertising revenue, many newspapers in the US were quick to recognize the threat from online publications, and equally quick to take remedial measures. They realised that classified advertising, which usually accounts for more than a third of their revenue, could be easily put online as searchable lists. Therefore, they invested in online sites meant exclusively for classified advertisements, such as employment sites, and also put classifieds on their own sites. The strategy proved successful.

Boynton writes that book publishing is the "least efficient and most outdated" of all the media. Despite the use of advanced management techniques, publishers have to take back about 30 percent of the printed copies from booksellers, giving them a full discount. Digitized books – e-books that can be downloaded from the internet, or in the print-on-demand (POD) system, a small number of copies can be printed from the digitally stored books on POD machines as and when required – are seen as a solution to this problem. While eliminating the problem of unsold copies, digitization is also a way to preserve books that would be otherwise out of print.

Before ending this chapter, I would like to trace the reasons for the 'dotcom crash' – the collapse of the internet economy, or the 'new economy' – which took place in 2000 and 2001.

## Why the 'Bubble' Burst

The crash occurred in March–April 2000 when the index of NASDAQ, the US stockmarket for high-tech companies, began to fall sharply. By the end of November, it was down by 40 per cent from its record high of 5,123, which it had reached in March.[22] Markets around the world were affected, and several Indian companies also suffered. For instance, IndiaInfo, earlier valued at Rs 1,000 crore ($222 million), was rumoured to have been available for sale for Rs 60 crore (less than $13.3 million).[23]

Those who are conversant with the 'new economy' have offered several explanations for the crash. One of these is that a dominant market position in the high-tech sector does not ensure profits for a company if it fails to put up substantial barriers to the entry of potential competitors, and such barriers are difficult to create.[24]

Another explanation is that companies in net-based businesses were spending much beyond their means. There may be some truth in this, at least for the Indian media. In the heady months of the internet boom, many internet start-ups were paying several times the salaries being paid by their counterparts in the print media, which were almost invariably lower than those earned by white-collar workers at comparable levels in other industries, and sometimes even in government departments. As a result, many journalists left established newspapers and magazines to join the online media.

But these journalists were sorely disappointed, as many online media outlets were soon in deep trouble, having failed to earn the kind of revenue they had expected from advertising, which had to be their main source. The other potential source – subscription – was not feasible to implement on the net on account of its culture of free information sharing, carried over from its origin as a tool for cooperation among members of the scientific community.

The third explanation[25], which is related to the second (above) and seems to be particularly appropriate in the Indian context, is the following: Since the internet costs only about a tenth of the investment required to enter the older media and there is no complicated government regulation to negotiate, too many companies were vying for the small online share of the advertisers' total budget, which was only about Rs 25 crore ($5.6 million) out of Rs 9000 crore ($2 billion) or so in 1991. Sampat believes the main reason for the share being so small is that 'interruption-based' marketing is largely ineffective on the net.

While watching a TV serial, the viewer cannot avoid the intervening commercials. But the technology of the internet allows its user to assume a more active role, since she has to click on links on the page she is viewing, in order to go to a different page, and most users choose to ignore links for advertisements. Some sites have started experimenting with interruption-based advertising by placing pages with advertising content between pages with editorial content, so that the user has to pass through the advertisements while moving from one editorial page to the next.

But these are exceptions that prove the rule that the online user is generally not keen to click on ad links. Moreover, the dynamic and distributed nature of web technology development ensures that as soon as advertisers introduce some new type of advertising technique, for example, pop-ups, scores of programs designed to defeat these techniques, for example, pop-up blockers, appear on the web and many of these are available free of charge. In fact, some of these are even incorporated in new versions of operating systems – Windows XP has the pop-up blocking feature.

Yahoo!, Sampat points out, was valued in excess of $100 billion at one stage (equivalent to more than Rs 4,51,000 crore at exchange rates prevailing in mid-November 2004), but its value fell as the 'click-through rate' (the percentage of those visiting a page, who also choose to click on links to ads appearing on that page) declined from over 2 per cent to below

0.5 per cent and it became clear to advertisers that users were ignoring advertisements.

But we need to note that the viewership rate for advertisements is likely to improve to some extent in India as it enters the era of cheap dialup and broadband connectivity, especially the latter.

## Factors Favouring Online Advertising

Cost has been an important factor responsible for the low click-through rate. When the user is obliged to pay for one telephone call every three minutes in addition to the ISP charge, and the narrow-band telephone line forces her to spend a long time on the net for even relatively simple tasks, the resulting cost burden discourages her from spending even more time for clicking and viewing image-heavy advertisements that take a long time to load on her computer and may not contain anything of use to her in any case. (Some of these advertisements, a matrimonial site's for instance, even have short video clips.) Here, the limiting factor is the telephone charge, which works out to more than Rs 24.00 (53 c) per hour, while the other component of the cost, namely, the ISP charge, has been typically in the range of Rs 7.50 (17 c) to Rs 9.00 (20 c) per hour.

Now that internet connectivity is available at a fixed monthly charge, the only component of the cost that increases in direct proportion to the time spent online is the ISP charge. The telephone charge per hour, on the other hand, decreases in inverse proportion to the time spent online, and can be as small as Re. 0.74 (less than 1.7 c) in the extreme case of a subscriber who decides to keep her computer connected to the internet 24 hours a day, for a whole month. For BSNL's ADSL broadband connection after the tariff cut introduced in late 2005, the corresponding charge per hour would be a consolidated total of about Re. 0.35 or 0.75 c, which does not have separate telephone and ISP components.

This is clearly an incentive for subscribers to increase internet use, but even more tariff cuts cannot be ruled out in the coming months and years. For the increasing number of users who avail of broadband, its high connection speed is an added incentive to spend time on the net, not only to read the news but also to click and view advertisements.

Therefore, even though the nature of the web rules out a captive audience and makes interruption-based advertising a difficult proposition, online advertising seems to have a secure future in India. This, as we have noted, is cause for confidence in the world of Indian online journalism.

Note: *For further material on the history and evolution of the internet  you can visit the following websites:*
*http://www.let.leidenuniv.nl/history/ivh/chap2.htm*
*http://www.zakon.org/robert/internet/timeline.*

# References

[1]  Leiner, Barry M. et al, 'A Brief History of the Internet', *The Internet Society website*, accessed 18 March 2004 on http://www.isoc.org/internet/history/brief.shtml.

[2]  Bardini, Thierry, 'A Utopia Realized: Cyber for All', *ctheory.net,* vol. 27, no. 3, article 146, accessed 11 November  2004 on http://www.ctheory.net/text_file.asp?pick=433.

[3]  Hauben, Ronda, 'The Evolution Of Usenet News: The Poor Man's Arpanet', speech presented at MACUL on 12 March 1993, accessed 18 March  2004 on http://wuarchive.wustl.edu/doc/misc/acn/netbook/ch.1_poorman_ARPA

[4]  Mehta, Raj, *Internet Guide for VSNL's Gateway Internet Access Service*, (Videsh Sanchar Nigam Limited, 1997), pp. 1.5–1.7.

[5]  Zakon, Robert H., 'Hobbes' Internet Timeline', accessed 10 November 2004 on http://www.zakon.org/robert/internet/timeline/.

[6]  Chairman's Report, workshop on Internet Governance, International Telecommunication Union, Geneva, 26–27 February 2004, accessed 6 December 2004 on http://www.itu.int/osg/spu/forum/intgov04/workshop-internet-governance-chairmans-report.pdf.

[7]  Dharmadhikari, Abhijit, 'Internet in India – An Infotech Tiger!', *NetNacs!NetNews!*, accessed 18 March  2004 on http://www.netnacs.com/news/archive/nnas-0002.htm.

[8]  The Indian Telecom Services Performance Indicators, April–June 2004, the Telecom Regulatory Authority of India, New Delhi, September 2004,  pp. 31–34.

[9]  *The World Factbook*  (USA, Central Intelligence Agency), accessed 9 December 2004 on http://www.cia.gov/cia/publications/factbook/geos/in.html.

[10]  United Nations Millennium Indicators, accessed 18 March 2004 on http://millenniumindicators.un.org/unsd/mi/.

[11] Baijal, Pradip, Preface to Consultation Paper on 'Accelerating Growth of Internet and Broadband Penetration', the Telecom Regulatory Authority Of India, 28 November 2003, p. 3. accessed 8 December 2004 on http://www.trai.gov.in/ Internet%20and%20Broadband%20Consultation%20Paper%202003-11-28%20FINAL.pdf.

[12] 'Internet economy in India', *exchange4media.com*, accessed 18 March 2004 on http://www.exchange4media.com/e4m/izone/I_economy.asp.

[13] Broadband Policy 2004, Government of India, accessed 27 November 2004 on http://www.dotindia.com/broadbandpolicy2004.htm.

[14] Arrived at by dividing the number of net users in 2002 (Table 2.4) by the number of subscribers in March 2002, which was 1.5 million according to the above article.

[15] Consultation Paper on 'Accelerating Growth of Internet and Broadband Penetration', the Telecom Regulatory Authority of India, p. 22.

[16] Ibid., p. 5, etc.

[17] Bhatnagar, Akshay, 'Pepsi Releases its TVC Exclusively on Yahoo! before breaking it on TV', *exchange4media.com*, 22 May 2003, accessed 18 March 2004 on http:// www.exchange4media.com/e4m/izone/izone_fullstory.asp? section_id= 4&news_id=8038&tag=261.

[18] Bhatnagar, Akshay, 'Internet advertising in India Expected to Grow to $100 million in 5 years - MSN India', *exchange4media.com*, 21 May 2003, accessed 18 March 2004 on http://www.exchange4media.com/e4m/izone/izone_fullstory.asp? section_id=4&news_id=8027&tag=2660.

[19] Kumar, Ashu, 'E-commerce Bounces Back', *ZDNet India* (Source: *The Financial Express)*, 26 August 2004, accessed 11 November 2004 on http:// www.zdnetindia.com/biztech/ebusiness/ecomm/stories/108763.html.

[20] 'Internet economy in India', *exchange4media.com*.

[21] Boynton, Robert S., 'New Media may be Old Media's Savior', *The Columbia Journalism Review*, July/August 2000, accessed 18 March  2004 on http:// www.cjr.org/year/00/2/boynton.asp.

[22] Krishnan, Reshma, 'Nasdaq Crash Contagion', *The Hindu Businessline*, 10 December 2000, accessed 12 November 2004 on http://www.blonnet.com/iw/ 2000/12/10/stories/0610f251.htm.

[23] Sampat, Jay, 'Why Online Advertising was Bound to Fail', *ComputersToday*, December 2001, accessed May 2003 on http://www.india-today.com/ctoday/ 20011201/net.html.

[24] Summers, Lawrence H. and J. Bradford DeLong , 'Anatomy of the NASDAQ Crash', 20 April 2002, accessed 12 November 2004 on http://www.j-bradford-delong.net/ movable_type/archives/000772.html.

[25] Sampat, Jay, 'Why Online Advertising was Bound to Fail'.

# 3.
# Multimediality, Interactivity and Hypertextuality

This chapter looks at the net as a medium of communication for the mass media, that is, online journalism. The online news media offered little more than written text and pictures at the initial stage, but numerous sites currently offer audio and video content, including streamed and real-time signals. Examples of Indian sites of this type are those of Doordarshan and NDTV (for a fee).

Globally, there are a large number of such sites, especially 'web radio' channels, which can be found through indexes like web-radio.fm (http://www.web-radio.fm/fr_list.cfm). However, it is virtually impossible to receive these streams properly with the slow dial-up internet connections that are still extensively used in India. Therefore, the online journalism one comes across in this country, and in any country that still relies on slow dial-up access, is mostly based on text, images and graphics, much like the print media.

## Features of Online Journalism

Online journalism has three defining characteristics – hypertextuality, interactivity and multimediality. These make it quite different not only from print but also from radio and television.

To effectively utilise the net's potential in online journalism or associated fields like online advertising, the practitioner needs to understand these characteristics and the way these change the nature of writing, authorship and reading, including the way meaning is produced when a reader 'reads' the text, which may be written text, image, graphic, etc.

Media practitioners – journalists, advertising and public relations professionals, layout artists, web developers and others – usually develop an intuitive understanding of the way narratives work in different media environments, including the online one.

But such an understanding has at least two weaknesses – since it is not logically thought through, at least in a conscious way, it has a strong likelihood of being flawed and because it is deeply rooted in the individual's personal experience, it is difficult to teach, that is, to pass on from one person to another. Hence the need for a more theoretical or 'scientific' approach, which I seek to introduce in the following pages.

## Hypertextuality

As we move the cursor across web pages on a computer screen, and sometimes also across documents that are not on the internet, the 'I'-shaped line of the cursor changes to a hand with extended index finger as it passes over certain words or blocks of words (usually highlighted with a different font colour or underscoring or both), icons, images, graphics or parts of graphics (such as major cities or specific areas in a map).

If we click the mouse when the pointing finger is positioned over something, a different text opens up. This may consist of writing, graphics, images or any combination of these, either at a different location on the same page as before or on a different page altogether. The new 'text' may also be an audio file or a video file.

Thus, the hand with a pointing finger indicates the existence of a link between two documents or parts of documents – the original one, over which the user had been moving the cursor before clicking the mouse, and the new one that opens as a result of the clicking action. This link, which is implemented through a programming language called HTML (Hypertext Markup Language) is known as a hyperlink.

The word or block of words over which the cursor changes into a hand, that is, in which the link is embedded, is known as hypertext. The word hypermedia is sometimes used in place of hypertext when the linked items are not just written words but also include audio or video files. However, hypertext, said to have been coined in 1962 by Theodore (Ted) Nelson, one of internet's pioneers, remains by far the more widely used term. Landow quotes Nelson as defining hypertext in the following way[1]: "By 'hypertext,' I mean non-sequential writing – text that branches and allows choices to the reader, best read at an interactive screen. As popularly conceived, this is a series of text chunks connected by links which offer the reader different pathways."

A simple illustration is the web page in Figure. 3.1 (http://www.hypernav.com /hn04_history/). The underlined words and phrases in the three icons near the top of the page with the captions 'Hypertext', 'Hypertext Systems' and 'Hypermedia', and the links in the left-hand frame of the page for 'World Religion CD-ROM', 'Philosophy CD-ROM', et cetera, all have hyperlinks embedded in them. Clicking on these links takes the user to other pages.

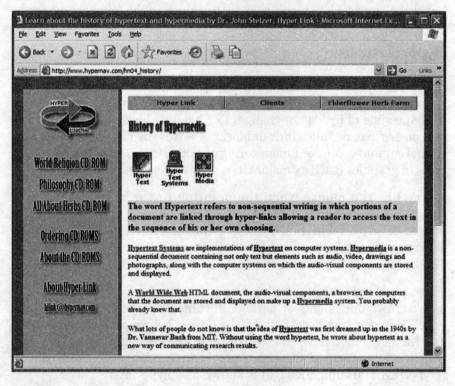

FIGURE **3.1** A web page on the history of hypermedia

The hypertext appears in blue when the page first opens on the computer screen but changes to purple when the corresponding linked pages are visited.

When the phrase 'Hypertext Systems' is clicked, a page opens at http://www.hypernav.com/hn04_history/hist02_hyptxsys.html and clicking on the word 'Hypermedia' opens a page at http://www.hypernav.com/hn04_history/hist03_hypermed.html. Each of these two pages in turn contains links to other pages, for example, 'Cow Creek Band of Umpqua Tribe of Indians' at http://www.cowcreek.com/. Thus, depending on the links she chooses to click on, the user finds different paths that take her to different texts.

## Origins of Hypertext

As we will see, this apparently simple innovation in the technology of writing or, generally speaking, of information management has far-reaching consequences for culture. Perhaps as a portent of this cross-fertilisation between technology and culture, the idea of hyperlinks and hypertext was put forward for the first time not by a cultural figure but by an engineer, who was writing not in a technical journal but in a respected literary magazine.

In his article 'As We May Think', published in *The Atlantic Monthly* in 1945, Vannevar Bush, an engineer, described his vision of an interactive mechanism he called memex. It would reflect the human mind's tendency to think in a nonlinear associative way (as opposed to a linear hierarchic way) by storing for retrieval, whenever needed, vast amounts of information linked together according to the user's requirements. The following passage[2] from the article clearly anticipates the internet as we know it:

> (The memex) affords an immediate step ... to associative indexing, the basic idea of which is a provision whereby any item may be caused at will to select immediately and automatically another. This is the essential feature of the memex. *The process of tying two items together is the important thing* [emphasis mine].

According to Ridgway[3], Theodore Nelson and Douglas Engelbart were the other main contributors to the idea of hypertext. In the early 1960s, Engelbart with his visualisation of an oN Line System or NLS or

Augment (1963)[4] and Nelson with his Xanadu[5] (about the same time as Engelbart's NLS/Augment) developed the concept of computer systems that incorporated hypertext. Landow writes that the emergence of these ideas marks a paradigm shift that was taking place not only in computer engineering (Bush, Engelbart, Nelson, etc.) but also in critical theory (Derrida, Barthes and others). This shift was from "conceptual systems founded upon ideas of center, margin, hierarchy, and linearity ... (to) ones of multilinearity, nodes, links, and networks."[6] As we have noted in an earlier chapter, this shift is in fact also evident in many other disciplines today.

Before we discuss the implications of hypertext for reading and writing, we should note that this type of arrangement is not unique to electronic documents but are to be found in print and even in oral cultures. As Landow has pointed out, annotations like footnotes and endnotes, found mostly in scholarly writing and journals, perform a function similar to hypertext. In these cases the reader leaves (or at least is invited to leave) the main text when she encounters a numeral or symbol denoting the note, reads the note and perhaps also another text if it provides a reference to that, and returns to the main text. Others have noted that there are parallels in oral cultures – storytellers often deviate from the main storyline into subplots and return to the main story after some time.

## Narrative Properties of Hypertext

Since the journalist is a storyteller, she needs to know how the story changes when the medium changes. Here, we are reminded of McLuhan's famous aphorism, "The medium is the message". The following are the narrative properties of hypertext.

## Multilinearity

As printed texts without annotations are read in one direction only – from top to bottom – a characteristic of such reading is linearity. One of the effects of hypertext is to abolish this linearity. Since the reader is able to choose from a number of alternative paths by selectively clicking the hyperlinks she encounters in the text, reading becomes multilinear or multisequential. Some authors, such as Josephine Wilson and Linda Carroli in *Water Always Writes in Plural* (http://www.hypertxt.com/sh/hyper98/water/index.html) and William Powhida in *Projection* (http://www.hypertxt.com/sh/hyper98/projection/projproj1.html), have attempted to construct innovative hyperfiction by utilising this effect of hypertext.

However, this may be a problem for the journalist. Since links turn the text into a multilinear entity, her story (news report, feature, etc.) lacks closure and she may be unable to ensure that the reader stays with the storyline she wants to present. It is not surprising, therefore, that news sites rarely provide hyperlinks in the body of a story.

## Multivocality

A related consequence of hypertext is multivocality. Since links take the reader into different texts authored by different people, hypertext becomes the product of a number of consciousnesses rather than that of a single consciousness. Landow writes: "(H)ypertext does not permit a tyrannical, univocal voice. Rather the voice is always that distilled from the combined experience of the momentary focus, the lexia[*] one presently reads, and the continually forming narrative of one's reading path."[7]

## Active Reading

Since the reader chooses the reading path by choosing the links to be followed, 'reading' – which may actually include listening to audio files or watching video clips – becomes a far more active process than it is in print, radio or television. And since the concatenation of texts encountered along each individual reading path can be viewed as a separate text, in a way the reader of hypertext also becomes a writer or author. Thus, we find here a certain blurring of the distinction between the activities of reading and writing that is characteristic of print and broadcast. This implies a partial loss of control on the part of the author and a corresponding gain of control by the user or reader.

It is possible to draw a different conclusion if, on the other hand, the 'text' is taken to be the aggregate of all possible readings or of "the written signs forming the common source of these readings".[8] Ryan notes that in this case the author remains "the hidden master of the maze". This is because the configuration of the "maze" itself remains the same irrespective of the order in which the user visits different lexias by clicking various links. However, one can easily see that even if the reader/user

---

[*] Derived from the Greek 'lexeme', which is the basic unit of a language consisting of one or more words that do not convey its meaning when taken individually. The term is used here to denote a block of text that has meaning as part of a larger text – for instance, as part of a certain web page.

does not gain complete control over the text and its reading, she does gain a certain degree of control, and this in itself sets online journalism apart from print and broadcast.

## Decentring

One important consequence of hypertext is that it decentres the text. Landow writes[9]: "As readers move through a web or network of texts, they continually shift the center – and hence the focus or organizing principle – of their investigation and experience." Thus, hypertext provides an 'infinitely re-centerable' system, whose point of focus at any point of time depends upon the reader. Here we again encounter the active nature of reading. The 'metatext' or 'document set', that is, the collection of lexias that would be called a book, work, or single text in print, has no centre. Landow notes that while this absence of a centre can create problems for both readers and writers, it also means that the user of hypertext makes his or her own interests the actual organising principle for whatever he or she happens to be 'reading' online at any given point of time.

## Explicitly Intertextual

Yet another consequence of hypertext is that it emphasises intertextuality, makes it explicit.[10] Landow notes that poststructuralist theorists like Derrida and Foucault have stressed the open, intertextual nature of all texts, meaning thereby that a text cannot be self-contained but is always related to other texts, since its words and ideas have to refer to other texts (in this sense, everything that exists in the world is considered a 'text') in order to mean something. Thus, intertextuality is usually implicit in texts, except for such things as annotations, which make it explicit. By establishing a tangible, almost physical link between two texts that are related in some way, hypertext makes intertextuality explicit just as annotation does.

## Uses of Hypertextuality

The simplest use of hypertext is in navigating the web. This may be for moving among different websites, among different pages on the same site (through links like 'Next' or 'Next Page', 'Previous' or 'Previous Page', 'More', etc.), or within the same page (with links like 'Top of Page'). This function of hypertext may be viewed as analogous to turning the pages of a book or a newspaper, or retrieving books and other printed matter from a shelf.

But it is the other uses of hypertext – its ability to link the main text with other websites and any number of supplementary texts of various kinds – that makes it the powerful technology it is. This characteristic, when utilised properly, can enrich journalism to a level it cannot reach with the print and broadcast media because of the inherent limitations in their technologies.

### What Readers Want: A Study

A study conducted by Robert Huesca and Brenda Dervin on the way readers responded to hypertext versions of conventional linear news items originally published by *The Los Angeles Times* comes to some interesting conclusions. It may be useful to keep these findings in mind when one is preparing online news packages.

Those who took part in the experiment were evenly divided between strong preferences for the hypertext and linear narratives, respectively. Several readers felt that both had advantages and disadvantages, and preference for one or the other depended on the context and purpose of reading. Those who did not favour hypertext, cited its inherent characteristics (fragmentation, absence of authorial voice) among the reasons for their dislike.

It should be noted that the experiment involved only twenty volunteers, who read the linear and hypertext versions of the news items. This being a very small number in terms of sample size, no statistically valid conclusion for the entire population could have been drawn from it. Therefore, one cannot conclude that the entire reading population is evenly divided between those with positive and negative attitudes to hypertext.

However, qualitative studies involving small samples can bring out the issues involved more effectively than quantitative studies involving larger samples. The authors interviewed the participants, therefore, to explore their responses in a qualitative manner instead of attempting a quantitative exercise using statistical procedures. Although their findings may not be statistically valid for the entire population of newspaper readers, they are still valuable for journalists, journalism educators and communication scholars, because these bring out the attitudes that readers bring to hypertext, as well as the reasons behind these.

## Interactivity

The second characteristic of online journalism, which decisively sets it apart from print and broadcast, is interactivity. Virtually any feature of a website that requires or allows the user to become an active participant in the communication process is referred to as interactivity. It is advanced by sponsors of many web pages, as well as publishers of material like interactive CD-ROMs of various kinds, from computer games to encyclopedias, as a major selling point. Examples of such features include navigation links/buttons that have to be clicked in order to move from page to page, and the readers' opinion polls that are provided on many news sites.

According to its function, interactivity has been classified as navigational, functional and adaptive. Navigational interactivity, as the name suggests, is the function of such buttons as 'Next Page' and 'Back to Top', and of scrolling menu bars. Functional interactivity is that which is achieved through direct 'mailto:' links to the email addresses of staff provided on some news sites, moderated discussion lists, bulletin board services, etc. The most complex type of interactivity is adaptive interactivity, which refers to the facility of personal customisation offered by such sites as *The Washington Post* and Yahoo!.

At its most sophisticated, a website that incorporates adaptive interactivity would allow itself to adapt, ideally in real-time, to the surfing behaviour of the individual user. An example would be a site that changes itself to give salience to sports news and sports-related advertisements on a particular user's computer screen when it senses that this user is taking a greater interest in sports news than in other areas of news. We should note that in almost every case, interactivity is achieved by the use of hyperlinks. Therefore, while hypertextuality is the core principle of online media, interactivity can be conceived as a function of it.

Since the term 'interactivity' has become so commonplace today, most of us have an intuitive understanding of its meaning. However, it is a complex concept, which calls for a formal definition. Rafaeli has noted[11] the difficulty in defining interactivity, and proposed a solution.

"Some of the dimensions that go beyond surprise and novelty, but still do not capture interactivity, include *bidirectionality, quick response, bandwidth, user control, amount of user activity, ratio of user to medium activity, feedback, transparency*[†], *social presence*[‡], and *artificial intelligence...*" [emphasis as in original]. This being the case, he feels, the most helpful definition for interactivity would be one that focuses on responsiveness. While quasi- and fully interactive communication requires that sender and receiver roles be interchangeable with each subsequent message, non-interactive communication sequences do not. According to Rafael, the conditions for full interactivity are fulfilled when any given state in a message sequence depends on the reaction in earlier transactions, as well as on the content exchanged.

While Rafaeli is often quoted in the literature on interactivity because his explication lists some of its attributes (as in the first paragraph), it is somewhat problematic. It does not make a clear distinction between interactivity as a property of a medium that *necessarily* arises from the specific nature of its technology (first paragraph) and interactivity as a purely *contingent* characteristic of communication between two individuals (third paragraph) dependent upon their volition.

In our case, the focus being on interactivity as a feature of the internet, and more specifically of online journalism, a more appropriate and powerful definition is that offered by Steuer and quoted by several scholars, including Hall[12] : "(T)he extent to which users can participate in modifying the form and content of a mediated environment in real time".

## Dimensions of Interactivity

There are six dimensions of interactivity noted by Heeter and quoted in Kenney, et al[13] :

- complexity of choice available to users
- effort that must be made by users
- responsiveness to the user
- ease of adding information

---

[†] Transparency refers to a situation in which the user is unable to notice that the information she is receiving is coming through a medium. That is, the presence of the medium is not noticeable or barely noticeable.

[‡] Social presence of a medium is defined as "a compendium of impressions regarding warmth, sensitivity, sociability, familiarity, and privacy" (Rafaeli).

- facilitation of interpersonal communication, and
- facility for monitoring use of information.

The first five are seen from the perspective of users and the sixth from that of news organizations.

The first dimension is almost axiomatic, since the greater the number of hyperlinks provided on a web page, quite obviously the greater the range and complexity of choice available to the reader. As for the second dimension, which concerns effort, newspapers and other printed material that do not contain annotations like footnotes and endnotes, require the minimum amount of effort from the reader. Radio and television call for slightly more effort, as the viewer has to choose the station or channel she would like to listen to or view.

Websites require much greater effort (the exact degree of which depends on their design) as the reader has to choose not only the 'channel', that is, the website she would like to visit, but also the particular items she would like to read on the chosen site, and often, also, the related stories and other material she would like to read, view or listen to (audio clips) along with each story. A mathematical definition of interactivity, proposed by Paisley in this sense is "the ratio of user activity to system activity" (Kenney, et al).

Responsiveness to the user is achieved by inviting queries from her by providing email addresses of editorial and other staff or links to web forms on websites, and responding to queries received through these. As for the facilitation of interpersonal communication, providing email addresses makes communication easy between users and news site staff. Discussion forums and live chat areas perform this function not only between readers and staff, but also among readers.

The facility of adding information by the reader, listener or viewer is practically non-existent in the print and broadcast media. In contrast, some online news sites allow users to add various types of information, including the announcement of births, marriages and deaths, and reviews of films, plays and other cultural and entertainment events. A handful of sites actually allow readers to make a contribution to news reports and features produced by the editorial staff.

As for monitoring use, this refers to means of recording the (online) identities of those who visit a site and sometimes also the specific parts of the site they visit. Kenney et al point out that in addition to providing a measure of the attention a site attracts from users, such monitoring can also be used for billing the user according to her usage details and for programming the site's content to meet her interests.

## Factors Constituting Interactivity

Lotrmbard and Ditton[14] have listed five main factors that determine the degree to which a medium can be considered interactive. In that sense, the six dimensions listed above are functions of the following factors.

1. The number of inputs from the user that the medium accepts and to which it responds. We are familiar with what are known as 'haptic' inputs – commands given by the user to the medium by manipulating certain objects, for example, knobs and buttons in the case of radio and television, and the mouse, joystick, touchpad, et cetera, in computers. Other possible types of inputs include the following: voice/audio (speech recognition systems that allow computers to respond to voice commands); kinetic, that is, body movement and orientation (data gloves, body suits, and exoskeletons that translate body movements into electronic signals which a computer processes in order to place or fit the user in a virtual environment); facial expressions and eye movements; and psychophysiological inputs like heart rate, blood pressure, muscle tension, skin resistance, and brain waves which could be fed into a computer to manage the user's mood or enhancing mediated interpersonal communication (say, provide a user with the feel of the other person's hand on hers, simulating a handshake).

2. The number and type of characteristics of the mediated environment (the website in our case) which can be modified by the user. Among these are temporal ordering (order of events within the mediated experience), spatial organization (placement of objects), intensity (of volume, brightness, colour, etc.), and frequency characteristics (timbre, colour, etc.), size, duration, and pace.

3. The range or degree of change that can be brought about in each of these characteristics.

4. The degree of naturalness to which the response of the medium corresponds to the user's input. For instance, let us assume that a web page contains a map of India flanked by a row of buttons for different states, clicking on which opens detailed maps of the corresponding states. Such a page would be less interactive than one in which the links are embedded in the states on the map itself.

5. The speed with which the medium responds to user inputs. The ideal is 'real time' response, that is, when the time lag between a change in the mediated environment and the user's input that caused it is too small to be noticed. By this measure, all other factors being equal, a website that takes a long time to load would be less interactive than another that is quick to load.

## Narrative Properties of Interactivity

Just as we noted the manner in which the use of hypertext changes 'the story', that is, the narrative properties of text, we need to understand how interactivity changes these properties. Scholars like Heeter[15], Lombard and Ditton, and Nolan[16] have written on this issue, mainly in the context of virtual reality.

Nolan has addressed online journalism, but her focus is on a rather extreme type of interactive journalism which incorporates features of computer games and virtual reality, and is being experimented with in the USA. It requires the reporter to carry equipment that recreates for the 'reader', through virtual reality technology, the environment in which the reporter finds herself. The main issue in such interactive media environments is that of 'presence', that is, the creation of sense impressions in the user that she is present or 'immersed' in the space and time of the news event, though she is in reality removed from it spatially, temporally or both.

At the present time, however, the interactivity one encounters in online journalism is mostly limited to its navigational and functional uses and less frequently to adaptive uses of a limited type, in which the website can be adapted to the user's interests. The immediate need, therefore, is to understand the effect of these on the story.

As far as navigational interactivity is concerned, since it is a simple function of hyperlinks, the effects are those that have been discussed in the context of hypertextuality – multilinearity, decentredness, multivocality, explicit intertextuality and active readership. These lead to a blurring of the distinction between reading and writing if the collection of lexias selected by the user along the path of her choice is viewed as a text. In this sense, as we have already noted, navigational interactivity implies a partial loss of control for the author and a corresponding gain of control for the user or reader.

The functional uses of interactivity introduce a different set of complexities. Ordinarily, the printed newspaper can be read only by one individual at a time. Sometimes the reader may choose to read out items of interest to others, but newspaper reading is essentially an individual activity. So is reading news online when one is not interacting with other readers. However, when a news site offers discussion forums like chat rooms and bulletin boards so that readers can discuss issues and events of the day among themselves and perhaps also with the news staff, reading the news online becomes a communal, social activity.

This has important implications for opinion formation and for democracy in general. This feature helps news sites at least approach, if not fully achieve, Habermas' ideal of a public sphere in which citizens can freely discuss important issues without being hampered by barriers of class and other determinants of social status. Since the reader is under no obligation to reveal her true identity and can assume any identity she pleases in chat rooms and on bulletin boards, explicit markers of class, religion, ethnicity and other divisive factors are absent and the discussion can be less inhibited than it is in most face-to-face interactions.

As for the kind of interactivity in which readers are invited to contribute to the main text, the obvious effect is that of a blurring of the distinction between reading and writing to a much greater degree than is the case for navigational interactivity. Here, we encounter once again a loss of control over the text on the part of the journalist and a corresponding empowerment of the reader. It is not surprising, therefore, that most news sites do not incorporate interactivity beyond the navigational and functional levels. We will have an opportunity to discuss this issue later in the next chapter.

## Multimediality

The third distinguishing characteristic of online journalism is multimediality. Like 'interactive' or 'interactivity', the term 'multimedia' has also become rather common. However, this is probably the least discussed of the three in the academic literature on journalism. As the word suggests, it refers to the coexistence of different media in a single package, which for our purpose is a website.

While multimedia can take several forms, such as computer games, digital art and reference works like encyclopedias, the form in which it appears in online journalism is known as hypermedia. It has been characterised by Nadin as that which exists "(a)t the intersection between multimedia-integrated data and non-sequential data structures" and illustrated with the Venn diagram in Figure. 3.2. [17] In other words, these media packages are those which not only contain elements in multiple media (text, image, sound, video, etc.), but are also structured in a nonlinear or multilinear (non-sequential) way through the use of hypertext.

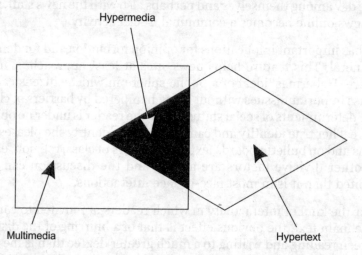

**FIGURE 3.2** Visualisation of hypermedia

(Source: Nadin)

The coexistence of different media is possible because digital technology reduces every type of content into the same binary stream of 1's and 0's, and this allows the use of images (photographs, sketches, etc.), graphics (maps, charts, etc.), animation, audio and video content along with written text in any conceivable combination.

Thus, multimedia, as we know it, involves visual and aural information. However, attempts are being made to enable the technology of virtual reality to also reproduce data from the senses of touch and smell, and it is possible that these will become part of the conceptual space of multimedia in the future. One does not hear about computer-generated sense of taste, but this, too, may become a reality one day – after all, many features of the media that we take for granted today were unthinkable even half-a-century ago.

The following definition of multimedia is suggested by Rockwell and Mactavish[18]: "A multimedia work is a computer-based rhetorical artifact in which multiple media are integrated into an interactive whole." It is a 'rhetorical artifact', the authors explain, because its purpose is not administrative or technical but "to convince, delight or instruct in the classical sense of rhetoric". This fits into our scheme, since journalism is a rhetorical process or activity in the same sense, its purpose being to inform, and sometimes also to instruct and/or entertain.

The authors further note that a multimedia work is not a random collection of different media but an integrated whole, because it is the result of "deliberate artistic imagination aimed at producing a work that has artistic unity". This means the creators or authors of multimedia treat each work as a unified whole and users or readers also view such works in this way. "The art of multimedia", Rockwell and Mactavish say, "consists in how you integrate media."

A point worth noting is that the authors have included interactivity as a defining feature of multimedia. In their view, even if a work consisting of several media is designed as an integrated whole, it does not qualify as true multimedia unless it also incorporates interactivity. This is because interactivity is the factor that "helps weave the multiplicity into a whole ... (and) is thus important to the artistic integrity of multimedia." In fact, the authors privilege interactivity even more by stating that, "in the sense of the programming that structures the work, (interactivity) is the form that integrates the others."

Although print journalism usually involves two media – written text and images (photographs and cartoons) – and sometimes also a third, namely graphics (maps, charts, etc,), it falls short of multimediality in one crucial aspect, namely, its lack of interactivity. As for assemblages that include sound and visuals (including motion), Benazet points out that in the absence of interactivity, these become mere audio-visual works rather than multimedia.[19]

We may note here that the weaving together of different media elements, as also interactivity, is achieved by the use of hyperlinks. Therefore, multimediality can be seen as a function of both hypertextuality and interactivity.

Another point I would like to stress is that students of journalism should not be deterred by the talk of 'artistic imagination', 'artistic unity', etc.

These issues are as relevant to journalists as they are to new media artists and authors of hyperfiction, because the craft of journalism includes the art of storytelling. In the context of multimedia it involves the telling of a story through two or more media elements woven together into an integrated and interactive whole instead of through plain text.

### Meaning in Multimedia

Just as we have discussed the way in which hypertextuality and interactivity change the 'reading' of texts, it is also necessary to present at least a rudimentary discussion on the aesthetics of multimedia in order to understand the way such works act upon the senses and are 'read' by users. Or to put it in the everyday language of journalists, it is essential to understand how the 'story' changes when it leaves the domain of plain written text in print or even on the computer screen, and enters that of multimedia. But this is not an easy task, and scholars have pointed out the complexities involved. Lichty writes[20]:

> Possibly more than at any time in history, the technological society is constantly cross-referencing the information it takes in and reprocesses it in the form of media texts. For example, as the words I speak trigger off mental images or sounds from past experience, they are reassembled into new configurations, frequently shaped by mass media architectures. This is not to say that this particular effect is new in itself, but the unprecedented amounts of data that the citizen of the mediascape is required to assimilate creates these ontological shifts.

Understanding these 'ontological shifts' is not easy. As Petty observes[21], citing Sean Cubitt, multimedia remains 'forever elusive', because it involves the coexistence and interaction of different media in every imaginable combination: "(H)ow does one adequately structure an analytical framework for a form that may contain video streaming, sound collage, photographic elements, graphic design, print text, interactivity and any number of other elements in a kaleidoscope of varying degrees?" We should note that for any given 'channel' (in our case a website), the combination itself may be fluid, changing on its own (if this is how it has been designed) or as a result of the choices the reader makes by clicking on links as she interacts with the site.

Another dimension is added to the complexity by the fact that the different media that can go into the making of a multimedia work are fundamentally different. As Borchardt[22] points out, all media (including the verbal, that is, written words) are visual with the sole exception of sound. Sound is also the only medium that cannot but exist in a diachronic manner (has to unfold with time), because all the others can be presented synchronically or 'freeze-frame'. Even a video clip can be frozen at any given point but sound ceases to exist as soon as it is stopped, and cannot therefore be 'frozen'. Borchardt feels that sound is also the least developed of the different media, in terms of both the practice of and theorizing about multimedia.

While several writers, such as Lemke, Nadin, Mactavish, Rockwell, Benazet and Zbikowski have sought to address the way meaning is constituted in multimedia, most of them have taken a semiotic approach, and focused their attention primarily on verbal elements (written words), on the one hand, and pictorial elements (mostly photographic images), on the other. Apart from having the obvious shortcoming that it does not pay adequate attention to sound, their approach is also problematic in that it tends to treat each medium as a self-contained semiotic 'resource system' although in reality the user experiences any 'instance of multimedia' or IMM, that is, any multimedia work (indeed, the world itself) as an integral whole, the meaning of which arises from the interaction of the different media elements (involving the different senses) contained in it.

The significance of this can be appreciated if we keep in mind the fact that human perception is originally synaesthetic, that is, the stimulation of any one of the senses produces sense impressions not only on that particular sense but also on the others. (A literal example is a condition found in some individuals, whereby they see certain colours when they hear certain sounds or read certain words.) Therefore, the meaning of a given situation encountered by an individual derives from a complex synthesis of impressions on all of her senses.

If we are today accustomed to thinking of our senses in isolation from one another, this is because we have internalised over many generations an analytic orientation to the world, which Western science has adopted as part of the psychological landscape of modernity.[23] However, if synaesthesia is an innate characteristic of human perception, it must be present at a subliminal level in spite of these cultural changes. It follows that the meaning we derive from a multimedia work (and the world itself) is not a mere sum of impressions on all the senses corresponding to the different media elements that make it up but a complex synthesis of these, resulting from their interaction.

Hence, we need to look elsewhere to understand the way meaning is produced in multimedia and Zbikowski's work holds promise in this respect. Not only does he take sound into account, what is more important, his method is also able to account for the interaction taking place among the different senses. Figures 3.3 and 3.4 are diagrammatic representations of his method, known as a conceptual integration network (CIN). It is meant to show the manner in which the interaction takes place. In formulating his approach, Zbikowski draws on the works of Mark Turner, George Lakoff, Mark Johnson (contemporary theories of rhetoric and metaphor), Nicholas Cook (analysis of musical multimedia), and Gilles Fauconnier (linguistics).

### Conceptual Integration Network (CIN)

The CIN involves three types of interconnected mental spaces – input space, generic space and blended space. Zbikowski illustrates the method by analysing a metaphor-rich passage from the writing of Marcel Proust. In the passage the description of some lilac trees almost invests them with the character of intelligent beings, thus blending the domains of trees and intelligent beings (input spaces) into a single, hybrid domain of meaning[24]:

> We would leave town by the road which ran along the white fence of M. Swann's park. Before reaching it we would be met on our way by the scent of his lilac-trees, come out to welcome strangers. From amid the fresh little green hearts of their foliage they raised inquisitively over the fence of the park their plumes of white or mauve blossoms, which glowed, even in the shade, with the sunlight in which they had bathed.

The solid double-headed arrow linking the two input spaces is meant to show that elements within them serve as 'structural correlates': 'tree' with 'being', 'giving off scent' with 'animate', and 'shape of foliage' with 'inquisitive nature'. The process of correlation ('mapping') between these spaces is controlled by the conceptual framework of a generic space, which contains their common feature – in this case, a living being that can be known through certain characteristics – and the resultant meaning is projected into the blended space.

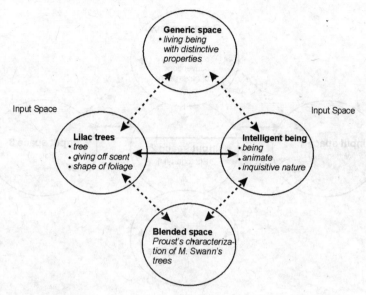

Figure **3.3** CIN for the passage from Proust

(Source: Zbikowski)

This method can be applied in order to understand the interaction that takes place among the different senses corresponding to different media in a multimedia work. Let us say this work is an online news package about a football match, a political rally or a riot, and consists of written text (report on the event), photographs and sound files.

In this case, the CIN would be three-dimensional, consisting of two layers. The surface layer, shown in Figure 3.4, would have three input spaces corresponding to the three media elements of the package. Its generic space would consist of the feature common to all three, namely the situation or event being represented, viewed according to the generic code (conventions) of news production for example, a football match as a contest between two sides as opposed to, say, an event that throws light on the particular society's cultural life. (The situation that makes up the generic space is actually the 'reference' part of meaning. As Ricoeur has pointed out, drawing on the work of Gottlob Frege, the meaning of discourse consists of the unity of 'sense', that is, what is being said, and 'reference', that is, about what it is being said.[25])

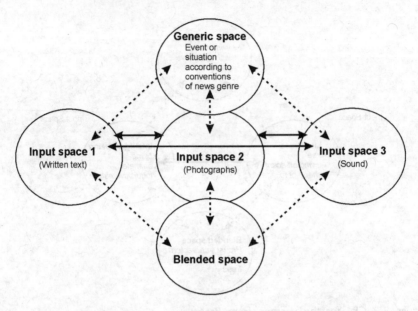

FIGURE **3.4** Surface-layer CIN for an online news package

The solid lines among the three input spaces can then stand for the following correlations:

1. Between text and photographs: On the one hand, highlights of the event, such as those usually found in the first one or two paragraphs of news reports structured in the traditional 'inverted pyramid' style. On the other, photographs of goals being scored, important speakers on the dais and/or participants at the rally, or scenes of violence and arson, as the case may be.

2. Between text and sound: Highlights of the event (as above) and sound of the crowd cheering (football match); a speech and/or sound of clapping/booing/slogan-shouting (political rally); shouting, bombs exploding, shots being fired (riot).

3. Between photographs and sound: Highlights, as noted above, recorded in photographs and sound recordings, respectively.

It should be noted that each of the three media – text, photographic image and sound – is effective in representing the situation in a way peculiar to itself. Broadly speaking, writing (text) helps an analytical representation, in which metaphor has a key place (since language is fundamentally metaphoric) even though the conventions of news discourse favour a literal reading.

The photograph, at least news photograph, can be viewed primarily as a metonymic device as it attempts to represent events and situations, which have necessarily taken place over a period of time, by the image captured at a single moment. However, 'reading' (interpreting) a photograph may also require the 'reader' to engage with the visual metaphor created by the setting, framing, camera angle, depth of focus, shutter speed, lighting and other devices.

For instance, a news photograph of a speaker at a rally shot from below would connote high stature. In an advertisement or a public relations package about a particular make of car, a photograph of a well-dressed young person in an affluent setting would point to the idea that owning that particular car would place the owner in that person's social category with its attendant privileges. A photograph of a casually dressed person on a rugged landscape would point to the idea that the car should be owned by those who wish to lead a life of healthy outdoor adventure.

Sound files, too, are metonymic in that the sound that has been recorded perhaps over a few tens of seconds or a few minutes is called upon to represent the entire event, which might have unfolded over hours, days or months, even years. However, sound also does not entirely escape the metaphoric mode of meaning production. A few seconds of recorded clapping would connote an exciting match or an appreciative crowd at a rally, even though both might have been listless affairs on the whole. In advertisement and public relations works, fast-paced music is often used to connote happiness, affluence, youth, upward mobility and modernity, while sad violin music may be used to connote tragic situations.

Thus, none of the media elements of a multimedia package yields its own, individual meaning in a literal way even though news discourse traditionally privileges literal use of the medium over metaphoric use. It is easy to see that this is even more true in the case of advertising and public relations work, which are genres in which the code (conventions) privileges the metaphoric over the literal rather than the other way.

Therefore, underneath the surface-level CIN shown in Figure 3.4 there would have to be a second layer of CINs. One CIN for each of the three top-level input spaces, showing what conceptual domains are mapped within it and in what way, and each of these deeper-level CINs would be structured in the manner of Figure 3.3. The two layers together make a complex structure, the complexity of which would increase with every increase in the number of different media elements.

Journalists, advertising professionals and public relations professionals, who are required to prepare or even contribute to multimedia packages, would need to keep these considerations in mind, as it is essential that they avoid any dissonance between any two input spaces on either of the two levels. Such a dissonance at any point would place the entire package in jeopardy.

## Exercises

1. Read the day's lead news item in your favourite newspaper. Then read the same item on the website of the same newspaper.

   a. Note the links, if any, which have been provided in the body of the online version and along with the item but outside its body text. Follow all these links individually. Write a detailed account of the way each path produces a separate narrative, and how each differs from the narrative in the print edition.

   b. Repeat the above exercise for other newspapers, but the same news story. Then compare the way in which they deal with hyperlinks, and the effect of this on their respective narratives.

2. a. Visit the website of your favourite newspaper. List the different interactive features you find, and classify these under the navigational, functional and adaptive heads. Discuss the way the interactive features have affected the narrative in the day's lead story.

   b. Repeat the above exercise for other newspapers and compare your findings.

3. a. Visit the website of your favourite newspaper. List the multimedia elements used in the day's lead story, and discuss the way meaning arises in the story with the help of CIN diagrams.

   b. Visit the website of your favourite television channel and repeat the above exercise. Compare the way the two websites (the newspaper's and the TV channel's) use multimedia, and the way this difference is reflected in the different meanings yielded by the same story on the two sites.

# References

1. Landow, George P., *Hypertext: The Convergence of Critical Theory and Technology* (Johns Hopkins University Press, 1992), pp. 3–4, accessed 13 March 2005 on http://www.cyberartsweb.org/cpace/ht/jhup/history.html#1.

2. Bush, Vannevar, 'As We May Think', *Computer Media and Communication: A Reader*, ed. Paul A. Mayer (Oxford, and New York, Oxford University Press, 1999), p. 34, reprinted from *The Atlantic Monthly* 176 (1945).

3. Ridgway, Neil, 'Hypertext and Hypermedia', accessed 11 March 2005 on http://www.mmrg.ecs.soton.ac.uk/publications/archive/ridgway1998/html/node18.html.

4. Engelbart, Douglas C., 'A Conceptual Framework for the Augmentation of Man's Intellect', *Computer Media and Communication: A Reader*, ed. Paul A. Mayer (Oxford and New York, Oxford University Press, 1999), pp. 72–96, reprinted from Howerton and Weeks, eds., *Vistas in Information Handling* (Spartan Books, 1963).

5. Nelson, Ted, 'A New Home for the Mind', *Computer Media and Communication: A Reader*, ed. Paul A. Mayer (Oxford and New York, Oxford University Press, 1999), pp. 120–128, reprinted from *Datamation* (March 1982).

6. Landow, George P., *Hypertext: The Convergence of Critical Theory and Technology* (Johns Hopkins University Press, 1992), pp. 1–3, accessed 13 March 2005 on http://www.cyberartsweb.org/cpace/ht/jhup/parallels.html.

7. Ibid., p.11, accessed on http://www.cyberartsweb.org/cpace/ht/jhup/multivoc.html.

8. Ryan, Marie-Laure, 'Immersion vs. Interactivity: Virtual Reality and Literary Theory', *Postmodern Culture*, vol. 5, no.1, 1994, accessed 16 March 2005 on http://www.humanities.uci.edu/mposter/syllabi/readings/ryan.html.

9. Ibid., pp.11–13, accessed on http://www.cyberartsweb.org/cpace/ht/jhup/decenter.html.

10. Ibid., pp.10–11, accessed on http://www.cyberartsweb.org/cpace/ht/jhup/intertext.html.

11. Rafaeli, Sheizaf, 'Interactivity: From New Media to Communication', *Sage Annual Review of Communication Research: Advancing Communication Science*, vol.16 (Beverly Hills, Sage, 1988) pp. 110–134, accessed 14 March 2005 on http://gsb.haifa.ac.il/~sheizaf/interactivity/.

12 Steuer, Jonathan, 'Defining Virtual Reality: Dimensions Determining Telepresence', *Journal of Communication*, vol. 42, no. 4 (1992), p.76, quoted in Jim Hall, *Online Journalism: A Critical Primer* (Virginia, Pluto Press, London & Sterling , 2001), p.49.

13 Kenney, Keith et al, 'Interactive Features of Online Newspapers', *First Monday*, vol. 5, no. 1 (January 2000), accessed 16 March 2005 on http://firstmonday .org/issues / issue5_1/kenney/index.html.

14 Lombard, Matthew and Theresa Ditton, 'At the Heart of it all: The Concept of Presence' , *Journal of Computer Mediated Communication*, vol. 3, no.2, September 1997, accessed 16 March  2005 on http://www.ascusc.org/jcmc/vol3/issue2/ lombard.html.

15 Heeter, Carrie, 'Interactivity in the Context of Designed Experiences', *Journal of Interactive Advertising*, vol.1, no. 1, Fall 2000, accessed 18 March 2005 on http:/ /jiad.org/vol1/no1/heeter/.

16 Nolan, Sybil, 'Journalism Online: The Search for Narrative Form in a Multilinear World', *Fineartforum E-zine*, vol. 17, no. 8, August 2003, accessed 18 March  2005 on http://www.fineartforum.org/Backissues/Vol_17/faf_v17_no8/reviews/ nolan.html.

17 Nadin, Mihai, 'Visible Signs – the Language of Multimedia', *Signs and Systems: A Semiotic Introduction to System Design* (Cambridge University Press, 1997), accessed 22 March 2005 on http://www.nadin.name/pdf/visisign.pdf.

18 Rockwell, Geoffrey and Andrew Mactavish , 'Multimedia', accessed 18 March 2005 on http://www.humanities.mcmaster.ca/~hccrs/IHC/multimedia.pdf .

19 Benazet, Patrick, 'Multimedia Evaluation by Semiotics Approach', *Journal of International Forum of Educational Technologies & Society* and *IEEE Learning Technology Task Force*, accessed 22 March  2005 on http://patrick-benazet.chez.tiscali.fr/semiocom/travaux/ifets1.htm.

20 Lichty, Patrick, 'Speaking the Multimedia Culture: Art, Pedagogy, and New Technologies', accessed 23 March 2005 on http://www.voyd.com/voyd/ speaking.pdf.

21 Petty, Sheila, 'New Technologies and New Forms of Expression: Towards an Aesthetics of New Media', accessed 23 March 2005 on http:// www.neutralground.sk.ca/artistprojects/sheilapetty/index4.html.

22 Borchardt, Frank L., 'Toward an Aesthetics of Multimedia', 8 January 1999, accessed 24 March 2005 on http://www.duke.edu/~frankbo/edtech04/frame/ EDUC113_PPT/exeter8.PDF.

[23] Boucher, Marc, 'Kinetic Synaesthesia: Experiencing Dance in Multimedia Scenographies', *Contemporary Aesthetics*, vol.2 (2004), accessed 23 March 2005 on http://www.contempaesthetics.org/pages/article.php?articleID=235.

[24] Zbikowski, Lawrence M., 'Music Theory, Multimedia, and the Construction of Meaning', accessed 23 March 2005 on http://humanities.uchicago.edu/faculty/zbikowski/COOK_Rev.pdf.

[25] Ricoeur, Paul, *Interpretation Theory: Discourse and the Surplus of Meaning* (Fort Worth, Texas Christian University Press, 1976), p.19.

# 4.
# Annotative Reporting and Open-source Journalism

Now that we are familiar with hypertextuality, interactivity and multimediality, and the way they change the character of the text it is time to discuss the way these characteristics can be utilised to give the reader (user), and society in general, more than what they get from print or broadcast journalism. The two main ways of doing this are: annotative reporting and open-source journalism. The terms hyperadaptive news and participatory journalism are also sometimes used.

## Annotative Reporting

According to the *Concise Oxford English Dictionary*, to 'annotate' is to "add notes to (a text or diagram) giving explanation or comment". Therefore, this word and its derivative, 'annotative', presuppose the existence of other texts. In the case of online journalism, these other texts are the immense and ever-growing number of web pages and databases on every conceivable subject that are available on the internet.

Deuze notes[1] that the term 'annotative reporting' was coined in the mid-1990s when media commentators realised that since news sites constituted a very small fraction of all existing sites, these were far from being the only sources of information for the public. They saw that in the new situation, the reporter's role would have to evolve beyond the traditional one of a mere provider of information to that of a facilitator of interactive media environments in which readers (users) would construct their own 'news' from material present on the net with the help of hyperlinks. Journalists would provide guidance in this activity through commentary and explanatory entries (annotations). Such guidance had become necessary, because scarcity of information had given way to an information glut with the advent of the internet. The reader was at risk of missing the really significant facts because of this overabundance of information on the net.

Hence, analysis becomes an essential part of the journalist's responsibilities in the new situation. Deuze says that many journalists in the west are aware of this change in their role. But the new environment requires a change on the part of users as well. They need to be more active and also more skilled as information seekers than they needed to be with the print and broadcast media, which served information in neat, easily digestible packages.

*Kuro5hin*.org, a US-based news site specialising in technology, politics and culture, can be seen as an example of annotative reporting. Figure 4.1 shows the page that has a story on the alleged suicide of Gary Webb, a Pulitzer Prize winning reporter of *The Mercury News*. It was published from San Jose in Silicon Valley of California in December 2004. This story is an excellent example of annotative journalism. Incidentally, Webb himself was a pioneer of annotative reporting.

Gary Webb (1955–2004)

In 1996, Gary Webb had authored 'Dark Alliance', a three-part exposé of the links that had existed among the CIA, the Contra rebels of Nicaragua, and large-scale drug peddling in Los Angeles in the 1980s. The text of the *Kuro5hin* story on his death contains links (in blue letters, underlined) to pages from which the information has been culled. The first link, from 'the finest journalist ... the truth', is to a report on Webb's death which appeared on counterpunch.org. In the second paragraph, the title of Webb's series, 'Dark Alliance', is linked to an Amazon.com page on the 608-page book that was published by Webb on the same subject. The link from 'CIA knowledge ... in L.A.' is to an article, 'How John Kerry Exposed the Contra-Cocaine Scandal', published on truthout.org and originally on the webzine *Salon.com*. The second last link in the second paragraph (not seen in the figure), from 'verifies that the CIA ... and ignored them', is to an online press release of the US House of Representatives, titled 'CIA Confirms It Allowed Contra Drug Trafficking: Rep. Waters Calls On Committee to Hold Hearings In 106th Congress'.

Thus, the writer of the *Kuro5hin* story presents the reader not just with a report as would have happened in the print medium, but with a report that guides the reader, with the help of hyperlinks, to sources of information which the writer (who identifies herself/himself only as 'badtux') finds important enough to be read. And while doing so, the author provides the reader with an explanation of, or a commentary on, the role Webb played as a journalist in the political life of the USA. The importance

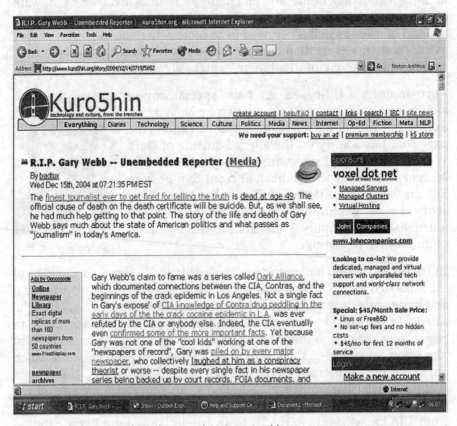

FIGURE 4.1 The *Kuro5hin* obituary for Gary Webb

of such a guiding role can be appreciated from the fact that a Google search for 'Gary Webb' turned up about 1.25 million results and when the search was narrowed to 'Gary Webb and Dark Alliance', it still turned up an unmanageable number of results – about 50,200. Webb himself may be regarded as a pioneer of this type of journalism. One of the links provided by the writer of the *Kuro5hin* story is to a web log entry, apparently posted by a reporter who identifies herself as Lisa. Speaking of the manner in which Webb's 'Dark Alliance' series of investigative reports were published in *The Mercury News*, she writes[2]:

> Accompanying the stories, for a journalistic first, were scans of court documents, audio files of testimony, pages from notebooks, and all kinds of supporting documentation. It was truly wonderful. For once, the public didn't have to take on faith what a reporter said. He shared his best evidence with everyone in the world who had Internet access.

Lisa's observation clearly explains the way annotative reporting, enabled by the internet, can take journalism beyond its traditional form. It is not difficult to see that, had badtux been a print or broadcast journalist, the inherent limitations of these media would have prevented him/her from providing the readers/listeners/viewers with anything remotely approaching the amount of material the *Kuro5hin* story provides, or the interactive reading experience it affords.

## Open-source Journalism

According to *Wikipedia* (http://www.wikipedia.org), a multilingual and free online encyclopedia, the term 'open source' refers to "projects that are open to the public and which draw on other projects that are freely available to the general public." *Wikipedia* itself is an open-source project, as it draws on the contributions of readers, and can be edited by them. However, the term is most commonly used for referring to software such as the GNU-Linux operating systems whose source code (that is, blueprint) is freely available to users, so that they can modify it if they wish. Users are also free to redistribute such software.

As *The Economist* noted[3], the open-source concept is not new. Since 1857, the *Oxford English Dictionary* has been relying on readers to provide it with word definitions, so that the editors may keep themselves updated on the contemporary usage of words. Science, too, has been advancing through an open-source process – the publication of research done by scientists after peer review. But the use of the term in the context of journalism is new, and refers to a completely new phenomenon, namely, that of allowing readers/users to write/construct the story (package if it is in multimedia) and then making it available for modification by other readers or users.

The *Kuro5hin* and *Slashdot* (a website specialising in technology news) sites are organized on an open-source principle. The latter's readers submit stories they would like to post on the site, and its editors select the ones they consider fit to be posted. When a story goes up on the site, comments received from readers are posted along with it.

*Kuro5hin* follows the open-source principle in a purer form – while its readers are its 'reporters' as in *Slashdot*, stories are selected on the basis of readers' preference. Readers submit new content for the editors' consideration by filling out an online form that opens when the appropriate link is clicked. The submission does not appear on the public pages at this stage, but enters a list that can be accessed by all registered users. These users can read the submission and vote in one of three ways – in favour of posting it on the public pages, or against this, or indicating their lack of preference in the matter. They can also attach comments to their respective votes. If and when the vote reaches a certain percentage of the total number of registered users, the story is posted on the public pages along with readers' comments. The editors occasionally correct grammatical or typing mistakes, but the final decision on 'publishing' content is left to the readers (users) through the system of voting.

## Criticism of Open-source Journalism

Open-source journalism has had its share of criticism. The following example[4] illustrates this. In October 1999, Johan Ingles-le Nobel, deputy editor of the reputed international publication *Jane's Intelligence Review*, posted an article on cyberterrorism (meant to be ultimately published in *Jane's*) on a private preview page of *Slashdot* along with a request for feedback from its readers on certain points. There were over 250 responses, the majority of which were negative. Nobel decided to discard the original text and wrote a fresh one, incorporating material from the feedback.

Some journalists felt that this process overturned certain basic principles of journalism. By having *Slashdot* readers preview his story and changing it in light of their criticism before final publication in *Jane's*, Nobel opened his own work to censorship. Robert X. Cringley, a columnist of the online edition of PBS (the US Public Broadcasting Service), wrote[5]: "The only way to write the news is to write the news ... You have to do it the best that you can, then take the heat, because the censorship of the nerderati is still censorship. That's why newspapers make corrections."

Nobel's response was that he had merely checked facts with knowledgeable people and incorporated their input, as was already the norm in gathering information. The managing editor *of Slashdot*, Robin Miller, said he felt that *Jane's* was a scholarly publication, not one in the popular category, and Nobel had followed a standard practice of scholarly journals, whereby articles are subjected to expert peer review before publication.

We may note that the type of open-source journalism that is practised by *Slashdot* and *Kuro5hin*, circumvents these criticisms. Since the stories they post (publish) are contributed by readers and are reviewed by other readers and the editors, the question of journalists subjecting themselves to censorship by readers does not arise. In the case of *Kuro5hin*, censorship on the other side – by the editors – is also reduced to a minimum by leaving the decision to readers through a mechanism of voting.

## Practical Considerations

There are certain practical considerations which should be kept in mind by anyone wishing to practice this type of journalism.

*Slashdot* and *Kuro5hin* have been extremely successful with open-source journalism because their readers are a more or less well-defined group sharing a common cultural background (predominantly American) and a common knowledge base – mostly information technology (*Slashdot* calls itself 'news for nerds') – as a result of which they are able to collectively create appropriate content.

But the process may be less effective with a more heterogeneous readership, as is the case with general-interest news sites. In such cases it may be harder to find a significant number of readers who are both able and willing to create content of value on specific topics.

Andrew Leonard of the *Salon* webzine points out a practical difficulty. Having a story previewed by a large number of readers may be impossible, since deadline pressure often leaves insufficient time even for proper copy-editing and proofreading. If we pay attention to the procedures followed by *Slashdot* and *Kuro5hin*, we will see how these effectively tackle this problem in two areas – content generation and publication.

Since stories are submitted by a large army of readers, who are specialists in their chosen fields, these sites have a steady supply of updated content to work with and there is no question of a delay in content generation. As for publication, the practice of posting readers' comments along with the selected stories rather than rewriting these to incorporate comments takes care of such issues as updates, correction of errors and analysis, but does not hold up the publication process.

This illustrates the fact that adherence to democratic ideals need not be a drag on the efficiency of a news site, nor does it add to expenses. In fact, it saves money as much as it saves time. Those who contribute stories to *Slashdot* and *Kuro5hin*, do so not for money but as unpaid volunteers, out of an interest in the subject and to promote discussion on it.

The software needed for such applications is not particularly expensive, and is usually free software or open-source software (which are very similar). These are sometimes, though not always, available free of cost, and by definition are open to alteration and/or redistribution by users.

*Kuro5hin* uses the Linux operating system, Apache server, Perl programming language and the Scoop collaborative media application which combines features of a content management system, a bulletin board system and a weblog. All of these are in the FOSS (free/open-source software) category.

We should note that the special characteristics of internet technology constitute the key factor in making practices like open-source journalism possible. Because of their inherent constraints, neither print technology, nor broadcast could have given rise to this type of journalism. It is not possible to work within the time frame of typical journalistic deadlines if one wishes to first print or air a story, as the case may be, for preview by readers/listeners/viewers, then read/hear their comments, then rework the piece to incorporate the comments or simply append these to the story to save time, and finally print or air the finished version, which is actually far from finished as the audience usually continues to send responses well after the final publication.

If dictionaries have succeeded in working on the open-source principle in the print medium, it is because journalistic deadlines do not apply in such projects. The same holds true for science and scholarly work in general as publishing in these areas is not always subject to explicit institutional deadlines though there are implicit ones arising from requirements for career advancement and competition with peers. Even when deadlines exist, explicitly or implicitly, these are usually quite long and bear no comparison with those which apply in day-to-day journalism.

As a postscript, I would like to mention an interesting attempt to use the open-source method for writing about open-source, participatory journalism. This has been done by Dan Gillmor, who was a technology columnist with the San Jose *Mercury News* (USA) until 2004. (Coincidentally, this is also the paper that had employed Gary Webb.) While writing a book titled *Making the News*, Gillmor posted outlines of the chapters on his blog (web log) (http://weblog.siliconvalley.com/column/dangillmor/archives/000924.shtml#000924) and invited readers' comments through direct mailto: links to his email address, so that he could incorporate the feedback in the book. This approach, Gillmor writes, elicited an enthusiastic response from the readers of his blog.

## Participatory Journalism

The phenomenon we have discussed as open-source journalism shades into what has come to be known as participatory journalism or citizen journalism, and sometimes also as 'we journalism'. Bowman and Willis[6] define it as, "The act of a citizen, or group of citizens, playing an active role in the process of collecting, reporting, analyzing and disseminating news and information."

*Wikipedia*, which is itself an open-source participatory project,[7] points out that an important aspect of citizen/participatory journalism is its stress on empowering ordinary people, including those who belong to traditionally marginalized sections of society, to perform functions that are the province of professional reporters in the traditional media. This definition covers more than the type of journalism that is practised by sites like *Slashdot* and *Kuro5hin* and includes the 'blog' phenomenon which will be discussed in detail later on in the chapter.

As Bowman and Willis have noted, news and views flow from the audience in participatory journalism, rather than in the top-down manner typical of conventional news organizations. Moreover, unlike the conventional media, it involves little or no editorial control or the formal journalistic hierarchies that dictate editorial decisions.

Instead, participatory journalism is produced by 'many simultaneous, distributed conversations' that either develop or fade away within a short time in the social network created by the web. Viewing it from another angle, we may see that participatory journalism is an exemplar of post-modern culture. It bears at least two of the marks – fragmentation and decentredness – that characterise postmodernism.

According to *Wikipedia*, this type of journalism has its roots in the 'public' or 'civic' journalism movement, which took shape in the USA after the 1988 presidential election. It was a reaction to the people's declining faith in the media and their disillusionment with politics and civic affairs. That election was held at the end of President Ronald Reagan's second and final term, and George Bush emerged the winner.

The Bush victory was a traumatic development for liberal Americans, who had been hoping to see the Democrat, Michael Dukakis, installed in the White House after eight years of President Reagan's conservative right-wing presidency. Many journalists working for the mainstream media, including senior figures, felt the need for a more activist approach and embraced civic journalism. Although the movement lost much of its steam by 2003 its spirit had found an anchor in the web-based technologies of public discussion, such as web logs, chat rooms and message boards that had become popular since the late 1990s.

Participatory journalism is the result of the marriage of the spirit of public journalism with the internet's technology. According to US-based writers like Bowman and Willis, as well as Gillmor, the turning point at which this new journalism began to flourish was 11 September 2001, when terrorists flew passenger airliners into the World Trade Center and the Pentagon. Many mainstream news sites found it difficult to cope with the massive internet traffic generated by the attacks as people continuously sought the latest information.

This, and the personal touch provided by citizen channels – email lists, web logs, bulletin boards, et cetera – increased their attraction. People needed to talk to one another in order to grasp the meaning of events. "Everything from eyewitness accounts and photo galleries to commentary and personal storytelling," Bowman and Willis write, "emerged to help people collectively grasp the confusion, anger and loss felt in the wake of the tragedy." This led to the proliferation of what the authors call 'do-it-yourself journalism'.

## OhmyNews and South Korea Show the Way

In South Korea, however, participatory journalism had come into its own a year and a half before it did in the USA. This had happened through the launch of the *OhmyNews* site in February 2000 with the motto "every citizen is a reporter". As in the USA, the urge for democracy and opposition to extreme right-wing rule was the driving force in this case.

Oh Yeon Ho, founder and Chief Executive Officer of *OhmyNews*, is a journalist educated in South Korea and the USA. He had taken part in student protests against the South Korean government in the turbulent 1980s when the country was making the transition from a military dictatorship to a parliamentary democracy. He joined the alternative monthly magazine *Mahl* in 1988 and served as a reporter and director of its news department until 1999. Oh describes *OhmyNews* as a "marriage of democracy and technology"[8] that came about in the following way[9]:

> In Korea, readers' dissatisfaction and distrust with the conventional press had considerably increased. Citizens' desire to express themselves greatly increased. Thus, on the one hand, discontent with the conventional press, on the other hand, citizens desire to talk about themselves. These two things were joined together.

> The reason the Internet was highly attractive was that I had little money and the Internet meant launching was relatively easy at first – easier than paper newspapers. So I thought the Internet was the space where

a few people who possessed nothing could bring about results using guerrilla methods.

I thought up our motto, slogan, or concept – 'every citizen is a reporter' – when I was a reporter for the monthly, Mal. Because the magazine Mal was not mainstream media but alternative media, I had to have that kind of determination or attitude. Only when I was armored with the philosophy of 'every citizen is a reporter' could I equally compete with the reporters of the mainstream media.

The motto 'every citizen is a reporter' has modesty as well as confidence. That is, no matter how small the alternative media I was working for as a reporter, I could be arrogant because of the fact that I was a reporter. And, even though I had a reporter's license, it had the meaning that I was not above a general citizen. So 'every citizen is a reporter' means on the one hand, confidence, and on the other hand, modesty.

By January 2005, *OhmyNews* had more than 35,000 registered citizen writers, who were contributing more than 70 per cent of the news.[10] In addition, it had some 40 staff reporters. It had reached break-even point in 2003 [11] and has been making a modest profit since then. The major part of its income, about 70 per cent, comes from advertising and the rest from the sale of news to other publications, etc.

In 2004, the organisation was paying the citizen reporters a small fee – between $5 and $20 per item, depending on the importance assigned to it by the editors. It also has a system in which a reader can pay a small fee to a reporter if she likes the latter's story, and in this case *OhmyNews* receives a commission on the fee. Readers can also contribute a voluntary subscription fee to *OhmyNews* by paying through their mobile phones or credit cards.

For those of us who are accustomed to practices followed in the conventional media, the idea of ordinary citizens contributing news may seem alarmingly anarchic. But *OhmyNews* has put in place alternative practices to ensure that accuracy is not compromised.

It has a number of copy-editors who check the stories for factual errors, and since the citizen reporters are all registered with their real names, social security numbers and addresses, they can be easily contacted for verifying the correctness of their stories. As is the case with any news organisation, items published on *OhmyNews* also, sometimes, result in disputes with people who feel aggrieved by their content, but a relatively small number of these are serious enough to reach the courts.

However, commercial and operational success within a short time is not the only achievement the site can boast of. It is widely recognised as having been instrumental in bringing the liberal politician Roh Moo Hyun to power as President in December 2002 after years of conservative rule. It marked what *The New York Times* saw as a transition "from conservative to liberal, from gerontocracy to youth culture and from staunchly pro-American to a deeply ambivalent ally all seemingly overnight"[12]. The events, in Oh's own words[13], are given in the box on p. 72. It has been given in some detail because it can be instructive for practising journalists and those aspiring to be journalists.

## The Anatomy of Success

According to Oh, there are five reasons behind the success of *OhmyNews*. First, the mainstream conservative media had long disappointed readers, who yearned for alternative media. Second, South Korea's internet infrastructure is superior to most other countries. With more than 75 per cent broadband penetration, readers are able to access multimedia, always-on service and interactive news. Third, South Korea being geographically small, staff reporters are able to reach the news scene in a few hours to verify the correctness of a citizen reporter's story if necessary. Fourth, since Korean society is 'unipolar' rather than diverse, the entire nation can be quickly mobilized around one or two issues.

"But the most important reason," Oh says, "is that Korean citizens were ready to participate. Korea has a young, active and reform-minded generation, those in their 20s and 30s and early 40s." Koreans, he says, have paid dearly for this situation to come about, in the shape of the struggle against military dictatorship, the division of the country into North and South, the Korean War of 1950, and the Kwangju Massacre* of 1980. "The Korean War taught people to keep silent in order to survive," Oh says. "The Kwangju Massacre too. But there has been an endless struggle for democracy and liberating from keeping silent (*sic*)."

---

* In 1980, martial law was declared after student demonstrations. At least 200 people were killed by the army in the city of Kwangju.

## How *OhmyNews* Changed the Face of South Korea

"Let's look back to the last day of the 2002 Korean Presidential election campaign. Just eight hours before the start of voting, at around 10.30 p.m. on December 18th, Mr. Chung Mong Joon, Roh Moo Hyun's campaign partner suddenly withdrew his support. This astonished the whole nation. Mr. Chung's withdrawal was a kind of atomic bomb. Interestingly enough, the news provoked a last minute confrontation between Old media and New media. The conservative mainstream newspaper *Chosun Daily* changed its editorial and posed a question to voters along the lines of 'Mr. Chung withdrew his support for Roh, will you?'

But reform-minded netizens including *OhmyNews* readers quickly mobilized overnight to fight Mr. Chung's atomic bomb. They visited many Internet bulletin boards and posted urgent messages like "Mr. Chung betrayed his party, Roh Moo Hyun is in danger. Save the country, please vote for Roh." They even called their conservative parents to persuade them, crying "If Roh Moo Hyun fails, I will die." *OhmyNews* reported Mr. Chung's withdrawal and updated the story of netizens' reactions every 30 minutes, all night long. The number of hits for that main breaking story was 720,000 in just 10 hours. (Thanks to the nonstop reporting through the night, *OhmyNews* was the epicenter of reform-minded netizens). On the night of December 19th, when Mr Roh's victory was confirmed, I wrote on *OhmyNews*: "As of today, the long-lasting media power in Korea has changed. The power of media has shifted from conservative mainstream newspapers to netizens and Internet media."

Some critics said I exaggerated. Maybe that's the case. My declaration was made not by evaluating the last day's combat and the final results, but by two years of watching the Roh Moo Hyun campaign for the presidency. When Roh Moo Hyun began his bid for the presidency only one congressman supported him. And almost all conservative newspapers ignored or undervalued his campaign. But netizens were different. They strongly supported Roh because the young netizens, in their 20s to early 40s, wanted to reform Korean politics. The two-year process was a very significant example of the shift of media power."

If we look closely at *OhmyNews*'s success in influencing the political process in such a decisive way, we will notice that on the purely technical level, it is the specific nature of the internet that worked in its favour, especially because South Korea (as Oh acknowledges) is one of the most heavily wired countries in the world. The effectiveness of its strategy of mobilising voter turnout in favour of Roh Moo Hyun would have been greatly reduced if its medium had been print, in which case the question of updating content every 30 minutes through the final hours before polling would not arise. And since space is limited and fixed in a print environment, the kind of discussion that was posted throughout those crucial hours and ensured that liberal voters went to the polling stations, would have been impossible to reproduce in print.

South Korea's widespread broadband connectivity and wi-fi (wireless internet) infrastructure – as of April 2004, about a quarter of the world's total number of wireless 'hotspots' were located in this country alone despite its modest size – has helped *OhmyNews* start a web TV service called *OhmyTV* which serves news with citizen anchors just as *OhmyNews* serves news from citizen reporters. Todd Thacker, Editor of *OhmyNews International*, writes that citizen reporters and staff reporters are able to upload digital photographs and video feeds to the *OhmyNews* website in seconds through Korea Telecom's wi-fi network.[14]

While the specific nature of internet technology coupled with its quality and scale of expansion in South Korea has played an important role in ensuring the success of *OhmyNews* as an influential environment for participatory journalism, the site's policy on writing style is no less important. Unlike the traditional media, which tend to force reporters' 'voices' into a uniform mould by demanding standardisation, *OhmyNews* makes a conscious effort to keep citizen reporters' individual voices intact.

Stories submitted by contributors are often sent back and they are asked to write in their own personal styles instead of trying to imitate the conventional news writing style. As a result, not only is the journalism practised on this site a conversation rather than a 'lecture'[15] in substance, it also has the feel of a conversation in which citizens of all kinds – those who merely read the news and send feedback, those who contribute stories as citizen reporters, and those who are members of the site's own staff – share their concerns and aspirations with one another in their own voices.

The policy on style really is part of the site's larger policy of challenging the power of the traditional media. Oh says:

... (P)ower comes from established standards. Those who have power set the standards, and in this way are able to maintain their power. In the media market, too, they say 'this is the standard, follow me.' The standards of twentieth century journalism have been created and controlled by professional newspaper journalists. But these standards are challenged by new Internet journalists: the netizens or citizen reporters. They challenge the traditional media logic of who is a reporter, what is news, what is the best news style, and what is newsworthy.

Oh's words echo Foucault's thesis that power and discourse – the latter in the sense of forms of representation, codes, conventions and habits of language through which we define the world, including ourselves – are mutually implicated. In this view, power is about inclusion and exclusion, about designating certain things as acceptable and others as unacceptable, about enabling certain voices while silencing others.

In Foucault's view, 'discursive fields' (roughly coterminous with different social institutions), such as the law or the family, contain competing and contradictory discourses, some of which tend to curb the production of knowledge, dissent and difference, and others encourage these. In *OhmyNews*, Oh Yeon Ho clearly has created a vehicle for the second type of discourse in the discursive field of journalism.

## Blogs

The word 'blog' (popular abbreviation of web log) refers to online logs or journals, often maintained by individuals but sometimes also by corporate bodies and other organisations. The entries on these sites carry datelines and are usually arranged in reverse chronological order. Not all blogs are news-oriented, but some are, and these serve up analyses and opinion pieces in a format that is often akin to annotative reporting. Many of these focus on providing commentaries on news coverage in the mainstream media.

Blogs also post breaking news occasionally, and it was the blog-like *Drudgereport* site (www.drudgereport.com) that broke the Clinton-Lewinsky scandal. But this is relatively rare and the strength of blogs mainly lies in opinion and analysis. They have become a force to reckon with in the advanced industrial countries, so much so that a large number of news organisations today carry blog entries by their own reporters or editors on their web editions. *The New York Times* even has a section called *The Annotated Times* (http://nytimes.blogrunner.com/) in which it reproduces a selection of (external) blog entries that have commented on its own stories and also provides links to these.

A blog can be on any subject that is of interest to its author(s), but only those which have some relation to journalism – provide news, or analyses of/commentary on news, or commentary on news coverage in the media, or any combination of these – are relevant for the purpose of this book.

Just as access to online journalism is limited by the digital divide (discussed in chapter ten), it is natural that access to blogs also should be – and is – limited by this divide. Moreover, although blogs have proliferated over the last four or five years, they are still an overwhelmingly American phenomenon and relatively rare (though not negligible in terms of absolute numbers) in the Indian cyberspace.

If we still find it necessary to discuss this cultural practice, it is because blogs pose a challenge to the established power of the traditional media in a way similar to the challenge posed by open-source, participatory and citizen journalism.

Tim Wood notes[16] that blogs appeared mainly because of the people's frustration with the arrogance of the 'big media', on the one hand, and the nature of internet technology, on the other. "Bloggers quickly discovered that they could compete with and contest establishment reporting and commentary through the internet. The publishing medium is inexpensive and it provides access to facts and an audience not previously available." Bloggers took the major media organisations to task "for transparent distortions or juvenile logic" and even a newspaper like *The New York Times* has had to publish corrections in response to the commentary written by bloggers.

There are thousands of blogs today – probably even a million[17] or more. This explosion has come about because building and maintaining a blog is easy. There are several free blog building and hosting services available today. Among these are Livejournal (http://www.livejournal.com/), Google's Blogger or Blogspot (http://www.blogger.com/start), Lycos' Tripod (http://blog.tripod.lycos.com/), which also offers the Paypal credit card transaction service (http://blog.tripod.lycos.com/adm/redirect/www/build/paypal/) to those who would like to make commercial use of their blogs – say, offer content to others on payment.

## Some Important Blogs

The following are a few good examples of journalism-related blogs originating in the USA and UK:

- *InstaPundit* (http://www.instapundit.com/), maintained by Glenn Reynolds, a law professor at the University of Tennessee

- *AndrewSullivan* (http://www.andrewsullivan.com/), maintained by Andrew Sullivan, a columnist of *The New Republic* magazine

- *PressThink: Ghost of Democracy in the Media Machine* (http://journalism.nyu.edu/pubzone/weblogs/pressthink/), maintained by Jay Rosen, Associate Professor and former Chairman of New York University's Department of Journalism

- *DocSearls Weblog* (http://doc.weblogs.com/), maintained by Doc Searls, Senior Editor for the *Linux Journal*

- *Greg Palast: Journalism and Film* (http://www.gregpalast.com/blog.cfm), maintained by Greg Palast of the London *Observer*

## The Power of Blogs

The web logs mentioned in the box above, and many others – a list is available at http://www.cyberjournalist.net/cyberjournalists.php – are of high quality. However, the clearest indication that this type of practice has come to wield considerable influence over US media and politics came, not from one of these blogs but through the breaking of the Clinton-Lewinsky scandal on *Drudgereport* (http://www.drudgereport.com), a blog-like site maintained by a former Fox News correspondent, Matt Drudge.

According to Hall[18], a reporter of the *Newsweek* magazine was tipped off on acts of a sexual nature that had taken place between President Clinton and the White House intern, Monica Lewinsky. When *Newsweek* refused to publish the report, the story found its way to Matt Drudge in early 1998, and he posted the main points on *Drudgereport*. Since a large number of journalists in the USA are in the habit of regularly visiting this site for politics and media-related gossip and story tips, the scandal was immediately picked up by all the media, and the rest is history. Under these circumstances, *Newsweek*, too had no choice but to publish the story.

It is natural, therefore, that a section of the traditional media should try to blunt the edge that blogs have acquired. The manner in which they have done this, attests to the accuracy of Oh Yeon Ho's observation that those who have power, seek to perpetuate it by establishing standards to which others are required to conform. In the case of blogs, the attempt has been to put them – and anything else that is not published under the 'brand' of established media – outside the definition of journalism.

However, all blogs cannot be considered works of journalism by any stretch of the imagination. Many of them, perhaps the majority, are mere musings on bloggers' personal lives.

### Blogging vs. Journalism

The question of the relation in which blogging stands to journalism has assumed so much importance in the West that Harvard University's Nieman Foundation for Journalism devoted a sizeable section of its Fall 2003 report[19] to a discussion on this issue. Among the points noted in this section is the view, held by some, that the absence of editorial filtering before publication (posting) of content makes blogs unfit to qualify as journalism. The opposite view is that this filtering process kills much that is spontaneous and valuable in the content, in the pursuit of conformity with the established media's policy of legitimating only the discourse of the powers that be.

It is also noted that while bloggers who are not professional journalists, lack the training required to produce original reporting, their work can stimulate and catalyse reporting by the established media on issues left untouched or inadequately covered. In some circumstances, bloggers can even present readers/users with stories that professional journalists cannot.

Perhaps the most famous example of this was the blog maintained by a young Iraqi under the pseudonym Salam Pax from Baghdad during the second Gulf War in 2003. While the reporters who were 'embedded' with the attacking US forces were not free to move around and report as they pleased, the few that had remained in Baghdad were under surveillance by the Saddam regime. As such, Salam's blog was the only way for the rest of the world to have an eyewitness account of life in Baghdad during the war.

A large number of journalists in the West, especially the USA, have taken to blogging, mainly as a way of expressing themselves freely, without the usual constraints of editorial control. But this has not always been easy. Some news organizations have forced their reporters to shut down their blogs on the argument that these were in conflict with their professional duties. This was the case with CNN correspondent Kevin Sites, who had been reporting and blogging from Kuwait and later from Iraq before and during the war of 2003.

Realising the power of blogs, however, many other media companies have incorporated these in their operations. Among these are the *Guardian* (UK), *Malayasiakini* (Malaysia), the *Hindustan Times* (India), *The Washington Post*, *Newsweek*, the *Christian Science Monitor*, *MSNBC* and *USA Today* (all USA). But blogging on news sites is not necessarily as unfettered an activity as doing it independently, since some media organisations require their staffers' blog posts to be checked by editors before being uploaded.

There are now a large number of blogs maintained by Indians living both in India and abroad (a list is maintained by Anita Bora at http://indianbloggers.blogspot.com/). A handful of these for example, *Media Musings* (http://mediamusings.blogthing.com/) and Harini Calamur's *POV* (Point of View) (http://www.20six.co.uk/gargi) – focus on media and current affairs. Another such blog, *Mediaah* (http://mediaah.blogspot.com/), was reportedly shut down by its owner, Pune-based journalist Pradyuman Maheswari, after he received a legal notice from the *Times of India* over certain posts related to that newspaper.[20]

## Hyperadaptive News

This is the last of the concepts I shall mention with regard to online journalism. It refers to the use of all three characteristics – hypertextuality, interactivity and multimediality – while presenting news on the web. We should note that the term is useful only as a concept, and is not encountered on a day-to-day basis in the practice or even the study of online journalism.

# Exercises

1. Identify a news event or issue, which has been covered by a major newspaper in its print and online editions, and also by *Slashdot* and *Kuro5hin*.

    a. Discuss the differences among the four with reference to the core principles of journalism, such as fairness, accuracy and balance.

    b. Discuss differences among the four with reference to the depth and information content of their respective coverage.

    c. Try to find more examples of the type of journalism practised by *Slashdot* and *Kuro5hin*, and repeat the above exercises.

2. Repeat 1(a), (b) and (c) for *OhmyNews* and a major mainstream newspaper.

3. Choose an important issue or event and study the manner in which news-oriented blogs, both Indian and foreign, have discussed it. Compare this with discussions on the same subject taking place in the mainstream news media.

    a. Do you feel that the blogs offer information and/or insights not offered by the mainstream media? Do they present views from outside the elite?

    b. Identify and discuss the difference between the Indian and foreign blogs with reference to the above points.

# References

1 Deuze, M. 'Understanding the Impact of the Internet: On New Media Professionalism, Mindsets and Buzzwords', accessed 23 March 2005 on http://www.ejournalism.au.com/ejournalist/deuze.pdf.

2 Lisa, 'The Tragic Passing of Gary Webb', 12 December 2004, accessed 23 March 2005 on http://realhistoryarchives.blogspot.com/2004/12/tragic-passing-of-gary-webb.html.

3 'Hacker Journalism', *The Economist,* 4–10 December 1999, accessed 23 March 2005 on http://mailman.anu.edu.au/pipermail/link/1999-December/042308.html.

4 Moon, Jin, 'Open-source Journalism Online: Fact-checking or Censorship?', *Freedom Forum*, 10 October 1999, accessed 23 March 2005 on http://www.freedomforum.org/templates/document.asp?documentID=7802.

5   Ibid.

6   Bowman, Shayne, and Chris Willis, *We Media: How Audiences are Shaping the Future of News and Information* (Reston, VA, The Media Center at The American Press Institute, 2003), p.9, accessed 23 March 2005 on http://www.hypergene.net/wemedia/download/we_media.pdf.

7   Article on 'Citizen Journalism', *Wikipedia*, accessed 24 March 2005 on http://en.wikipedia.org/wiki/Participatory_journalism.

8   'OhmyNews a Marriage of Democracy and Technology', *OhmyNews International* accessed 6 April 2005 on http://english.ohmynews.com/articleview/article_view.asp?article_class=8&no=201599&rel_no=1.

9   'OhmyNews Makes Every Citizen a Reporter', interview with Yeon-Jung Yu, *Japan Media Review*, 17 September 2003, accessed 29 March 2005 on http://www.japanmediareview.com/japan/internet/1063672919.php.

10  Sanomat, Helsingin, 'In South Korea, Every Citizen Is a Reporter', tr. Antti Leppanen, *OhmyNews International*, accessed 6 April 2005 on http://english.ohmynews.com/articleview/article_view.asp? article_class=8&no=153109&rel_no=2.

11  Borton, James, 'OhmyNews and "Wired Red Devils"' *Asia Times Online,* 25 November 2004, accessed 10 April 2005 on http://www.atimes.com/atimes/Korea/FK25Dg01.html.

12  French, Howard W., 'Online Newspaper Shakes up Korean Politics', *The New York Times*, 6 March 2003 reproduced in *OhmyNews: Anatomy of a Full-fledged Multimedia News Service in Action* (Seoul, SeoulSelection, 2003), p.16.

13  'Korean Netizens Change Journalism and Politics', *OhmyNews International*, address by Oh Yeon Ho at Berkman Center, Information and Society Conference, Harvard University, 11 December 2004, accessed 10 April 2005 on http://english.ohmynews.com/articleview/article_view.asp?article_class=8&no=201423&rel_no=1 .

14  Thacker, Todd, 'Journalism's Ultimate Road Warriors', *OhmyNews: Anatomy of a Full-fledged Multimedia News Service in Action* (Seoul, Seoul Selection, 2003), p.11.

15  Dan Gillmor speaks of traditional journalism as the 'lecture' model of journalism, in his book - *We the Media: Grassroots Journalism by the People, for the People* (Sebastopol, CA, O'Reilly Media, Inc., 2004), p. 126, accessed 30 November 2004 on http://www.oreilly.com/catalog/wemedia/book/ch06.pdf.

16  Wood, Tim, 'Open Source Journalism is Here', *Moneyweb*, 13 September 2002 accessed 27 July 2003 on http://m1.mny.co.za/bb.nsf/0/C2256A2A005233 F985256C31007FFAAB?OpenDocument.

[17] Andrews, Paul, 'Is Blogging Journalism?' *Nieman Reports*, Fall 2003, p.63, accessed 7 May 2004 on http://www.nieman.harvard.edu/reports/03-3NRfall/63-64V57N3.pdf.

[18] Hall, Jim, *Online Journalism: A Critical Primer* (VA, Pluto Press, 2001), p.129.

[19] *Nieman Reports*, vol.57 no.3, Fall 2003, accessed 9 May 2004 on http://www.nieman.harvard.edu/reports/03-3NRfall/V57N3.pdf.

[20] Glaser, Mark, 'Indian Media Blog Shuts Down After Legal Threats From Times of India', *Online Journalism Review*, 15 March 2005, accessed 18 April 2005 on http://www.ojr.org/ojr/stories/050315glaser/.

# 5.
# Computer Assisted Journalism or Reporting

Today, it is difficult to imagine an Indian newsroom without computers, but this was not the case twenty years ago. It was in 1987, when I was a sub-editor with the Calcutta edition of *The Economic Times*, that I saw a few computers. They were Apple Macintosh desktops, commonly called 'Macs' now, and caused a great deal of excitement and bewilderment in our newsroom. Those days, even in places where computers had made an appearance, they were not connected to the internet as India was only taking its first tentative step towards the internet age. Newsroom computers were used mainly for writing and editing copy, and for preparing graphics.

The larger media houses, such as *The Hindu*, *The Times of India*, *The Indian Express* and the *Hindustan Times*, were the early adopters of this technology, and many smaller organisations went on with their old typewriters and ballpoint pens well into the 1990s. It goes without saying that the Indian media have come a very long way since then, and computers in today's newsrooms are extensively used not only for writing, copy-editing and graphics but also for performing the more complex tasks, which form the core of journalistic work.

These applications can be divided into two broad categories, namely, computers and the net as journalistic tools, and the net as a medium of mass communication. This chapter deals with the former through an account of the methods and consequences of what has come to be known as computer assisted reporting (CAR), and sometimes as computer assisted journalism (CAJ).

## The Four Rs of CAJ/CAR

As the name suggests, CAR or CAJ (I shall use the two abbreviations interchangeably.) is a matter of newsgathering and analysis. DeBrock writes[1] that it can be broken up into four Rs – reporting, research, reference and rendezvous. "Each of (these tasks)", he points out, "can be accomplished without a computer's assistance, but the use of a computer can speed up, simplify, and/or expand the range of the work."

Sometimes CAR is only seen as a matter of using email and listervs to identify and communicate with sources, and using the web for finding information. But it is much more than these in the scheme suggested by DeBrock. Furthermore, when the application of CAR is accompanied by an understanding of the *process* of communication on the part of the journalist, it can bring about certain qualitative developments in journalism that go beyond mere speed, simplification and enhancement of the range of work.

Speaking of the first R, DeBrock writes that reporting means "announc(ing) or relat(ing) the result of a special search, examination, or investigation". According to him computers can help reporters carry out such scrutiny through the use of spreadsheet programs for complex calculations, statistical programs for the analysis of large datasets, and database software for building their own repositories of information. It needs to be noted that by drawing the reporter's attention to trends that otherwise would have remained outside her knowledge, these exercises can lead to the production of important news or feature stories. They can also provide independent verification of information given to the reporter by sources. Common examples of spreadsheet, statistical and database programs are Microsoft Excel, SPSS (Statistical Package for the Social Sciences) and Microsoft Access, respectively.

Like reporting, research also involves a special search or investigation. The difference is that while reporting generally involves the use of primary sources, such as interviews, observation or data analyses conducted by the reporter herself, research uses secondary sources, that is, material derived from other material, such as reports, articles, and studies. A complete news report ideally consists of both reporting and research.

The third R stands for reference, which means consulting authoritative sources of information, such as dictionaries, encyclopedias, gazettes, almanacs and glossaries for checking facts, spellings, definitions etc. A vast number of such sources are available on the internet, some of which can be used free of cost while others are available for a fee. Many reference works, such as dictionaries and encyclopedias, are also available on CD-ROMs.

The fourth R stands for rendezvous, a place to which people "customarily come in numbers". Virtual communities on the net are electronic rendezvous spots, where journalists can communicate informally with other journalists, acquiring tips and ideas from one another. Anyone who has some experience of working as a reporter knows the importance of spending time with others of the profession in informal or semiformal settings, such as the press rooms or 'press corners' of secretariats, municipal bodies, police headquarters, offices of political parties, et cetera, or in the Press Club of the city or town in which one happens to be working. The journalist who avoids these places risks, among other things, missing major stories every now and then. In the internet age, listservs and websites meant for journalists, such as those of SAJA (South Asian Journalists' Association), are 'places' that are important in this respect.

## Precision Journalism

In DeBrock's definition of the first R, quantitative analysis of data is part of the reporting function of journalists. This is in conformity with the views of those like Philip Meyer who advocate what is known as precision journalism.[2] These journalists and teachers of journalism wish to see reporters use the quantitative research methods of social scientists in their own work, even to the extent of carrying out surveys and other types of quantitative research on their own rather than reporting on the research conducted by social scientists, market survey firms and other interested parties.

Most proponents of this type of precision journalism are to be found in the US. This is because the US has a strong quantitative tradition in social science, major linkages between journalism and mass communication research and social science research, and what are perhaps the world's most comprehensive databases on various aspects of the lives of individuals and society.

## Use of Email

In countries like India, journalism and mass communication research is far less developed, and so are databases. Moreover, most news organisations may not wish to, or cannot afford to spend resources on data analyses on a regular basis, not counting the election season polls sponsored by large media houses. As a result, it is the other aspects of CAR or CAJ that are gradually coming into use in countries like India. One of these is the use of email and email discussion groups or listservs by journalists.

For the reporter, email has the following advantages over the telephone as a medium of communication. (Here, we are mainly speaking of interpersonal communication between the reporter and her source.)

- Convenience: it shrinks distance and cuts the cost of communication. If the reporter knows the source's email address, expensive long-distance calls can be dispensed with, and this expands the horizon of possible sources geographically, to cover the entire globe. As a journalist, I have interviewed sources living in the USA and Sweden by email.

  Email also saves time and money in the transfer of text, graphics, formatted documents and multimedia content, all of which involved considerable shipping costs and delays before the use of email became widespread. For instance, to send a photograph to a journalist, a source not so long ago would have to either send the print by post or courier, or fax it. The former was time-consuming, as a result of which the immediacy of news would have been lost and faxing was expensive and often accompanied by serious degradation of image quality.

Today, the same picture can be sent, instantaneously, cheaply and without any degradation of quality, as an attachment with an email message.

- A major advantage of email as a medium of communication is that it allows the writer to edit the message before sending it. As every reporter knows, the most carefully planned interview conducted face-to-face or over the telephone can be marred by a single ill-conceived word or phrase from the reporter. This is usually sufficient to put the source on her guard or even make her hostile.

  Avoiding such pitfalls is not easy when one is working under pressure, especially for reporters who are new to the profession. If the interview or interaction is conducted by email, on the other hand, such situations can be largely avoided. Before sending the message, the reporter can take a little time to carefully consider the possible effect of her words on the intended recipient of the message.

  But this works both ways. Since the source also has time to weigh her words carefully before answering the journalist's questions, some of the spontaneity of the 'conversation' may be lost. As a result, bits of information which the source might have revealed on the spur of the moment during a spoken interview (without intending to do so), could be lost in an email interview.

- Furthermore, while a telephone conversation requires both parties to be available at one and the same time, they do not have to be online simultaneously in the case of an email interview, since email is asynchronous. A conversation can take place by email with each party reading and replying to the other's messages at her own convenience. While this does take away some of the spontaneity that is characteristic of face-to-face, and to a lesser extent, of telephonic interviews or conversations, it adds an important value – depth.

### Speech and Writing

Thus, in considering the consequences of email conversations or interviews we encounter an issue that has been debated at least since Plato's time, namely, the relative merits and demerits of orality and literacy. If we take this debate into account, it seems that as far as journalism is concerned, there aren't very solid grounds for privileging face-to-face interviews over email interviews across the board (see pp. 87–88).

## The Debate

In *Phaedrus,* one of Plato's *Dialogues,* Plato has Socrates tell the young Phaedrus[3] that writing is not truth, but "only the semblance of truth" and "even the best of writings are but a reminiscence of what we know". Writing, Socrates says, will engender forgetfulness, because learners "will not use their memories". Moreover, written works cannot defend themselves against questions: "(I)f you ask them a question they preserve a solemn silence ..."

It has been pointed out – by Ong[4], for instance – that Plato's critique of writing is weakened by the fact that it took the form of the very thing he was critiquing, namely, writing (in *Phaedrus*). It has also been argued that Plato's epistemology was in fact a rejection of the old oral culture, though not deliberately so.[5] Ong believes that writing has actually brought about fundamental changes in human consciousness. "(I)ntelligence is relentlessly reflexive," he writes, "so that even the external tools that it uses [in this case, writing – TR] to implement its workings become 'internalised', that is, part of its own reflexive process."[6]

But the most famous defence of writing in modern times has come from Derrida, whose deconstructionist work, *Of Grammatology,* challenges the Western tradition of treating writing as twice removed from thought, which originated in Plato and had been carried forward by scholars like Ferdinand de Saussure. Derrida's work is too complex and composed in too dense a style, typical of many poststructuralist thinkers, to lend itself to easy summarisation. However, an attempt to recount some of his arguments, though necessarily brief and simplistic, can help us appreciate from a new perspective what is involved in the use of email for interviews in the place of face-to-face meetings.

In Derrida's view the Western tradition is informed by the 'metaphysics of presence', which can be translated in crude terms as the assumption underlying Western epistemology that reality has an essence that is present behind the words used to describe or refer to it. Since thought is closest to this essence, that is, to the idea, which the speaker wishes to convey to the hearer, it is viewed as the term of central importance. Speech is seen as external to thought but an authentic expression of it. Hence, the actual, physical presence of the speaker near the hearer – which happens in spoken communication – is seen as the factor that ensures the value of the communication.

Writing is seen as external to and derived from speech, hence a type of communication of lower status. But, according to Derrida, words refer not to some essence of reality that is present but to other words, since a word's meaning can be grasped only with the help of other words. We can understand this idea if we think of the way we look up the meaning of a word in a dictionary.

Therefore, our quest for meaning leads us to the *difference* between words, and a continuous *deference* of meaning from word to word to more words. To signify this phenomenon that combines 'difference' and 'deference', Derrida coined the word 'differance'. The idea is also expressed by the aphorism, "There is nothing outside the text." If there is no way of getting to the essence (that is, to absolute truth) through words, there is no reason to privilege speaking over writing.

Moreover, according to Derrida, there is no language without writing, and speech is also a kind of writing[7]: "I believe that generalised writing is not just the idea of a system to be invented, an hypothetical characteristic or a future possibility. I think on the contrary that oral language already belongs to this writing. But that presupposes a modification of the concept of writing ..." Further, "(W)hat is natural to mankind is not spoken language but the faculty of constructing a language; i.e., a system of distinct signs corresponding to distinct ideas."

All this may sound like mere philosophical quibbling, but it has profound consequences for journalists. If it is unreasonable to give spoken, face-to-face communication a privileged position over written communication, there is no reason to see email interviews as being less authentic and less valuable than face-to-face interviews.

This, however, does not take anything away from the fact that much valuable aural and visual content, such as intonation, accent, body language and dress, are absent in written communication. It needs to be noted here that, generally speaking, journalism courses are excessively logocentric in that they concentrate on the words spoken by sources to the near exclusion of these non-verbal cues.

Even when dealing with verbal communication, their focus is rather narrow – it is not often that they train students to deal with anything but the mere surface meaning of spoken discourse. However, language being fundamentally metaphoric, as philosophers have often noted, this failure to engage with the issue of meaning, that is, to deal with the discourse of the subject/source on the rhetorical level – by such means as Kenneth Burke's 'dramatistic analysis'* in matters of special importance and at least in an intuitive way for day-to-day work – leaves many aspects of reality concealed behind the rhetorical content of the discourse.

The need for such an analytic engagement with language perhaps is even greater in the case of email interviews, because in this case the journalist has nothing but words to work with. Therefore, journalists in general and practitioners of CAR or CAJ in particular need some training in rhetorical analysis† if the meaning of things people say or write is to be probed to any depth.

But this requires on the part of teachers of journalism, and more importantly of editors, an acceptance of the view that interpretation is not necessarily bad for reporting. In any case reporting necessarily involves interpretation, as the very act of constructing a 'story' means imposing a pattern on discrete facts and events, and that in so-called straight reporting this act of pattern construction is merely masked by a minimalist style. My argument here is that email interviews conducted and analysed with even a moderate level of competence can be extremely productive from the journalist's point of view, and there is no need to consider them less valuable than face-to-face interviews. It is only that they require a different mix of skills from that required for face-to-face interviews.

---

\* Dramatistic and pentadic analyses are types of rhetorical analysis, which is the formal practice of reading texts in a critical manner, so as to bring out hidden meanings and motives of the speaker or writer. This is done by breaking up the text into its key parts and attending to the manner in which these relate to one another.

† See above.

### Problems with Email

However, like almost every technology, email is not an unmixed good. A study of journalists[8] in the US has found that they are concerned about several issues related to email. These are, in decreasing order of importance: junk mail (which clog users' inboxes and take up time to delete), loss of data due to viruses transmitted through email, damage to newsroom computer systems due to viruses, the lack of security of messages sent by them, the likelihood of their messages not reaching intended recipients, the possible loss of email messages, etc. Despite these worries, however, email has become a widely used mode of communication, obviously because its advantages outweigh its disadvantages.

Another issue that every journalist – indeed, every user – needs to keep in mind is that the net allows identity to be totally fluid and impersonation is an extremely easy thing to do. As Berkman and Shumway have noted,[9] "(The internet) ... makes it much more difficult – perhaps even impossible – to verify that a person's identity is really what he or she claims it is – age, sexual orientation, ethnicity, gender and all the other fundamental ways we categorize people become invisible online." As a dog tellingly remarked to another dog in a cartoon in *The New Yorker* magazine, "On the Internet, nobody knows you're a dog." The two animals were shown seated in front of a computer. This is why a large number of online crimes involving impersonation are being reported in which unsuspecting people are cheated. The reporter, therefore, has to exercise extreme caution while dealing with emails, especially from strangers.

## Use of Listservs and Newsgroups

The listserver, popularly known as listserv, is an important resource for the journalist. It is an email discussion group, in which subscribers can send messages to, and receive messages from, all other members of the group. The group has a collective email address and a message sent to this address goes to every subscriber. Therefore, listservs are an instance of many-to-many communication.

They are organised around particular fields of knowledge, profession or interest. For instance, the nettime list caters to people with an interest in the internet and the culture surrounding it. The US-based Cultstud and the India-based Sarai lists are for people with an interest in cultural studies. To be a subscriber of a listserv, one has to register with the computer server that maintains and supports that particular discussion group's list of email addresses and its activities, that is, the communication taking place among these addresses in accordance with rules set by a list administrator, who may be the person who 'owns' the list or someone who has been authorised by the 'list owner' to act as administrator.

Large lists of listservs – the number is in tens of thousands – are maintained by L-Soft International (http://www.lsoft.com/lists/listref.html), Meta-List.net (http://www.meta-list.net/query?acc=111en) and Tile.net (http://www.tile.net/lists/). These databases can be searched by anyone wishing to find listservs catering to the area of one's interest.

Newsgroups comprise another class of discussion groups. Unlike listservs, which function through email, newsgroups are web-based. Groups of one's interest can be found through various directories, such as Google (http://groups.google.com/advanced_group_search), Newsgroups.com (http://www.newsgroups.com/), and Tile.net (http://tile.net/news).

Discussion groups like listservs are valuable to the journalist in several ways. By 'listening in' on the discussion she can monitor public opinion on current events and issues, thus picking up important story ideas, and can identify potential sources for stories, as many listservs include academics and professionals. Public relations professionals can use listservs to send out press releases, thus making sure that these reach the targeted journalists almost instantly.

The importance of listservs to reporters can be illustrated with the help of my own experience. While lurking on a cultural studies list, that is, reading the messages being posted by members who were taking part in the discussion without taking part myself – I came across a message that interested me. It stated that a certain state government was about to sign a memorandum of understanding (MoU) with Microsoft for an e-governance package. The sender of the message felt that this would be detrimental to the people of the state, especially because India is a poor country and the government should opt, instead, for free software. Certain web addresses were given at the end of the message.

I had never heard of free software before. I searched the web for material on it and visited the sites listed in the message. From these, I learned what the term free software meant. I found out that an organisation called the Free Software Foundation, India, had its own listserv. I registered on that list and sent a message to it, expressing an interest in learning more about the subject and eventually writing a story on the state government's MoU with Microsoft. Leading members of the Foundation responded and, among other things, gave me the email address of Richard Stallman, a former scientist of the MIT Artificial Intelligence Laboratory, who is considered the father of the free software movement.

I emailed Stallman, Microsoft, the state government and others with questionnaires. Stallman responded and I wrote a story that appeared in the op-ed page of the newspaper I was serving at the time. The point I would like to stress here is that I would not have learnt of the issue, and my readers would not have become aware of some of the merits and demerits of proprietary software (sold by Microsoft and many other companies) vis-a-vis free software if I had not been reading the discussion on a listserv. Also, it is through a listserv that I identified and communicated with the sources.

### Ethical Issues

The use of listservs and other types of discussion forums presents the journalist with certain ethical dilemmas. Berkman and Shumway[10] point out that they raise the following questions:

> (S)hould journalists, academic researchers or public relations professionals gather information by lurking in chat rooms? If they do, what are their responsibilities with regards to the privacy of the other participants? Should journalists identify themselves accurately and state their purposes upon entering a chat room or logging on to a message board? Is it OK to lurk for a while before identifying oneself? Is it OK to quote from a message posted in a chat room?

The authors say that discussion forums often have their own rules of online behaviour and a journalist wishing to use such forums should abide by these. However, this may not be an easy task, as they have illustrated with the following case study.

In its 10 December 2001 issue, *The New York Times Magazine* published 'Lonely Gay Teen Seeking Same', an 8,000-word feature by Jennifer Egan, author and journalist. It was about homosexual teenagers interacting with others of their kind in internet chat rooms meant for people like them, and sometimes being pursued by older individuals impersonating as teenagers.

Egan, who was in her thirties, had been researching the story since 1999, and had initially gained access to several chat rooms by entering a false identity and age in their registrations forms. After lurking for several weeks to familiarise herself with the conversation, she had finally posted a message identifying herself as a reporter and inviting the teenagers to be interviewed. Although the initial response was poor, she eventually interacted with several teenagers by email and even met one of them in person. This is how she gathered the material for her story.

Since impersonation is usually viewed as an act of deception, Egan had to go through some soul-searching while passing herself off as a teenager. She did it because she realised that she might have been denied access if she had entered her true age and identity, thus losing an opportunity to identify and contact potential sources. Also, if she had identified herself as a reporter and posted her invitation for interviews immediately after registering instead of lurking for some weeks, she might have disrupted the conversation by putting the participants on their guard.

Egan felt that she had to be guided by the 'do no harm' principle, which judges the ethical value of an action by looking at its effect – if some harm is done to others, the action is considered unacceptable. In Egan's case, no harm was done. On the contrary, her work brought to light the ease with which nominally 'members only' chat rooms can be infiltrated by people who usually would not be welcome, and the way such chat rooms provide opportunities for older sexual predators to prey on lonely teenagers. Egan also confronted the problem of determining whether the sources she was interviewing were really the teenagers they claimed to be, and tried to solve this by talking to them over telephone and meeting them if possible (only one person agreed).

Apart from the propriety of impersonation, Berkman and Shumway write, there is also a debate over the nature of such online communities. Some feel that they are 'private spaces' as registration is required to become members, but others feel they are 'public spaces' since such registration procedures can be circumvented with ease, as Egan's case showed. Furthermore, the use of quotes from chat room conversations or bulletin boards without permission is considered improper and some believe it may be unethical for journalists, especially comments that are of a deeply personal nature and those made by minors.

Thus, there are quite a few grey areas in the ethics of using listservs and other discussion forums, especially because the internet is a relatively new medium of communication. The journalist has to deal with these case by case, with full regard to their concrete contexts.

## Searching the Web

As we know, the world wide web is a vast storehouse of information. But finding information that fits one's specific requirement demands certain background information and skills. There are two main ways in which one may search the web – by using directories and by using search engines.

## Directories

Directories are indexes of websites classified hierarchically, and different directories do this classification in somewhat different ways. Among the most popular are those of Yahoo!, Google and About.com. For instance, the Yahoo! directory (http://dir.yahoo.com/), which is perhaps the most popular directory, organises the web under the following headings on the first level: Arts & Humanities, Business & Economy, Computer & Internet, Education, etc. Each of this is further divided into sub-classes. Arts & Humanities is subdivided into Photography, History, Literature, etc. Under Literature come Authors, Awards, Banned Books, Chats & Forums, Classics, etc. For some reason, however, it is accessible through the 'Directory' link on the international site of Yahoo! (http://www.yahoo.com/) but not from that link on the Indian site of Yahoo! (http://in.yahoo.com/).

As for the Google directory (http://www.google.co.in/dirhp?hl=en) – which has merged with Netscape's dmoz Open Directory – its first level has Arts, Business, Computers, Games, Recreation, Reference, etc. Under Reference, one finds Education, Libraries, Maps, etc. Under Education are grouped Alumni Directories, Colleges and Universities, Distance Learning, Subjects, etc. The Subjects index has 38 entries, such as Archaeology, Arts, Earth Sciences, Philosophy, etc. The Philosophy index is divided into Categories and Web Pages. The first has Academic Departments, Ethics, Organizations, Philosophy for Children, and Writing Guides. Each of these in turn has its own sub-index. The 'Web Pages' head, as the name suggests, lists a number of websites that offer resources for studying and teaching philosophy.

## Search Engines

Perhaps the most powerful tool for searching the web is the search engine. It is a class of computer programs that search the web for sites matching keywords or key phrases typed in by users in their search fields. There are scores (probably several hundred) search engines, and there are sites such as Search Engine Colossus (http://www.searchenginecolossus.com/) and SearchEngineWatch (http://searchenginewatch.com/) that specialise in listing and providing news updates on search engines from across the world. Different engines often use different algorithms[‡] for searching the web according to the keywords provided by users and ranking the search results.

While it is to some extent a matter of personal preference – different people like different search engines – the most popular one today is Google. Many prefer Teoma, which is more recent than Google, and others continue to use older ones like Yahoo!, AltaVista, Lycos, Excite, NorthernLight, etc. Meta-search engines constitute a subclass of programs within this group. These engines – such as AskJeeves (http://www.askjeeves.com/), Dogpile (http://www.dogpile.com/) and MetaCrawler (http://www.metacrawler.com /) – send out queries to a number of normal search engines and present the results to the user.

However, the overabundance of information on the web presents the user with certain difficulties. Depending on the keyword(s) and the search engine used, a single search may yield anything from tens to millions of web addresses. For instance, a search for 'online journalism' with Google yielded about 5,020,000 results (URLs or addresses) in a mere 0.11 second. Obviously, the journalist (or anyone else) who wishes to use this powerful tool needs some way of separating the wheat from the chaff.

Before describing the evaluation process, however, it needs to be noted that the volume of search results can and should be limited by a careful selection of keywords. This vastly simplifies the task of elimination through evaluation. While the term 'online journalism' in Google's search field had been typed without the quotation marks, typing the same two words with the quotation marks brings down the number of search results to about 391,000 in 0.32 seconds. In other words, the new search returned less than a twelfth of the addresses and took almost three times as long as the first search.

---

[‡] An algorithm is "a process or set of rules to be followed in calculations or other problem-solving operations, especially by a computer" (*Concise Oxford English Dictionary*).

This happened because the use of quotation marks had limited the search to those pages on which the exact phrase was present, that is, the two words were present together and in the very order in which they had been typed. In the first search, carried out without the quotation marks, the Google search engine searched the web for pages containing either or both of the two words. Such strategies, and an understanding of the basic Boolean operations 'and', 'or' and 'not', which are needed for improving the search process, are available in the tutorial pages of most major search engines.

### Shortlisting URLs

Once the results list is returned by the search engine, the two-step elimination process begins. Since it would be impossible to check each of the 391,000 pages for suitability by clicking on the links given and viewing the pages that are thereby called up – for that matter, it would be very difficult to check even 391 pages in this way, not to speak of 391,000 – we need to reduce this number to manageable proportions. The first step therefore consists in eliminating individual results simply by looking at the URLs.

If the URL contains what appears to be a person's name, such as 'tray' or 'rayt', 'tapasray' or 'raytapas', sometimes (but not always) after a tilde sign (~), a percent sign (%) or words like 'user(s),' 'member(s),' and 'people', and the server belongs to a commercial ISP, it is likely that the page in question is someone's personal page. This is not sufficient ground for rejecting the page, but in such cases, the journalist (or any other user) needs to carefully investigate the identity and background of the page owner, because in such cases the domain owner – say, Yahoo!'s Geocities web hosting service or Lycos' Tripod service – does not claim responsibility for the information contained in the pages.

Next, one needs to look for a match between the kind of information source one is looking for, and the type of domain to which the page belongs. For instance, if one wants to find information on lung cancer, it may not be wise to choose a site in the .com (commercial) domain, because such a site could be linked to pharmaceutical companies or tobacco companies, both of which are likely to have their own agendas. It might be safer to use sites in the .gov (government), .edu (education), .ac (academic), .org (non-profit organisation) or the new and relatively rare .res (research) domains.

However, this presents problems in certain cases. In India, for instance, government websites are yet to be standardised in terms of domains. While sites of various ministries and departments of the Government of India are mostly in the .nic.in domain (National Informatics Centre, India), some state governments continue to maintain their websites in other domains. The address of the Kerala government site (http://www.kerala.gov.in/) gives a clear indication that it is a government site in India, but the West Bengal government site (http://www.wbgov.com/e-gov/English/EnglishHomePage.asp) is in the commercial domain.

The third point to note is whether the 'publisher' – the person or entity that owns the server – is appropriate for the kind of information source one is looking for. An example will be helpful in illustrating the point. Suppose a web search for news on the Ayodhya crisis[§] in *The Indian Express* newspaper turns up, among others, the link to a report titled 'Advani begs to differ, rules out apology for demolition' (http://www.hvk.org/articles/0198/0084.html).

The entry for the page on the results list mentions the Express News Service as the author of the contents of the page. However, it would be wrong to take it as authentic Indian Express content, as the server name in the URL is 'hvk', which is obviously not of the Express group of newspapers. If we truncate back the URL (deleting parts of the URL from the right) until we reach the domain (.org), we find that the page is part of the site http://www.hvk.org, which belongs to an organisation called the Hindu Vivek Kendra (Hindu Conscience Centre).

### Evaluating Pages

Once a shortlist of URLs has been made through this process of elimination, one needs to visit the pages on the shortlist by clicking on the selected links given on the results list and check the actual pages for suitability.

First, one needs to look for links that read 'About', 'About us', 'Philosophy', 'Background', 'Biography', 'Who am I', 'Who we are', etc. These usually appear on the periphery of the page. If none of these can be found on the page, the URL has to be truncated back step by step, that is, the strings of characters that appear after each 'back slash' sign ( / ) deleted one string at a time, and the pages that open with the truncated URL checked for the above links. This may have to continue until one reaches the back slash sign immediately after the domain, that is, .com, .edu, .gov, etc.

---

[§] The demolition of Babari Masjid by activists of radical Hindu organisations in 1992

If one of these links is found at any stage of the exercise, the page that opens with the link should provide some information about the identity of the author and/or publisher – these may be either individuals or organisations – and some indication of the reasons for putting up the page. In any case, someone should claim responsibility for the page. If no such name of a person or organisation can be found, it would not be wise to use the information contained in the page.

If some information on the credentials of the author(s) and/or publishers is found, the user needs to decide whether these qualify them to write on the subject matter of the page. Since publishing on the web is inexpensive, thousands of people put up pages on every conceivable topic, with diverse intentions or motives. Therefore, the intending user of such information has to be extremely careful in selecting the pages.

She should exercise at least the same degree of caution as she would with printed matter, perhaps even more. The Berkeley tutorial suggests that the user ask herself the following questions: Is the author simply a hobbyist? Is the content of the page merely some individual's or organisation's opinion? Is there any reason to believe its content more than that of any other page? Does it contain a diatribe against someone or something, or an extreme view, possibly distorting or exaggerating facts?

One also needs to look for a date with the words 'last updated' or something to that effect. Usually, these can be found at or near the top of the page or the bottom. This will tell the user whether the information in the page is current or dated. However, a page that has not been updated recently is not necessarily useless. It will be useful if one is looking for information on events that had taken place in the past.

For instance, a search for 'Ayodhya timeline' brings us to a BBC page titled 'Timeline: Ayodhya crisis' (http://news.bbc.co.uk/1/hi/world/south_asia/1844930.stm). An entry below the BBC masthead reads: 'Last Updated: Friday, 17 October 2003, 11:57 GMT 12:57 UK'. The last entry in the timeline is for September 2003.

Although this page has not been updated since 17 October 2003, it has several possible uses for anyone wishing to write on the Ayodhya issue. One of these is as a starting point for her research. But the writer must also look for other pages for information on developments that have taken place since 17 October 2003. The point I would like to stress here is that one needs to know *when* the page was last updated, and whether it is current or not; there should be a match between one's requirement and this date.

If a page has passed the above tests in the eyes of the user, the next step is to evaluate the quality of information it offers. An important indicator of quality is the presence of references to the sources from which the information has been culled, in the form of footnotes or links (appearing as 'links', 'additional sites', 'related links', etc.). According to the Berkeley guide the questions to ask here are: Are sources documented with footnotes or links? If there are links to other pages as sources, are they to reliable sources? Do the links work?

Though meant primarily for students using the web for research, the following explanation from the guide is also useful for journalists:

> In scholarly/research work, the credibility of most writings is proven through footnote documentation or other means of revealing the sources of information. Saying what you believe without documentation is not much better than just expressing an opinion or a point of view. What credibility does your research need? An exception can be journalism from highly reputable newspapers. But these are not scholarly ... Links that don't work or are to other weak or fringe pages do not help strengthen the credibility of your research.

If material is reproduced from other sources, the user needs to ensure that it is complete, has not been altered from the original, and is not fake or forged. The questions to ask here are: Is it retyped? (If so, it could easily have been altered.) Are permissions to reproduce and copyright information provided? If there are no links to the original source even though it is online, is there a reason for this? The tutorial explains that the user may have to find the original to satisfy herself on these questions.

If she finds a piece taken from a reputable media outlet (newspaper, magazine, radio station, television channel or website), journal or other publication reproduced on the page being evaluated, it should be accompanied by the copyright statement and/or permission to reprint. If there is no such entry, she needs to treat the page with suspicion.

If the page provides a reference link to another page as its source of information, but the URL of the latter is not of the original source, there is a possibility that it might have been illegally reproduced in the latter, and the text might have been altered, even if the copyright information is present.

The HVK page with a report purportedly from *The Indian Express* mentioned earlier in this chapter, is not the 'original source'. Nor does it contain any copyright or permission statement from *The Indian Express*. What it does contain is the following: 'Copyrighted ©1994-2003, HinduNet Inc.' As such, it would be unacceptable as a legitimate reference, and a page that uses this HVK page as a source of information – perhaps by providing a link to it – would be of no value to journalists and other researchers unless, of course, the topic of research is the improper practices of reproducing information, prevalent on the web.

If the user is satisfied that the references provided on the page under evaluation are original sources, she needs to check these for bias. The Berkeley guide states that the page being evaluated is likely to be balanced and unbiased if its reference (linked) pages represent a diversity of opinion and not just its own. However, we need to note that for journalists, the presence of bias cannot be a sufficient reason for rejecting a page. On contentious issues, a web page put up by any individual or organisation that takes sides – say, a political party or a religious organisation – cannot be expected to link to pages that represent views opposed to its own, except to show them in a poor light. Such pages would still be of value to a journalist as long as she uses these with an understanding of the context and motive, and does not assume the information to be balanced.

Next, it is important to check what others think of the page the user is evaluating. This can be done by finding out whether other pages, put up by other people, link to this page. This can be done by typing 'link:' (without the quotation marks) in the search field of Google or Yahoo!, pasting the page's URL after the colon mark ( : ) and pressing the Enter key.

By pasting the URL in the search field of alexa.com, the user may be able to find more information of this kind in addition to a list of sites that link to the page – traffic rank of the page, reviews on it, site statistics, and contact and/or ownership information. If the links are from the same site as the page being evaluated, obviously this should not count as a recommendation. However, the user needs to pay attention to external links, that is, links from other sites, even if these are from fans or critics.

One may also look up reputable directories, such as About.com and Infomine, for entries on the page. The Berkeley tutorial points out that since these directories mention a very small percentage of all existing websites, a mention is an indication of a certain degree of quality.

Searching for the author's name with Google or Yahoo! is also likely to unearth considerable information useful for evaluating the page.

After all the above steps, the journalist needs to add up her findings in her own mind, using the fine and indefinable sense called judgement. As I have mentioned earlier, a variety of intentions or motives are at work behind the billions of pages being put up on the web. The journalist needs to ask herself what the intention or motive of the author and/or publisher might be. Some possibilities are: to inform, give facts, give data, explain something, persuade someone about something, sell something, entice someone, share something, or disclose something.

The journalist also needs to be sensitive to the tone of the page and ask herself whether it is humorous, whether it might be a parody, whether it might have exaggerations or put forward overblown arguments. She needs to be careful to check whether it contains outrageous photographs or a juxtaposition of unlikely images. All these might work as red flags to the intending user. And finally, the user must look within herself to see whether she is being fair in judging the page, whether she is letting her personal biases colour her judgement.

## Exercises

1. Open an email account, if you do not already have one, and get accustomed to its use.

2. Identify a subject of interest, find listservs organised around it from websites mentioned in this chapter, join as many such listservs as you can, identify story ideas and possible sources from the discussion, interview such sources by email, and write a story on the basis of these.

3. Identify a subject of interest, carry out web searches with a few different search engines, identify the engine which serves your requirements best, evaluate the search results using the procedure described in the chapter, and write a story on the basis of information found on the selected pages.

4. Write a story on a subject of your choice after gathering information from both listservs and web searches, and then combining and cross-checking each with the other.

Note: *For further material on using search engines you can go to the following online tutorials:*

- *'Beyond General Web Searching,' http://www.lib.berkeley.edu/ TeachingLib/Guides/Internet/BeyondWeb.html.*

- *'Evaluating Information Found on the Internet,' http://www.library.jhu. edu/researchhelp/general/evaluating/–.*

# References

1   DeBrock, Ron, 'Computer Assisted Reporting Basics', *Reporters,* Illinois Press Association, 4 December 2000, accessed 9 January 2005 on http://www.il-press.com/main.asp?SectionID=44&SubSectionID=244&ArticleID =938&TM=46070.09.

2   Meyer, Philip, *The New Precision Journalism* (Indiana University Press, 1991), accessed 13 January 2005 on http://www.unc.edu/~pmeyer/book/.

3   Plato, *Phaedrus,* tr. Benjamin Jowett, Project Gutenberg Etext, accessed 20 January 2005 on http://www.gutenberg.org/dirs/etext99/phdrs10.txt.

4   Ong, Walter J., *Orality and Literacy: The Technologizing of the Word* (London and New York, Routledge, 1988), p. 79.

5   Ibid.

6   Ibid., p. 80.

7   Derrida, Jacques, *Of Grammatology* (Baltimore, Johns Hopkins University Press, 1974), accessed 21 January 2005 on http://www.hydra.umn.edu/derrida/ ofgramm.html.

8   Garrison, Bruce, 'The Use of Electronic Mail as a Newsgathering Resource', paper presented to the Newspaper Division, Association for Education in Journalism and Mass Communication, 10 August 2002, Miami Beach, Florida, accessed 21 November 2004 on http://www.miami.edu/com/car/miamibeach2.htm.

9   Berkman, Robert I. and Christopher A. Shumway, *Digital Dilemmas: Ethical Issues for Online Media Professionals* (Iowa, Blackwell Publishing, 2003), accessed 21 November 2004 on http://www.ojr.org/ojr/ethics/1065048923.php.

10  Ibid.

# 6.
# Preparing Online Packages

The previous chapters dealt with the way new forms of journalism are coming into being through the innovative use of the internet's characteristics. However, proper use of this technology requires knowledge of certain techniques, which will be discussed in the present chapter. This will be followed by examples of the successful application of these techniques, as well as instances of failure. The chapter will end with a brief discussion of news editing practices in the online media.

## Writing and Preparing Packages for the Web

### Main Considerations

There are two important considerations to be kept in mind while preparing online news packages.

### *Is it about Written, Visual or Aural Information?*

For a journalist who is required to perform the functions of a reporter or an editor for a news-oriented website, the first point to remember is that the web is neither mainly about writing as

is the case with the print media, nor purely about visuals and sound, as in television.

It is, or can be, a combination of writing with various types of visual elements plus audio, and this complex mix is given yet another dimension by interactivity. As Dube notes[1], "Online journalists must think on multiple levels at once: words, ideas, story structure, design, interactives, audio, video, photos, news judgment. TV is about showing the news. Print is more about telling and explaining. Online is about showing, telling, demonstrating and interacting."

This has to be a conscious activity on the part of the journalist, since most of those who work for news websites – especially in countries like India, where the online media have been late to develop – start out as print or broadcast journalists and are later assigned to the online editions of their respective news outlets, or move to web-only news organizations which in any case are extremely rare as far as India is concerned. In this context, Dube says:

> It's easy for online journalists, most of whom have been trained in traditional media, to stick to broadcast and print storytelling forms. But that would be a waste. In online journalism you have many more elements to choose from – so use them. Combine the best of each world:
>
> • Use print to explain
> • Use multimedia to show
> • Use interactives to demonstrate and engage.

## Reading Behaviour

The second point to remember is that people's reading behaviour on the web is substantially different from their reading behaviour in print:

1. The majority of web users scan web pages instead of reading every word according to the authors of a writing guide for the web, made available online by Sun Microsystems.[2] The same authors say that reading from computer screens is 25 per cent slower than in print.

2. Web users "tend to be more proactive than print readers or TV viewers, hunting for information rather than passively taking in what you present to them,"[3] according to the publisher of *Cyberjournalist*, a website of the American Press Institute dedicated to online journalism.

3. Online news readers "read shallow but wide, while at the same time pursuing selected topics in depth" concluded an eyetracking study jointly conducted by Stanford University and the Poynter Institute.[4] In the study web users wore a headgear that tracked their eye movements as they read web pages.

4. The eyes of the participants in the above mentioned survey systematically went over more than 75 per cent of the length of almost all the articles they read. This, the authors pointed out, might be a natural consequence of the fact that one has to take purposeful action to read an article online. A headline or 'brief' (summary of an item, usually two or three lines long, found on the main or 'front' page of a news website) has to be clicked to call up the full story on the screen.

   We should note that this action implies the investment of time, energy and also money, since use of the web usually involves a financial cost in proportion to the time spent online or to the amount of data downloaded and uploaded in the course of one's browsing or other online activity. In contrast, a reader may abandon an item in a print newspaper after reading a smaller portion. In this case reading often involves chance – the reader often starts reading an item when his eyes fall on it while reading another item or simply skimming over the page – and it does not involve any added cost over the price of the newspaper.

## Approach to Online Journalism

The task of online journalists may appear complicated in the light of the points discussed above, but several useful articles and guides available online provide a structured approach to the problem. Their recommendations are summarised below.

### Flexibility

Different stories call for different approaches, and the online journalist should not apply the same approach to every story. For instance, one particular story may be substantially improved if links to audio or video files are provided with the text, but this may be completely inappropriate for another story. Therefore, the journalist should not try to link audio and video files to every story.

## Creativity

It must be remembered, at all times, that the web can support a much richer form of journalism than either print or broadcast. This potential must be exploited to the maximum extent possible under the specific circumstances of any given story. This requires creative thinking.

## Intelligent Handling

Some stories allow a relatively long lead-time and the journalist can take the help of creative design professionals to implement innovative ideas. Other stories may have to be posted on the website as quickly as possible. In the second case, the journalist may have to take the 'shovelware' approach, that is, post the print edition's content online without rewriting it to suit the web or augmenting it in any way with hyperlinks to related material, multimedia content, interactive elements, etc.

## Planning the Package

Having adopted this orientation, the first step that is required is to plan the manner in which the story is to be presented, that is, the elements that will make up the online package. Rich[5] points out that because of the hypertextual nature of the web, news writers need to visualise their stories differently from print. The first step which needs to be taken before the reporting process begins is to decide on the format that would be appropriate for the story and to discuss the elements that might be linked to it. This is similar to the way one plans a feature story or a major news package in the print medium, as a main story with sidebars. The question to be asked and answered at this stage is: What is the best way to tell the story at hand?

Different stories call for different formats. While some may work well with a linear text format, that is, in a straight line from beginning to end like a common news report in a printed newspaper, others may not, and it needs to be kept in mind that the web is a nonlinear medium, that is, readers/users on the web access information in any order they choose. Some of the elements and features that should be considered at this stage are:

- Timelines: Is the nature of the story such that a background, created as a timeline, will enhance its value?

- Interactivity: Will the story go well with a discussion question, poll, quiz, searchable database or other information the reporter may need to gather in order to get the readers involved?

- Lists or data for full coverage: Will it be appropriate to provide with the story a complete list of contest winners, test scores or other information on the lines of the practice sometimes followed for sports stories?

- Mini-profiles: Will it be appropriate to provide short biographies of the sources? An example is an election-related feature, where a short biography of the candidates may enhance its value.

- Multimedia: Will a video clip go well with the story? If the answer is yes, a video photographer may have to be assigned. It has to be decided whether audio will go with the story, in which case 'sound bites' may have to be taped by the reporter.

- Related links: It has to be decided who should suggest or gather links to related material on the web.

- Email addresses of reporters: Will these be provided with the story? If so, will reporters respond to messages from readers?

## Forms of Online Packages

Once the above points have been considered, the appropriate form for the story or package can be chosen from the following options mentioned by Dube[6].

### *Print Plus*

This is the most common format. Its basic element is a text item, which is usually not written for the web – such as a newspaper story or one received from a news agency. Other elements, such as photographs, links and video clips, are added to the page containing the story. This is a relatively cheap and easy way of creating an online package from items that are already available, that is, of repackaging content produced by the traditional media. However, Dube points out, this method does not make full use of the web's potential.

### Clickable Interactives

The most common instances are interactive versions of traditional newspaper and TV graphics, such as maps, which are provided to supplement the information contained in a story. However, this method can also be used to construct whole stories. Such packages usually contain both linear and non-linear storytelling, and may use multimedia elements. The reader or user is given some choices, but is also guided along a path. Dube notes that such packages are time-consuming to construct, but have produced "some of the most innovative online journalism". His examples are, *Catastrophic Collapse* (http://www.usatoday.com/graphics/news/gra/wtccollapse/frame.htm), *Experience a Hacker Attack* (http://www.msnbc.com/news/437641.asp), *Market Map* (http://www.smartmoney.com/marketmap/), and *The Rise, Fall and Rebirth of AT&T* (http://abcnews.go.com/sections/business/popoff/att_timeline2_popoff/index.html).

### Slideshows

These can be used not only to present a number of images one after the other, but also to present whole stories by providing text-based information in the caption fields of the images. The images (usually photographs) have to be selected in such a way that they tell a cohesive story when placed in a certain sequence. Dube's examples are, the *NYTimes.com photographer's journals from Afghanistan* (http://www.cyberjournalist.net/news/000117.php#), the *WashingtonPost.com* feature, *U.S. Under Attack* (http://www.washingtonpost.com/wp-dyn/photo/dayinphotos/G17490-2001Sep12.html), the *MSNBC slideshows* (http://www.msnbc.com/news/173305.asp), and the *WashingtonPost.com CameraWorks* ([http://www.washingtonpost.com/wp-dyn/photo/index.html).

### Audio Stories

The use of audio can be extremely effective when one is able to use sounds that cannot be described in words. For instance, people sometimes say things in such a way that their manner of speaking adds meaning which the words themselves do not convey. Such sounds can make very good stories. Along with the sound file, the speaker's photo should also be linked with the text. Among stories that can be enhanced in this way are those containing quotations from ordinary people and experts. Dube's examples are: *Inside the Church of Bethlehem, Frontiers of War, 102 Minutes* (http://www.msnbc.com/modules/aa587/audio_reax/default.htm),

*Audio Man on the Street* (http://www.msnbc.com/modules/aa587/ audio_reax/default.htm), *Threats facing U.S. forces: Ask the experts* (http:/ /www.msnbc.com/news/642867.asp#audioapp), and *Forecasting the Future* (http://www.msnbc.com/news/siliconsummit_front.asp?launch=/ modules/silicon_summit2/predictions/).

### Narrated Slideshows

These combine slideshows, with audio and video. Photographs and audio sound bites are selected in such a way that they complement one another. As the images appear one after the other, the corresponding audio clips play automatically. Examples are, *Eyewitnesses remember Columbine* (http://abcnews.go.com/sections/us/DailyNews/littleton_eyewitness.html), *Voices of Columbine* (http://www.cyberjournalist.net/news/000117.php#), and *Casualties of War* (http://www.msnbc.com/modules/kosovorefugees/ default.asp).

### Live Chats

When chat sessions are moderated properly, they can be used as an interactive version of the question-answer story format, with readers asking the questions. This can be an effective way of conveying information, since the story is given direction by readers. Examples are, *Columbine High School shooting* (http:// www.abcnews.go.com sections/us/DailyNews/chat_dube990423.html), *The World Trade Organization protests* (http://www.abcnews.go.com/sections/ us/DailyNews/chat_wtoprotests120199.html), *On the scene in Pakistan* (http:/ /www.msnbc.com/news/647360.asp) and *Oscars wrap-up* (http:// more.abcnews.go.com/sections/entertainment/DailyNews/chat_oscarwrap .html).

### Quizzes and Surveys

These can also be used to tell stories by organising the information as a set of questions and answers. This can be effective, Dube notes, because it engages the reader. Examples are: *Choosing a console* (http://www.msnbc.com/ news/techgames_front.asp?launch=/modules/game_consoles/ game_plan), *Invasion of Privacy* (http://www.msnbc.com/news/ TECHPRIVACYSERIES_front.asp?launch=/modules/privacy_online/quiz, and *Test Your Economic Literacy* (http://www.cyberjournalist.net/news/ 000117.php#).

### Animated Stories

This is an effective visual method to be used when photographs or video clips are not available or not possible. However, animation should be used sparingly, as it often diverts the user's attention from the story proper. Animation can be used to make newspaper infographics lively, to recreate an event that has motion or action, and to explain an event or a process. They can also be used for cartoons and other humourous items. Examples are, *The Enemy Below* (http://www.msnbc.com/news/NW-SHOWCASE_Front.asp?launch=/modules/newsweek/enemy_below/), *Molecular Motors* (http://www.msnbc.com/news/techfrontier_front.asp?launch=/news/wld/graphics/molecular_motors_dw.htm), *Race in Southern California: 1940-2000* (http://www.latimes.com/news/nationworld/census/la-census-race-anim.graphic), and *Hurricanes: How They Happen* (http://www.guardian.co.uk/flash/0,5860,773980,00.html).

### Interactive Webcasts

Links to related stories and other material like chats and polls can be provided with streaming video, making the experience richer than mere webcast, that is, TV on the web. There are even more sophisticated techniques, such as those in which text, links, et cetera, can be accessed at certain points in the video stream. MSNBC.com offered such content during the 2000 US presidential debates – along with the video of the debate, a Debate Monitor panel appeared on the user's computer screen and was continuously updated with facts related to the statements each candidate made, in real time. Examples are, *Yahoo! Finance Vision* (http://financevision.yahoo.com/) and *MSNBC's Silicon Summit* (http://www.msnbc.com/modules/silicon_summit2/default.asp).

### Multimedia Interactives

Sometimes various formats are combined to construct news packages. A sophisticated way of doing this is to use the Flash animation technology to weave together some or all of the following – text, clickable graphics, audio, photos, video, polls or quizzes –creating comprehensive and complex interactive packages. Examples are, *U Street in Focus* (http://www.washingtonpost.com/wp-srv/photo/blackhistory/), *Flash 9/11* (http://abcnews.go.com/sections/flash/morning/WNT_detect_morning.html), and *The Darkest Day* (http://www.msnbc.com/news/attack_front.asp?launch=/modules/wtc_terror_experience/default.asp).

In addition to these, Dube also mentions other forms of online storytelling, such as stories without words ('The Fall of the Twin Towers', http://www.washingtonpost.com/wp-srv/flash/photo/attack/sequence/tower_sequence.htm), surround photos and video ('Inside Space Stations', http://www.msnbc.com/news/537170.asp?launch=/modules/space_modules/surround_video/), and databases ('Crime Tracker', http://crimetracker.tbo.com/, and 'Does the IRS Owe You Money?' http://www.msnbc.com/news/572222.asp).

## Rules for Writing Online and Creating Packages

Once the most appropriate form for the online package has been identified, it is time to write the text and marshal the other elements that will go with it. Based on their empirical research on the usability of web pages, Nielsen, Schemenaur and Morkes have listed a number of rules that need to be followed at this stage.[7] Before presenting these, however, I would like to record a caveat on three counts.

First, treating journalism strictly as a craft with iron rules may sometimes produce technically sound but lifeless stories. But if journalism is treated as part craft and part art, in which rules can be broken to achieve desired effects, the stories can come alive. There are examples of brilliant online news packages that have broken many of the rules listed below. But the line between a brilliant story or package and a disaster is very thin, and treading it requires imagination and experience.

Secondly, the studies from which Nielsen and his co-workers have drawn their conclusions, seem to have focused on very small audience samples. This raises questions about the validity of their conclusions for the entire population of online news audience. Thirdly, since reading habits vary in some respects across different cultures, not all conclusions of the Nielsen studies, which were carried out in North America, may be valid for readers of online news in India.

With these things in mind, the following rules should be noted.

### Scannability

The majority of web users (79 per cent according to the studies mentioned above) seem to scan pages rather than read word-by-word. Hence, the web document should be made scannable. This can be done through the following ways.

### Highlighted Keywords

One way to make the document easy to scan is to highlight keywords. Coloured text or coloured backgrounds can be used for highlighting, but blue should not be used for words, as this colour is often used for hyperlinks.

Since hyperlinks stand out on account of being coloured, they should be selected in such a way as to serve also as highlighted keywords. Only key information-carrying words should be highlighted, and highlighting entire sentences or long phrases should be avoided, because a scanning eye can pick up only two – or at most three – words at a time.

Words that differentiate the page in question from other pages, and words that symbolise the content of a given paragraph, should be highlighted. For instance, Nielsen explains, the word 'Sun' should not be highlighted when one is writing for the Sun Microsystems website (on which his online writing guide is posted), since all the pages there are about Sun.

### Simple Headings and Sentences

Compared to print, the web has a greater degree of informality and immediacy. But informality does not mean one should use clever or 'cute' headings, because web users tend to scan the text to find its meaning and are not likely to dwell on or appreciate such headings. For the same reason, the use of metaphors should be limited, particularly in headings. Sentence structures should be simple. Convoluted writing and complex words are even harder to understand online than they are in print.

### Meaningful Subheadings

One way to increase scannability is to provide meaningful subheadings, so that the reader is able to quickly absorb the main points of the story without having to read the text. In case the subheadings indicate that the story contains information that is important to him, the subheadings allow him to focus on only the relevant portions rather than reading the entire story.

### Bulleted and Numbered Lists

Another way to increase scannability is to use bulleted and numbered lists, which slow down the scanning eye and can draw attention to important points.

### One Idea per Paragraph

Each paragraph should contain one main idea, since users tend to skip any second point as they scan over a paragraph.

### Splitting Documents

In print, the document forms a whole and the user is focused on the entire set of information. On the web, each document may have to be divided into multiple hyperlinked pages, as users are often not willing to read long pages that need to be scrolled down.

### Compact Pages

Since users can enter a site at any page and move between pages at will, every page needs to be made independent, to the extent possible, and its topic needs to be explained without assuming that the user has seen the previous page.

### Identifying People

The usual practice for naming an individual in print journalism is that the first time she is mentioned in a story, her full name – first and last names – are given along with a few words to identify her. Some publications also add a title to the name. For example 'the Prime Minister, Dr Manmohan Singh', or 'Prime Minister Manmohan Singh'. In references that appear after the first one, the individual is usually referred to only by the last name – in this case it would be simply 'Dr Singh'.

But in an online story that is broken up into two or more pages, the references to the individual (in our example, Dr Manmohan Singh) should be limited to the first page only as far as possible, and if references cannot be avoided in subsequent pages, he should be identified afresh (for example as Prime Minister Manmohan Singh).

The reason for this repetition is twofold: (1) the reader may have reached the second or third page directly through a web search, and in that case a simple 'Dr Singh' will not immediately convey to her the identity of the person being written about. (2) Even if the reader has been reading the story from the beginning, for a variety of reasons she may still be confused about the identity of a 'Dr Singh' or a 'Mr Bhattacharya' in a later page. In either case (1 or 2), she will have to click back to the first page to find out the identity, and this may be a slow process if the internet connection is through a telephone modem.

### Inverted Pyramid Style

Many users do not like to scroll through large masses of text. Therefore, the most important information should be put at the top of a page or story, and other information added in decreasing order of importance. This is the inverted pyramid style prevalent in writing print news.

### Uncomplicated Style

Web users seem to have an impatient and critical nature. Therefore, news should be presented in an uncomplicated style, so that users can find the information they want quickly and without difficulty.

## Hyperlinks

We have seen earlier that the most fundamental difference between the print and broadcast media, on the one hand, and the internet, on the other, is that the latter is hypertextual in nature. This carries over into the realm of news package design, and one of the most important things to remember is that hyperlinks add immensely to a story, and must be provided wherever possible.

This does not mean that links have to be provided without regard to their relevance to the story at hand, or their quality. A link that takes the reader to a page that is not very relevant to the main story, or one that takes the reader to a page containing material of poor quality, will only waste his time and annoy him. Moreover, too many links with a story may overwhelm, even if they are relevant and of high quality. Therefore, while the journalist should be liberal with the use of links, she needs to be judicious as well.

The following are the two most obvious uses of hyperlinks.

### For Depth and Interactivity

It is necessary to provide links to background, explanatory and related information. While this will illuminate the topic of the story for those users who do not know enough about it, it will also be useful to those who already have a fair amount of knowledge, and would like to know the subject in greater detail or depth than that which is afforded by the main story. The following are some of the material that can be usefully linked for this purpose, as mentioned earlier in this chapter:

* primary sources of data and other information used in the story
* timelines
* mini-profiles of important personalities mentioned or quoted in the story
* related stories
* multimedia, such as video clips of news events or audio files of speeches, interviews, etc.

Apart from helping the user obtain more information on the topic, links to discussion forums and reporters' email addresses also introduce interactivity.

But the practice of including reporters' email addresses has both advantages and disadvantages.[8] While it sometimes enables reporters to receive important tips from readers, very often it subjects them to a deluge of useless, even abusive mails. Responding to such mails, or even reading and deleting them, takes up considerable time that could have been spent in a more useful way. However, some reporters and editors feel that the pros of this practice outweigh the cons.

### For Credibility

Credibility is important on the web, since users often deal with unknown sites, whose servers are at remote locations. Hence, the online journalist has to make an effort to earn the user's trust. Hyperlinks to other sites (external links) with supporting information increase the credibility of a page.

## Story Length

The word count for the online version of a given story should be about half the word count of its print version. This is because users find it hard to read too much text on screens, and reading from screens is about 25 per cent slower than reading from paper.

## Pictures and Graphics

Graphics and text should complement each other. Words and pictures can make a very effective combination, but they must work together. Pictures must have captions. Graphics must be related to the text, and must add to it. They must not be used merely for ornamental purposes, since they will then serve to distract the reader and waste his time.

## Updates

Since the web is a fluid medium, pages should be frequently updated so as to reflect all changes. Statistics, numbers, and examples all need to be recent. In the absence of this, the site is bound to lose credibility.

## Meta-tags

The online journalist can, and should, make an effort to increase the visibility of his story or package, that is, the probability that it will be found by a web user who tries to obtain information on the relevant topic with the help of a search engine. For this, he needs to include in a keywords meta-tag for each page, all possible query terms that can be used to search for the topic of the page.

This meta-tag should include all such keywords plus all their common synonyms (even words not included in the body text). For instance, the Morkes and Nielsen article (http://www.useit.com/papers/webwriting/writing.html) has the following keywords in the meta-tag: "online reading, Web writing, usability tasks, scanning, skimming, scan text, word count, concise writing, scannable page layout, scannability, objective language, promotional style, marketese, hypertext, credibility, illustrations, humor, inverted pyramid structure". The tag can be found by clicking the 'View' option at the top of the page's browser window and then clicking on the 'Source' option.

## Online Media and the Tsunami

Now that we are familiar with the thumb rules for writing online news stories and preparing news packages, we will see how a few prominent news sites have handled a major news event, namely, the Asian tsunami of 26 December 2004.

Figure 6.1 shows the main page of the *BBC News* website at 07:07 GMT (12:37 p.m. IST) on 27 December, that is, the day after the tsunami. The title of the main story, 'Asia wakes to tidal catastrophe', serves as a link to the story proper, posted on another page.

This title is followed by four lines of text (18 words) summing up the situation. Below this summary are three links, 'At-a-glance: Countries hit', 'Your experiences: Asian disaster', and video clips of *BBC TV* reports. Next to this block is a bank of links to more material, under the title 'Asia Quake Disaster: In Depth'.

FIGURE **6.1** The main page of the *BBC News* website the day after the Asian tsunami

This has the following links: to a picture gallery titled 'In pictures: Devastation across Indian Ocean', to a page containing reporters' logs, 'Chaos as Britons stranded in Asia', 'Disastrous scenes in Phuket', 'In quotes: Witness accounts', and 'Earthquake explained'. The last one takes the user to a page with animation showing how earthquakes take place. These pages also have links to more stories, such as reports from individual countries like Indonesia, India, Sri Lanka and Thailand.

*Guardian Unlimited*, online edition of *The Guardian* newspaper of the UK, had the following links (in italics) on its main page at about 8:30 a.m. IST on 27 December:

> ### Thousands swept to their death
> · Giant waves kill 12,600 in Asia
> · Calls for warning system ignored
> *'It tossed boats around like toys'*
> *Out of the blue, a deadly wall of water*
> *Leader: Tsunami terror*
> *Audio: John Aglionby in Jakarta*
> *In pictures: the aftermath*
> *Special report: natural disasters*

As we can see, two bulleted points (total of 11 words) were provided below the link to the main story at the top, and these were followed by six links to more stories, an editorial, an audio file, a picture gallery and special reports on natural disasters. This block of links and text was flanked on the left by a photograph showing a house floating in the sea as a man walks by debris in Sri Lanka.

It is worth noting that although the main story (http://www.guardian .co.uk /naturaldisasters/story/0,7369,1380040,00.html) as updated at 8 p.m. GMT on 26 December (that is, 1:30 a.m. IST on 27 December) consisted of a photograph of the devastation in Sri Lanka and as many as 1,179 words, it was presented on a single page instead of being broken up into three or four pages as our thumb rule would have required. (As we will see, *The Guardian* online attracts a very engaged readership in spite of this practice.)

This lengthy story was accompanied by a number of links to special reports on natural disasters, as well as archived articles on such disasters, including earthquakes, typhoons, floods and volcanic eruptions from around the world. The archived version of the main story has been reduced to 842 words and the photograph has been removed.

The second story linked from the main page, consisting of eyewitness accounts (http://www.guardian.co.uk/naturaldisasters/story/0, 7369,1380036,00.html), was accompanied by 14 links (in italics) grouped under four heads as shown below:

> **Special reports**
> *Natural disasters*
> *Weather watch*
> *Global warming*
>
> **Interactive guides**
> *Earthquakes*
> *Mount Pinatubo: draining the volcano*
> *Inside Mount Etna*
> *The Indian earthquake*
>
> **Photo gallery**
> *Congo volcano*
>
> **Useful links**
> *Disasters Emergency Committee*
> *International Red Cross*
> *Natural Disaster Reference Database*[*]
> *Natural Hazards*
> *Global tectonic activity map*
> *Explorezone.com – earthquakes*

Figure 6.2 shows the contents of the *Guardian*'s page on global warming (http://www.guardian.co.uk/globalwarming/0,7368,395145,00.html) reached from the 'Special Reports' group of links (above), as it appeared on 27 December. The text in italics indicates links. The contents of this page, and those of other pages on the *Guardian* site, given above, are intended as examples to help the student form an idea of the wealth of information that can be provided on major issues in online journalism. The nature of the print and broadcast media prevent them from serving information of this magnitude.

---

[*] This NASA database at <http://ndrd.gsfc.nasa.gov/> contains information on all types of natural disasters.

*America's war on itself*
**December 21, George Monbiot:** 'Bushs wrecking tactics over climate change follow an established pattern of self-destruction
**Global warming**
*US deal offers climate change action*
**December 19:** Worldwide efforts to put a cap on global warming edged forward yesterday when the United States agreed to participate in a seminar to discuss climate issues.
*Set back for Blair on climate change*
**December 18:** Tony Blair's push for US engagement on climate change suffered a fresh set-back today when an international conference ended without agreement.
*Damage litigation*
**December 15:** We know that human behaviour is leading to global warming, but what if the companies responsible for changes to the weather in specific areas could be identified? **Peter Roderick** examines the growth of climate change lawsuits.
*Warming may turn coral white*
**December 15:** Scientists have identified early warning signs of rising ocean temperatures which threaten to drain Australia's Great Barrier Reef of its vibrant colours.
*Climate forecast soars into the red*
**December 14:** By 2050 heatwaves like that of 2003, which killed 15,000 in Europe and pushed British temperatures above 38C (100F) for the first time, will seem 'unusually cool', the Hadley Centre for Climate Change says.
*Sea level rise 'will hit poor most'*
**December 11:** Rich nations are prepared to spend up to $32bn to protect the European coastline from sea level rise - but have promised only $0.41bn to help poor nations confront climate change, according to a new report launched yesterday.
*Jurassic Park author pours cold water on global warming*
**December 11:** Michael Crichton's new techno thriller fantasises a world free of the pall of greenhouse gases.

FIGURE **6.2** Links on global warming in the *Guardian Unlimited*

It should be noted that while *The Guardian* newspaper (print edition) is not one of the largest circulating newspapers in the UK, its online edition, *Guardian Unlimited*, perhaps is the most thoroughly browsed site among mainstream British newspapers. According to data provided by the UK's Audit Bureau of Circulation (ABC)[9] *Guardian Unlimited* was in May 2005 ahead of the online edition of every British newspaper with the sole exception of the tabloid *Sun* in terms of page impressions. Page impression as defined by the ABC is "A file, or combination of files, sent to a valid USER[†] as a result of that USER's request being received by the server." (Since an interested or highly engaged user is likely to click on a large number of links on a site, the number of page impressions can serve as an indication of the degree of users' interest in or engagement with the content.) Among the different media, however, the *BBC* held sway, followed by the *Sun* and the *Guardian*.

---

[†] The ABC defines a 'unique user' or simply 'user' as "a unique and valid identifier." Explaining that websites may determine the number in three ways – IP+User-Agent, Cookie and/or Registration ID – it indicates that there are certain grey areas in these calculations and suggests that these need to be resolved through discussion with the ABC by individual sites.

At about the same time – on 17 June 2005 – the print edition of the same *Guardian* newspaper found itself at the fourteenth place in terms of average total circulation (multiple copy) and at the twenty-first place in terms of average net circulation.[10] It is reasonable to argue that the success of *Guardian Unlimited* in inducing users to browse or read its content (hence page impressions) – in spite of breaking rules, such as presenting a 1,179-word story on a single scrolling page instead of breaking it up into three or four chunks on as many pages – arises at least in part from its policy of providing a large number of links to high-quality source of information, which enables the reader to gain a very broad knowledge of a topic and a deep insight into it.

Indian news sites, by and large, do not seem to favour this approach. As of 18 June 2005, the website of *The Hindu*, a newspaper widely respected for its serious and comprehensive coverage of issues and events, had as many as 194 stories posted between 27 December 2004, and 25 February 2005 in a special section on the tsunami given below (Figure 6.3) linked from its main page.

These stories provide an almost minute-by-minute account of tsunami-related developments and significant human interest content. But, unlike *The Guardian*, they do not help the reader gain a comprehensive understanding of the linkages among global warming, climate change, natural disasters and other processes taking place in the natural environment, or the political processes surrounding these phenomena.

- Eviction of tsunami-affected residents stayed (20050225) New
- State Government unveils revised relief package for fishermen (20050225) New
- Rs. 1 crore more for Andamans from 'The Hindu Relief Fund' (20050224)
- New headquarters hospital for tsunami-hit Nagapattinam (20050224)
- FIEO contributes Rs. 51 lakhs for tsunami relief (20050224)
- 'Indian tsunami warning system will be superior to the Pacific variety' (20050224)
- Alternative habitats for tsunami-hit people (20050224)
- MLA donates Rs. 20 lakhs for tsunami relief (20050224)
- Rebuilding lives in Andamans (20050223)
- 'Andamans, Tamil Nadu coastline vulnerable' (20050223)
- WHO to fine-tune services in affected areas (20050223)
- More casuarina plantations along Tuticorin coast planned (20050223)
- U.P. donates Rs. 9 crores to PM's Fund (20050223)
- USAID team meets tsunami-hit families (20050221)
- '1,000 SSIs were hit by tsunami' (20050221)
- Training for tsunami affected youth (20050221)
- 'Families of missing persons entitled to all benefits' (20050217)
- Tsunami fund crosses Rs. 1.5 crores in Erode (20050217)
- They are still like fish out of water (20050216)
- Fishermen prefer direct grants to loans (20050216)
- Ramakrishna Math to give house sites for fishermen (20050216)
- Tremors in Sumatra (20050216)
- Quakes rock Assam (20050216)
- Tsunami relief (20050216)

contd.

- Centre to relax rules on missing persons in tsunami-hit areas (20050213)
- Earthquake magnitude was 9.3 (20050211)
- Ocean floor images offer tsunami clues (20050211)
- Tsunami-affected block NH at Karunagapally (20050211)
- Resettlement policy by month-end (20050208)
- Was Manmohan's letter deliberately delayed, asks Jayalalithaa (20050208)
- Raise compensation, demands DMK (20050208)
- Temporary shelters for Andamans' tsunami-hit before onset of monsoon (20050128)
- Tamil Nadu still awaits Centre's relief package (20050128)
- Rains have to reduce salinity in tsunami-hit areas (20050128)
- In the same boat, they pull together (20050128)
- Aftershocks (20050128)
- 'No pro-MNC approach to rehabilitation' (20050127)
- 'Extend Central subsidy to tsunami-hit fishermen' (20050127)
- What kept Nagapattinam healthy, safe (20050127)
- Contributions to relief work highlighted (20050127)
- A castaway on his home island (20050127)
- SAARC to discuss tsunami warning system (20050127)
- Rebuilding beaches the French way (20050127)
- Tsunami victims remembered (20050127)
- Additional cash relief for affected fishermen (20050127)
- The tale of a camera and the tsunami (20050125)
- 'Car Nicobar Air Force station will be fully restored in 6 months' (20050124)
- FCI augmenting foodgrain supply to tsunami-hit States (20050124)
- UNCTAD suggests steps to help tsunami-hit countries (20050124)
- Tirunelveli fishermen await assistance (20050124)
- Doctors set up camps in tsunami-hit areas (20050124)
- Temporary houses for tsunami victims (20050124)
- NYK told to give psycho-social counselling to tsunami victims (20050124)
- Oceanic survey to be made in Kanyakumari dt. (20050124)
- 'U.N. should help small countries install tsunami-warning systems' (20050124)
- Soil reclamation project for tsunami-hit paddyfields (20050124)
- Tsunami warning centre likely in Hyderabad (20050123)
- Rs. 75 lakhs for Andhra Pradesh from ' The Hindu Relief Fund' (20050123)
- "Our little bit" for tsunami relief (20050123)
- Tribal rescued weeks after tsunami (20050123)
- Housing scheme for fishermen getting ready (20050123)
- Mere seawalls won't do, keep natural cover: experts (20050123)
- UNDP to help State in rehabilitation of tsunami-hit (20050123)
- Navy studying effect of tsunami on sea (20050123)
- Nursing students to counsel tsunami victims (20050123)
- Tsunami-hit fisherfolk coming to terms slowly (20050123)
- Tsunami takes centre-stage at International Berlin Farm Week (20050122)
- Navy downsizes tsunami relief operations (20050122)
- Mega concert for tsunami victims (20050122)
- Tsunami victims in need of provisions (20050122)
- Three-tier counselling for victims in Nagapattinam (20050122)
- Rs. 2,731 crores for tsunami relief work (20050120)
- Kerala gets Rs. 1.5 crores from 'The Hindu Relief Fund' (20050120)
- Psychological trauma a serious problem in tsunami-hit areas: WHO (20050120)
- More relief sent to Andamans (20050104)
- Burning midnight oil for relief work (20050104)
- Operation Andamans in full flow (20050103)
- Quake warning in Assam (20050103)

FIGURE **6.3** *The Hindu's* tsunami section on 18 June 2005

Figure 6.4 shows the main page of the *Times of India* group's *Indiatimes* portal as it appeared at 6:30 p.m. on 27 December 2004. The main page has links to two tsunami stories – the main story, 'Tsunami toll over 5,700, rescue efforts on', and a human interest story, 'They honeymooned on tsunami waves'. The main story appears in two parts, at the following URLs – <http://timesofindia.indiatimes.com/articleshow/972296.cms> and <http://timesofindia.indiatimes.com/articleshow/msid-972296,curpg-2.cms>.

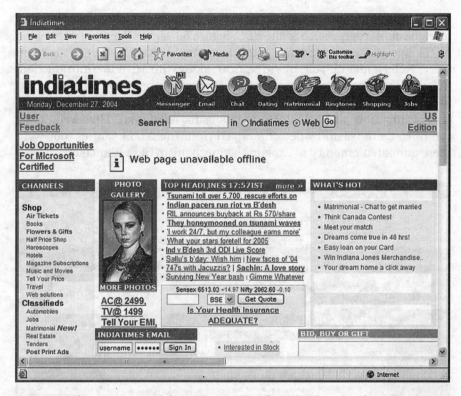

FIGURE **6.4** The main page of the *Indiatimes* portal on the day after the Asian tsunami

On each of these two linked pages, the text is accompanied by 21 links to related stories: 'Tsunami claims over 5,500 lives in India', 'Nuke scientist among Tsunami victims', ' "God saved me but why?" ', 'PM announces ex-gratia of Rs 1 lakh', 'Andaman tsunami toll feared at 3,000', ' "We don't know where to go ... how to begin" ', 'A honeymoon on tsunami waves', 'Sonia leaves for Andaman', 'Tsunami tragedy: Prime Minister's Relief Fund', 'UN warns of post-tsunami epidemics', 'India at sea about tsunami', 'Devastation in South India', 'Patil visits TN, offers central aid', 'Moderate quake rocks Andamans', 'Tsunami toll rises to 4,000 in India', 'Toll reaches 2500 in TN', '1,000 feared killed in Andaman and Nicobar', 'Port Blair runway submerged', 'Key installations safe', 'The wave train that chugs in death and destruction', and somewhat inexplicably, 'Credit Rao for Pokhran II: Atal'. Clearly, this event-oriented treatment of the disaster lacks the breadth and depth to be found in *The Guardian*'s issue-oriented coverage.

Among television channels, too, Indian websites were left behind by their foreign counterparts, such as the *BBC*. Figure 6.5 shows the main page of the *NDTV* site at about 7:22 p.m. on 27 December. It had the link to the main story, 'Killer tsunami: Toll rises to 24,000', along with a five-line introduction, followed by links to four more tsunami stories: 'Tsunami toll touches 6,000 in south India', 'Wake-up call: India to monitor tsunamis', 'Andamans toll mounts to 3,000', and 'PM urges donations for relief fund'. However, unlike the *BBC*, there was no video clip linked from the *NDTV* stories, nor were there animated graphics to explain the mechanism of earthquakes.

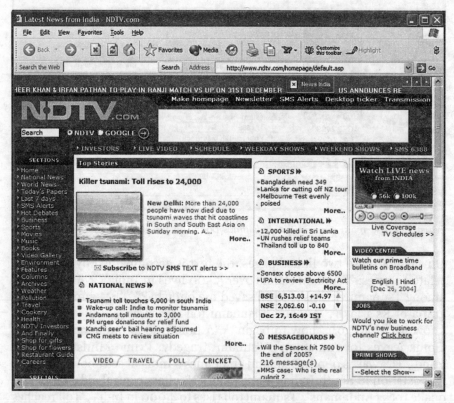

FIGURE **6.5** The *NDTV* home page a day after the Asian tsunami

## News Editing in the Online Environment

At first sight, editing in the online media would seem to be no different from editing printed newspapers and magazines, and this is what many journalists believe – especially those who have learnt their trade in print newsrooms. The fact is that online journalism has certain requirements in terms of editing and production practices going beyond those of the older media. These considerations can be divided into two broad groups – those which editors need to keep in mind, and those which can be built into the technology used for implementing news sites.

## Considerations for Online Editors

Janice Castro[11], assistant dean and director of graduate editorial programs at Northwestern University, Chicago (USA), has noted a few such factors:

- Preparing online news packages requires flexibility. "An editor could start the shift editing a story for the newspaper," Castro says, "incorporate that story into a multimedia package for a partner television or radio station by lunch and end the day by putting that same report on the Web."

- In India, news desk staff usually would be dealing with two media, not three – either print and web or TV and web – as cross-media ownership is still limited in this country though it is changing: witness *India Today's* Aaj Tak and Headlines Today TV news channels or the Ananda Bazar group's recently launched Star Ananda channel.

- In the online media, news has to be constantly updated, as readers expect this. This continuous news cycle of the web creates a culture clash: "Online is urgent; copy editors are methodical." Castro feels that the next generation of online editors should learn how to work like a news agency, and to balance speed and accuracy, among other things.

- Castro stresses the fact that websites have a global reach. Online editors need to remember that their sites are being simultaneously read by people in different countries, time zones and cultures, and learn to tailor their practices accordingly. For instance, references to 'the country' may be confusing to some readers and it would be better to name one's country explicitly.

- The role of headlines in the online media is different from print, as on the computer screen, they have to vie for the reader's attention with icons, links, advertisements and other marketing tools. Therefore, online headlines have to be shorter and crisper.

- Castro believes online news needs its own stylebook. For example, percentage signs should not be used online, because these often cannot be read clearly on the computer screen. Also, it is better to use acronyms without periods (BSNL instead of B.S.N.L.) as these are easier to read.

- Convergence is a major area of confusion. Castro says the question, whom the staff of online editions should report to, has been a major issue in the USA, and points out that at some of the most respected newspapers, online staff used to report to marketing departments!

  However, she believes the online newsroom will occupy centrestage in news organizations in future, since digitization turns story elements into 'liquid' form, which can be 'poured' into any number of delivery devices, such as printed newspapers, e-newsletters, cell phones, websites, radio and television channels, and syndication. "The copy desk can be not only the quality control system", Castro says, "but also the thinking editor that thinks about the form."

- Castro feels that online news editors need to think more visually than their print colleagues. People grew accustomed to 'seeing' their news with the advent of television, and the internet, being interactive in nature, reinforced this trend. But interactivity also implies that readers or users have a greater tendency to leave the story and click on something else.

  This increases the pressure on news providers to persuade readers not to stray from the story, perhaps to a different site altogether. Castro believes that editors will have a better chance of retaining their readers if they learn 'visual grammar'. Every element on the screen will have to be attractive to the reader, as online news providers have to "buy (the readers') attention one page at a time."

## Technologising the News Editing Process

In the print or broadcast newsroom, the sources of news are limited to the organisation's own reporters and correspondents, and news agency feeds. But in the online environment, the number of sources is extremely large, since hundreds of thousands of news-oriented websites and millions of other types of websites can serve as sources of news. Therefore, allowing technology to perform, or help editors perform some of the traditional functions of news editors – selecting and presenting timely and relevant information – is a necessity in the online environment.

Such systems are already being used on some news sites, for example, Topix.net, which uses NewsRank technology to categorise stories according to relevance, accuracy and magnitude.[12] The front page of the site "uses a complex set of semantic story filters to govern news selection." The fully algorithmic editing process takes into account the magnitude of the story, as well as its topic, as determined by an artificial intelligence based categorizer from a 'knowledge base' of 150,000 topics.

Technology companies and research laboratories have been working on such systems for some time. IBM and the MIT Media Laboratory's News in the Future research consortium have supported the development of a complex system called ZWrap by scientists D. Gruhl and W. Bender.[13] The system uses "richer representations of texts within a corpus of news".

These representations are composed by a collection of 'expert' software, which examine news stories using various methods ranging from statistical examination to natural-language parsing to "query expansion through specific-purpose knowledge bases". They examine both the text of the story and the annotations placed by other 'expert' software. ZWrap "provides a structure for the sharing of knowledge with human editors and the development of a class of applications that make use of article augmentation", write Gruhl and Bender.

## Exercise

Compare the coverage of an important issue or event in your favourite Indian news website with that in major British and US sites with reference to the considerations and rules of writing and preparing online news packages. Point out instances of deviation from these rules, and the effects of such deviations on the quality of the packages.

## References

[1] Dube, Jonathan, 'Online Storytelling Forms', *Cyberjournalist.net*, accessed 23 May 2005 on http://www.cyberjournalist.net/news/000117.php.

2   Nielsen, Jacob et al, 'Writing for the Web', *sun.com*, accessed 24 May 2005 on http://www.sun.com/980713/webwriting/.

3   Dube, Jonathan, 'A Dozen Online Writing Tips', *Cyberjournalist.net*, accessed 23 May 2005 on http://www.cyberjournalist.net/news/000118.php.

4   Accessed 26 May 2005 on http://www.poynterextra.org/et/i.htm.

5   Rich, Carole, 'Writing for the Web: Different, But How?', Archives of the American Society of Newspaper Editors, 1 August 2001, accessed 21 November 2004 on http://www.asne.org/index.cfm?ID=3354.

6   Dube, Jonathan, 'Online Storytelling Forms'.

7   Nielsen, Jacob et al, 'Writing for the Web', *sun.com*. Also, Morkes, et al, 'Concise, SCANNABLE, and Objective: How to Write for the Web' (1997), accessed 23 May 2005 on http://www.useit.com/papers/webwriting/writing.html.

8   *Nieman Reports*, vol.54, no.4, Winter 2000, pp.28–30.

9   Accessed 17 June 2005 on http://www.abce.org.uk/cgi-bin/gen5?runprog=abce/abce&noc=y.

10  Accessed 17 June 2005 on http://www.abc.org.uk/cgi-bin/gen5?runprog=nav/abc&noc=y.

11  Castro, Janice, quoted in *Preparing for Online News*, report on conference on 'Editing the Future: Helping Copy Desks Meet the Challenges of Changing Media', 20–22 November 2003, at Freedom Forum Diversity Institute, Vanderbilt University, Nashville, Tennessee, accessed 19 July 2007 on http://www.scripps.ohiou.edu/news/editfuture/EditingTheFuture.pdf.

12  'Topix.net: The Best Algorithmic News Editing in the Business', *Topix.net Weblog*, 1 August 2004, accessed 19 July 2005 on http://blog.topix.net/archives/000025.html.

13  Gruhl, D. and W. Bender, 'A New Structure for News Editing', *IBM Systems Journal*, no.s 3 & 4, 2000, accessed 21 December 2004 on http://www.research.ibm.com/journal/sj/393/part1/gruhl.html.

# 7.
# Web Authoring and Publishing

According to CERN, web authoring is the process of creating web documents, that is, web pages or collections of such pages on the same or related subjects that can be displayed on a screen using a program called a web browser. Web publishing is the process of making web documents available to the public on web servers[*].[1]

Several excellent articles and tutorials on this subject are available online, free of charge. Two particularly useful ones are: *Web Style Guide* (www.webstyleguide.com) by Patrick J. Lynch and Sarah Horton, which is also available in book form, and John Shiple's tutorial on information architecture on the *Webmonkey* site for website development (http://hotwired.lycos.com/webmonkey/design/site_building/tutorials/tutorial1.html). The topic which both of these stress as being of particular importance in web authoring is information architecture.

---

[*] The server computer is so called because it serves up these digital files when any other computer connected to the web (using the TCP/IP protocols) sends it a request for the page.

# Deciding the Information Architecture

The first step in designing a website should be deciding its information architecture (although this has often not been the case in practice, especially outside the advanced industrial countries). In Shiple's words:

> Information architecture is the foundation for great Web design. It is the blueprint of the site upon which all other aspects are built – form, function, metaphor, navigation and interface, interaction, and visual design. Initiating the IA process is the first thing you should do when designing a site.

The term information architecture (IA) refers to the structural design of shared information environments or spaces. Its aim is to enable users to access desired content in an intuitive way and to complete their respective tasks with ease. In the case of websites, this involves a combination of organisation, labelling, and navigation schemes for various pages and smaller elements within the site.

Kimen explains[2]:

> At its most basic, information architecture is the construction of a structure or the organization of information. In a library, for example, information architecture is a combination of the catalog system and the physical design of the building that holds the books. On the Web, information architecture is a combination of organising a site's content into categories and creating an interface to support those categories.

Myers[3] writes that the difference between IA and web design is analogous to the difference between the work of an architect and that of an interior designer.

The construction of IA involves the following steps:

1.  The first step in the IA approach is to define the site's goals. Shiple suggests that every department of the organisation that owns the site should be involved in drawing up this definition and each participant should answer the following questions: What is the mission or purpose of the organisation? What are the short and long-term goals of the site? Who are the intended audiences? Why will people come to the site? These answers have to be collated to prepare a document with a list of the site's goals.

2. The next step is to define the audience, its needs and goals. For instance, if the site is intended to be used for selling automobiles, the audience categories would be buyer, seller, dealer and other. For a news-oriented site, the audience will consist of readers – not only readers, viewers or listeners of the print or broadcast counterpart (if there is one) of the site, but also others.

   For sites like *Guardian Unlimited* of the UK's *Guardian* newspaper those who have never read the print edition constitute a large audience category. Since a number of their readers belong to the Indian diaspora, the *Hindustan Times* and *Indiatimes* websites have sections specifically designated as UK and US editions, respectively.

3. Next, 'scenarios' have to be written for each category of audience. A character is created to represent each category, given a fictional name and background, and a task to accomplish on the site chosen from the list of audience needs and goals. Using one's imagination, a scenario is then written in the form of a narrative about the manner in which this character uses the site to complete the task. (This will be important later, too, when the content and functional requirements of the site are defined.)

   Once this is done, the websites of competitors are evaluated for a set of chosen criteria, including download time, page size, layout, and look and feel. The site being designed and the other ones are compared in table form. This step ends with the preparation of a document on user experience, which includes the definition of audience, scenarios and comparative analysis of sites.

4. The next step in the IA process consists in identifying and listing the site's content elements and functional requirements. Content elements include static, dynamic, functional, and transactional ones. Among possible static content are copyright notices, privacy statements, and membership rules. Interactive elements, on the other hand, are dynamic. So are functional ones, such as members' logon pages, and signup pages for email newsletters. Pages involving forms or transactions are dynamic, functional and transactional.

   Once the lists are complete, content elements are divided into groups according to one's understanding of functionality. These groups will comprise separate sections of the site. This step ends with the preparation of a site content document consisting of a section on content grouping and labeling, another on functional requirements, and an appendix consisting of a content inventory.

5.  The next step is metaphor exploration. Three types of metaphor are possible in IA – organizational, functional and visual. Many news sites are organised to reflect the way content is organised in the different pages of newspapers – the front page, city, regional, national and international pages, the editorial page, the sports page, etc. This is an example of organisational metaphor.

    Examples of functional metaphor are to be found in functions like 'Cut', 'Copy' and 'Paste' in the user interfaces of Microsoft Word, Adobe Photoshop and other programs. Visual metaphors depend on the use of graphic elements familiar to most people. For example, some websites use small icons depicting an audio speaker and a video camera to denote links to audio and video files, respectively.

6.  Now that one has the rationale for a site structure, it should to be put down on paper for the sake of a better understanding, starting with a text-based one if necessary, and then moving to a diagrammatic representation. A text-based structure may look like the one below:

```
Section 1
        Section 1.1
        Section 1.2
Section 2
        Section 2.1
        Section 2.2
                Section 2.2.1
                Section 2.2.2
                Section 2.2.3
        Section 2.3
        Section 2.4
    Section 3
```

A diagrammatic representation will look like Figure 7.1. Most news-oriented sites have a rather complex structure that is difficult to depict with accuracy through a two-dimensional diagram, *Guardian Unlimited* being a case in point. In such an event, one may visualize the site as a three-dimensional structure and create diagrammatic representations for each plane. Figure 7.1 is a very small portion of one such representation of the *Guardian*'s structure.

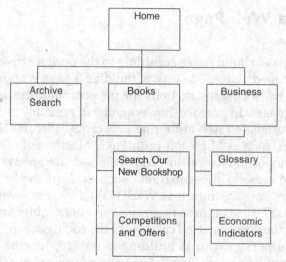

FIGURE **7.1** Diagram representing a portion of the *Guardian Unlimited's* information architecture

7. Once this structure is in place, the site navigation system is defined in order to ensure clarity and convenience for the user. The major sections listed in the site structure should be designated as buttons or links for the global navigation system, which appears on every page and enables users to move between sections of the site with ease. According to Shiple, the number of global navigation elements should be limited to between five and seven, if possible.

For local navigation, there are several options to choose from. For news sites, perhaps the most appropriate is a list of topics, such as that found in *Guardian Unlimited* or *cnn.com*. Depending on the nature of the site, one may also have a menu of choices like the one in the GeoCities members' area, or a list of related items. Once these choices have been made, a list is drawn up of the global navigation system and as many of the local navigation systems as possible.

8. The next step is to prepare the visual design, which should incorporate the site's structure in such a way that at every point, the user has a mental map of where (on the site) he is, where he has been and where he would be able to go from his present location. This part of the design is done with the help of layout grids, which are templates for pages that show the position, shape and size of each element on a page. These can be made with pen or pencil and paper, or with a graphics programme on the computer. The process is similar to making page dummies for print newspapers.

## Building a Web Page

The next step is to build pages according to the design arrived at through the steps outlined above. The task of building a page is accomplished by coding, that is, writing instructions for the computer in what are called markup languages. In practice, however, one may simply use any one of a number of automated web authoring programs called HTML editors or page builders, such as Microsoft FrontPage, Macromedia Dreamweaver, Netscape Composer, Nvu or BlueVoda (the last two are available free of cost). Even Microsoft Office programs, such as Word, can be used to build simple pages. They are known as WYSIWYG packages – what you see is what you get. The use of these programs does not require any knowledge of HTML, as the program itself carries out the coding according to choices made by the person who is building the page, leaving him free to concentrate on the design. Figure 7.2 shows a screen shot of the Nvu tool.

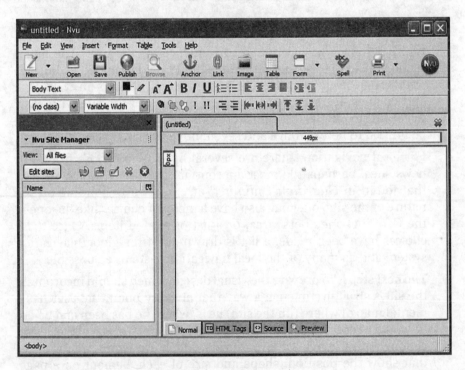

FIGURE **7.2** Screen shot of Nvu web authoring tool

## Markup Languages

Many of us are familiar with the term browser which refers to a type of software that enables us to view the contents of the world wide web. Many browsers are available, the most popular ones being Internet Explorer, Firefox, Netscape, Neoplanet and Opera.

Each web page is made up of digital computer files, whose number may be only one or as many as several dozens. The browser's job is to fetch (that is, copy) these files from the server that maintains the page online, and to open the files on the user's computer so that the page appears in its entirety on his terminal screen. This means the browser has to read the code written in a markup language, since files are computer programs made up of code.

Markup languages are a class of computer languages used to instruct browsers on the way the contents of a given web page should be displayed. These instructions pertain to such things as the colour of the background, the colours, types and sizes of fonts, paragraph breaks, emphasised text, whether a block of text will be treated as a heading, body text or list, et cetera, where an image will be placed on a page and whether the text will appear below, above or around it, what a table will look like, whether the page will be divided into frames and if so, what will be their dimensions, etc. According to *Wikipedia*, "A markup language combines text and extra information about the text. The extra information, for example about the text's structure or presentation, is expressed using markup, which is intermingled with the primary text."[4]

## *HTML*

While there are a large number of markup languages designed for specific purposes, such as geography, business, chemistry, mathematics, multimedia, spacecraft, and even one for the *Oxford English Dictionary*, the most common one is HTML (Hypertext Markup Language).

This language was originally defined by the British-born Tim Berners-Lee, who is considered the father of the web for the work he did at the CERN particle physics laboratory near Geneva. Berners-Lee combined the idea of hypertext with the ideas of TCP (transmission control protocol) and DNS (domain name server) to create the World Wide Web. The first website in the world was the one he built for CERN at http://info.cern.ch/.

It is now archived, and can be found at http://www.w3.org/History/ 19921103-hypertext/hypertext/WWW/News/9201.html.

For the web he was creating, Berners-Lee needed a language that would express hypertext and a browser that would read and 'render' hypertext. The language which came out of this need is HTML. He created it from another language known as the Generalised Markup Language or GML. GML was developed by Charles Goldfarb, Edward Mosher and Raymond Lorie for IBM in the 1960s. It was a metalanguage, that is, a language that could define other computer languages in a manner analogous to the way the grammar of a human language like English or Tamil defines the rules of that language.

Subsequently, SGML (Standard Generalised Markup Language) evolved from GML and took the latter's place as the standard metalanguage of markup languages. After Berners-Lee's initial work, HTML was developed by the Internet Engineering Task Force (IETF) of the Internet Society (ISOC) on the basis of SGML and its specifications were standardised. More recent specifications of HTML are maintained by the World Wide Web Consortium (W3C), headed by Berners-Lee. The W3C website (http:/ /www.w3.org/) contains a vast amount of documentation, news, status reports, announcements, tools and tutorials on markup languages, including HTML.

## XML

While HTML is often called the lingua franca of the web, XML (Extensible Markup Language) is becoming the standard metalanguage of the net and the web, as it has the ability to define markup languages for various kinds of data and for various systems. It is "a simplified subset of SGML"[5], that is, a metalanguage that incorporates some features of SGML while leaving out others. In this era of convergence, in which digital files are expected to be shared by diverse platforms or systems, from mobile phones to personal computers to web TV sets to 'smart homes' with internet-enabled gadgets, the importance of interoperability cannot be overstated.

XML is particularly important in the context of online journalism. Technological or 'device' convergence, among other types of convergence, is a major trend in journalism. The developing media scene requires the same content to be syndicated across diverse platforms. The user not only expects to listen to radio and watch TV on his personal computer but also to receive news updates, send and receive email, surf the web, record and send still or video photographs, and even watch films on his mobile phone. XHTML (Extensible Hypertext Markup Language), which is a version of HTML with stricter rules than the original, RSS (Really Simple Syndication) and Atom – all three based on XML – are the most common markup lanuages/file formats used for these purposes.

In March 2001, Nokia, Motorola, Ericsson, Siemens and several other major companies in the mobile communications and content industries announced that they were supporting XHTML as the format for the future evolution of mobile services and would develop products, content, and services based on this language[6]. In addition to handset manufacturers, several mobile operators also announced support for XHTML. Among them were the Vodafone Group, Orange, Radiolinja, Sonera, DNA, Telenor, Netcom, T-Mobil, TIM (Telecom Italia Group), RadioMobil and EuroTel Praha.

Most major news-oriented websites, many other sites, and many blogs today provide RSS or XML feeds (content) to users. By subscribing to such feeds, the user receives links to new content and one or two lines from this content with each link. In some cases, multimedia files are sent as attachments with RSS feeds. A user can also install a piece of software called feed reader or aggregator on his own computer. This program can search RSS-enabled web pages on behalf of the user and display any updated articles it finds.

## DHTML

An important language of the HTML family is Dynamic HTML or DHTML. It is used for creating interactive websites, and combines HTML with 'client-side scripting'[†] languages like JavaScript, the style definition language Cascading Style Sheets and the 'document object model'[‡].[7] Typical uses of DHTML are in creating interactive forms and browser-based video games.

---

[†] Client-side scripting refers to computer programs on the web that are executed by the user's browser and not 'server-side', that is, on the web server. This kind of programming enables web pages to be scripted, that is, to change their content according to input from users and other factors.

[‡] This is an application programming interface to access HTML and XML documents, and is independent of programming language and platform.

## Basics of HTML

A detailed account of any of the markup languages or metalanguages is beyond the scope of this book. In this chapter, I shall merely offer an introduction to HTML so as to give the reader the 'look and feel' of markup languages.

A good place to start acquiring a working knowledge of website building, including HTML, is the *Webmonkey* site (http://hotwired.lycos.com/webmonkey/). Here, I will demonstrate the process with a simple illustration, which is based on the tutorial[8].

HTML consists of a series of tags (computer commands) that are integrated with the text of a document. They instruct the browser what to do. Most tags are English words (such as 'blockquote') or abbreviations (such as 'p' for paragraph), but are distinguished from the regular text by being placed within angle brackets. For instance, the paragraph tag is <p>, and the blockquote tag is <blockquote>.

Some tags tell the browser how the page is to be formatted (for instance, <p> begins a new paragraph), and others indicate how words should appear (<b> makes text bold). Yet others provide information – such as <title> for the title – that is not meant to appear on the page itself.

Almost all tags occur in a document in pairs. This means every time a tag is used – say <head> (for the header field) – it must also be closed off with another tag containing the same command, preceded by a backslash (/). For example, the closing tag for <head> is </head>.

The basic HTML page begins with the tag <html> and ends with </html>. This tells the browser that everything that appears between these has to be treated as HTML. The contents of the document between <html> and </html> has two sections, namely, the header and the body. The header – which is placed between <head> and </head> – contains information about a page, such as the title, that does not appear on the page itself. (The title appears in the blue title bar at the top of the browser window.) The visible content of the page goes in the body, enclosed by <body> and </body>.

### Creating a Sample Page

To create a simple page, we need to create a new text document. It can be called 'sample.txt'. We want the page to have the title 'Sample' (to appear in the blue title bar at the top of the browser window) and a light yellow background. We want the sentence 'This is a sample page ... / made by Don Quixote ... / whose favourite online newspaper is *The Guardian* ...' written in blue letters with a line break at the first '/'and a paragraph break at the second '/'. We want the text *The Guardian* to serve as a hyperlink to the paper's website. We want the entire matter to appear under the heading 'Example' in darker blue letters.

For this, we need to write the code shown in the text document in Figure 7.3. If we save this text file as an HTML file, using the 'all files' option for file type and taking care to change the file name extension from .txt to .html, we will get the page shown in Figure 7.4 as it appears in the Internet Explorer browser in a Windows XP environment. The source code of the web page, that is, the text file, can be found by clicking on the 'View' link in Internet Explorer's main menu and then clicking on 'Source'.

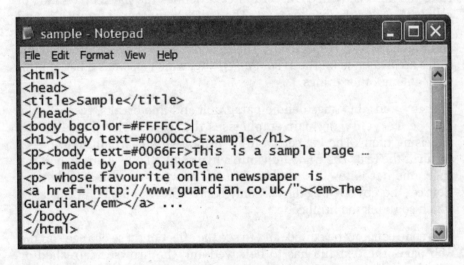

```
sample - Notepad
File  Edit  Format  View  Help
<html>
<head>
<title>Sample</title>
</head>
<body bgcolor=#FFFFCC>
<h1><body text=#0000CC>Example</h1>
<p><body text=#0066FF>This is a sample page …
<br> made by Don Quixote …
<p> whose favourite online newspaper is
<a href="http://www.guardian.co.uk/"><em>The
Guardian</em></a> ...
</body>
</html>
```

Figure 7.3 Text file 'sample.txt' as it appears on the computer screen

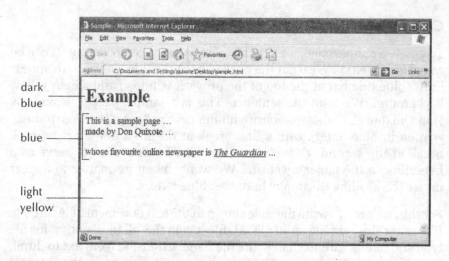

dark
blue

blue

light
yellow

FIGURE 7.4 HTML file 'sample.html' as it appears on the computer screen
(shown in single colour)

Here the tag <body bgcolor=#FFFFCC> defines the particular shade of
yellow used for the background. The tags <body text=#0000CC> and
<body text=#0066FF> define the two shades of blue used in the heading
and the main text, respectively. These, and a wide range of other colour
codes are available on the *Webmonkey* site, which also has a list of html
tags, among other things.

The <p> and <br> tags denote paragraph and line breaks, respectively.
The <em></em> tag pair emphasises the words 'The Guardian' by
italicising them. The tag set <a href='http://www.guardian.co.uk/'> </
a> turns the text *'The Guardian'* into a hyperlink. If one wants to edit the
page, one needs to click on 'View' in the browser's menu and then on
'Source', thereby opening the text-only 'source' file (sample.txt in our case),
which contains the html code.

This code can now be edited, and to see the effect of these changes on the
web page, the text file has to be saved and the browser refreshed or
reloaded – the two are different terms used in different browsers to denote
the same action.

## Design Considerations

Many books and free websites offer useful tips to help the website designer or developer arrive at usable and aesthetically pleasing designs. A few such tips from some of these sources, including the award-winning site www.colin.mackenzie.org, are given below. However, it should be remembered (as Mackenzie points out) that web development is a subjective process and opinions may differ. The tips, therefore, are meant not to establish 'right' and 'wrong' but to sensitise the reader to a few basic considerations.

### Layouts

Information should be divided into logical sections. The starting page (home page or main page) should be attractive and well-laid-out. There should be a consistent theme (as far as possible) throughout the site, and colours, styles and fonts should complement one another.

### Avoiding Clichés

One should try to avoid features that have been frequently used and are becoming clichés. According to Mackenzie, these might include page counters (found on some pages, usually near the bottom, purporting to show the number of times the page has been accessed), JavaScript text scrolling (found on some pages, and used for such things as displaying breaking news and welcome message from the page owner), excessive animated .GIFs, 'under construction' signs, page fade-ins, etc. Mackenzie feels that page counters, if needed, should be hidden because their display might look like arrogance on the part of the owner of a site that attracts high traffic. On the other hand, if the site is rarely visited, it might be unnecessary or unwise to let others know this fact. Mackenzie also feels that JavaScript scrolling and page fading have become so commonplace that they serve no purpose other than showing a lack of originality.

### Browser and Screen Compatibility

Different browsers and computer screens of different sizes and colour resolution settings often display the same page differently, and this fact should be kept in mind while building a page. The remedies are:

1.  Checking features intended for the page for browser-compatibility by referring to charts like the one on *Webmonkey* (http://hotwired.lycos.com/webmonkey/reference/browser_chart/)

2.  Using only valid HTML and testing the page for the smaller screens, as well as larger ones. Once the code is written, it should be validated using a service like the World Wide Web Consortium's 'Markup Validation' page (http://validator.w3.org/).

3.  Testing the page for both small and large terminal screens ($640 \times 480$, $800 \times 600$, and $1024 \times 768$ pixels)

### Using Novelties

Software developers constantly add new features to the web, but it may not be wise to use these too soon if a wider audience is to be reached. This is because many visitors may be unwilling or unable to download software components just to view one site. Some examples of such features are Java applets, activex controls, shockwave objects, tools that require plug-ins and specialized document formats.

### Usability

Ideally, the first page of a site should give the visitor the information he wants. If this is not possible, it should give him an idea of what the site is about. If a visitor has to navigate through several pages before reaching one that is useful to him, he may simply move away, midway, to a different site. Long scrolling pages are also annoying.

Making the site searchable is a good practice, but if this is not feasible, means of contacting someone who can provide information on the site, preferably mailto links to his email address, should be provided.

### Balance

Excessive use of graphics, frames, background images and other visual features makes a page flashy and tawdry. Their judicious use, on the other hand, improves a page's appearance and enhances its appeal.

### Freshness

Efforts should be made to make some changes in the appearance of a page from time to time. Otherwise it will become monotonous to repeat visitors.

### Graphics Quality

Mackenzie notes[9] that graphics quality can be a key factor in improving the appearance of a site, and subtle differences have a huge impact. He recommends the use of good graphics packages like Adobe Photoshop, Corel Photo-Paint or Microsoft Image Composer, or one of the many available freeware, shareware, and demo packages. Once a good program has been found, customized graphics should be created for the site, as this will lend coherence to the site's design.

### Page Size

Slow-loading pages are frustrating. File sizes should be limited in order to improve the speed of loading. Mackenzie recommends about 50 KB for a main page. Such a page will load quickly while allowing the use of some graphics. If the content has too much text, it should be split up into more pages.

Photographs should be in the JPEG format, as it allows limited file sizes. The GIF format is appropriate if a part of the image is to be made transparent or if it is required to be displayed with the exact same appearance always. High-quality graphics software packages allow the creation of smaller files while maintaining image quality.

## Hosting a Web Page

Now that Don Quixote has created his page, he needs to put it up on the web. This requires a server, and if he does not have one himself – which is usually the case for individuals – he needs to use a web hosting service. This may belong to the institution that employs him, or to a commercial ISP. There are also several free services, such as Yahoo!'s GeoCities and Lycos' Tripod, both of which have premium versions available for a fee. VSNL, too, offers its subscribers a small server space (memory) at no extra charge for hosting their own sites.

## Ensuring Visibility

It is not enough to build usable and aesthetically pleasing web pages and put them up on the web. Steps have to be taken to increase the site's visibility, and thereby the chances of it being visited by potential users. These steps are geared towards increasing a site's ranking in the list of results of web searches performed by users. As Bradley[10] points out, search engines are one of the most important tools for attracting new visitors.

"The vast majority of users will not know about your site at all," he writes, "but will be looking for sites that cover a particular subject area. They rely heavily on the results returned by the search engines ..." We should note that this may not be the case for well-known sites, such as those of the *Hindustan Times* or *BBC*. These are frequented by a large number of people as a matter of habit, and others seek them out for information on specific topics because of their reputation.

But for lesser known sites and new ones, ranking high on search results is crucial. As Bradley points out, users usually look at the first few results, and a very small proportion of users look beyond the first one or two pages of search results. Two methods for increasing visibility are the use of search engine optimisation and search engine submission, also known as search engine registration.

## Search Engine Optimisation

This means ensuring that the pages are "accessible to search engines and focused in ways that help improve the chances they will be found".[11] There are several resources on the web providing useful insights into the way search engines work in order to help owners of websites improve the search ranking of their sites. The strategy is to carefully choose and position target keywords including in the meta-tags. Naturally, these things have to be done at the page building stage. Sullivan offers some important tips in the *SearchEngineWatch*.

## Choosing Target Keywords

To choose target keywords, one needs to imagine how people may search for the page, that is, the words and phrases they are likely to type into the search field of a search engine in order to find this particular page. These words and phrases have to be chosen as target keywords.

If a page is about online journalism, its owner naturally would like it to be among the top ten results displayed by a search engine when a user types 'online journalism' in the search box. Therefore, 'online journalism' should be chosen as the target keywords for the page. Each page in a website will have a different set of target keywords reflecting the contents of that page. These keywords should be at least two words long. A large number of sites are likely to be relevant for a single word like 'online' or 'journalism' and a page with either of these as the keyword therefore will have a small chance of ranking high in a search. Combining two or more words decreases the competition and thus increases the chance of success. Therefore, even if the body text of this page mentions 'online' or 'journalism', so long as it is about online journalism, the keywords should be 'online journalism'.

## Positioning Keywords

It has to be ensured that the target keywords appear in crucial locations on the web page, of which the most important is the HTML title tag. The text used in this tag appears in the title bar at the top of the browser window (along with the names of browsers like Microsoft Internet Explorer and Mozilla Firefox) and often also determines the rank given to the page by search engines. If the target keywords are not included in the title tag, a page may receive a low ranking in a search even when its body content is highly relevant to the search terms typed in by the user. Moreover, this text also appears as the title of the entry for that page in search result listings, as we can see in Figure 7.5b. Figure 7.5a shows the HTML head tag of the home page of the Indian Institute of Management, Calcutta, and an entry for this page in a Google search results list.

As the title plays a crucial role in searches, it should be composed around the two or three most relevant key phrases for which the site owner would like the page to be found in a search. Moreover, it should be short and attractive like newspaper headlines.

Search engines give priority to a page where the keywords appear in its upper part. Therefore, target keywords should be included in the page headline, if possible, and in the first paragraphs. When a page is divided into sections with the help of a table – usually to accommodate a menu of links in the left-hand column and the body text in the right-hand column – search engines read the menu first, and the body text later.

Thus, tables push the keywords down the page in the 'eyes' of the search engine. This should be kept in mind while designing pages.

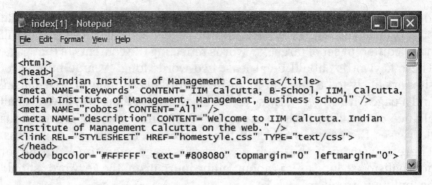

Figure **7.5a** Head tag of IIM, Calcutta's home page

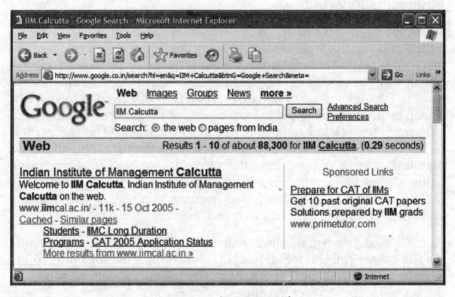

Figure **7.5b** Google search results for 'IIM Calcutta'

The presence of large blocks of JavaScript may have the same effect. As search engines read JavaScript first, the HTML body text appears lower down the page. Therefore, the script should be placed in the lower part of the page, if possible.

## Relevance of Content

Page titles with carefully chosen keywords alone will not enable a page to earn high search ranks. The body text must have content relevant to the topic. In other words, keywords need to be reflected in the content. A point that follows from this is that the content of the page should be entered in HTML text. Some sites present large amounts of written content through graphics due to aesthetic considerations, but search engines cannot read such graphics. As a result, the search ranking of such pages suffers.

Another popular method of search engine optimisation is the use of keywords in meta-tags, which are inserted into the 'head' area of a web page's source code in order to convey information to the computer. However, Sullivan writes, many search engines do not take note of meta-tags. (Words entered in the head area remain invisible, with the sole exception of the title tag.)

There are different kinds of meta-tags with different functions. One of these is the meta keywords tag, in which target keywords are sometimes entered in an effort to improve page rank. This tag is also useful for helping the page show up in searches for synonyms of keywords or unusual words that are closely related to the content of the page but do not appear on the page itself. This is why, in Figure 7.5a, we see that the IIM Calcutta home page has a keyword meta-tag with the phrases 'IIM Calcutta', 'B-School', 'IIM', 'Calcutta', 'Indian Institute of Management', 'Management', and 'Business School'.

Another meta-tag is the description tag, which allows the site owner to influence the description of his page in the crawlers that do read this tag. As we see in Figure 7.5b, the content of the description meta-tag – 'Welcome to IIM Calcutta. Indian Institute of Management Calcutta on the web.' – appears in the Google search results list.

## Search Engine Submission or Registration

Search engine submission or registration refers to having a website listed on the directory of a search engine. Unlike search engine optimisation, which is done at the page building stage, submission or registration has to be done after the site is online. The act of registering or submitting does not automatically ensure a high search rank for a site, but it is still an important step towards ensuring visibility. "Think of it like a lottery," writes Sullivan. "Search engine submission is akin to you purchasing a lottery ticket. Having a ticket doesn't mean that you will win, but you must have a ticket to have any chance at all."[12]

The site can be registered with directories or crawlers or both. Directories are subject-wise, hierarchically arranged indices (lists) of websites prepared by editors. The directories of Yahoo!, Google and Netscape's dmoz Open Directory (www.dmoz.org) are examples. It is important to have a site listed with the major directories, as their lists are viewed and consulted by a large number of web users. Moreover, it increases the probability of crawler-based search engines, that is, the services that are simply called 'search engines' in everyday parlance, finding the site and adding it to their own lists at no charge to the site's owner.

To prepare for the registration or submission, the site owner needs to write a short description (25 words or less) of the site. This text should use two or three keywords or phrases for which the owner wishes the site to be found by users. The description should be informative and to the point, and should avoid marketing language, as directory editors tend to dislike this.

The next step is to visit the directory's website and select the category which corresponds most closely to the topic of the page or site. Submit the URL and the short description through its 'suggest a site' link after checking that the site is not already listed. Yahoo! currently has two options for submissions – a paid option, costing $299, and a free option. The paid option is mandatory for commercial sites but open to all, and guarantees consideration of the submission within seven working days. The free option carries no such time guarantee. The Google directory accepts submissions through the dmoz site.

As for crawler-based search engines, Sullivan writes that the best way to get listed with engines like Google is to 'build links' to the site concerned. "Crawlers follow links, so if you have good links pointing at your website, the crawlers are more likely to find and include your pages." Thus, Google and other crawlers are almost sure to pick up the URL of a site if it has been submitted to the major directories and listed by at least one of them.

## Exercises

1. Create the information architecture (complete with diagrams) for a website on online journalism in India.

2. Study the *Webmonkey* tutorials and create the above site with four or five linked pages, using frames, images and a small amount of dynamic content. Put it up on the web using any hosting service of your choice.

3. Using major search engines like Google, Teoma, Yahoo!, et cetera, and keywords related to your site, find the search ratings for the site. Submit the above site to several directories, including Yahoo and dmoz, and then repeat the exercise after waiting for a few days. Discuss any changes that you may find in the ratings.

# References

1  'What is Web Authoring? What is Web Publishing?',*CERN Web Services Documentation,* accessed 11 October 2005 on http://webservices.web.cern.ch/WebServices/docs/AuthDoc/WebAuthTutorial/.

2  Kimen, Shel, '10 Questions About Information Architecture', *builder.com*, 29 September 2003, accessed 11 October 2005 on http://builder.com.com/5100-31-5074224.html.

3  Myers, Thomas, 'Information Architecture Concepts', *IBM developerWorks*, 1 July 2002, accessed 11 October 2005 on http://www-128.ibm.com/developerworks/usability/library/us-inarch.html.

4  'Markup language', *Wikipedia*, accessed 9 October 2005 on http://en.wikipedia.org/wiki/Markup_language.

5  'XML', *Wikipedia*, accessed 9 October 2005 on http://en.wikipedia.org/wiki/XML.

6  'Nokia, Motorola, Ericsson and Siemens to further advance the development of personal mobile services through XHTML', Nokia Press Release, 21 March 2001, accessed 10 October 2005 on http://press.nokia.com/PR/200103/813123_5.html.

7  'Dynamic HTML', *Wikipedia*, accessed 12 October 2005 on http://en.wikipedia.org/wiki/DHTML.

8  Monkey, W. T., 'Intro to HTML', *Webmonkey: The Web Development Resource,* 22 February 1999 accessed 11 October 2005 on http://hotwired.lycos.com/webmonkey/96/53/index0a.html?tw=authoring.

9  Mackenzie, Colin, 'Graphics Quality', *Web Design Tips*, accessed 12 October 2005 on http://www.colin.mackenzie.org/webdesign/quality.html.

10  Bradley, Phil, *Getting and Staying Noticed on the Web*, ( London, Facet, 2002), p. 64.

[11] Sullivan, Danny, 'Intro to Search Engine Optimization', *SearchEngineWatch*, 14 October 2002, accessed 13 October 2005 on http://searchenginewatch.com/webmasters/article.php/2167921.

[12] Sullivan, Danny, 'Intro to Search Engine Submission', *SearchEngineWatch*, 5 July 2004, accessed 13 October 2005 on http://searchenginewatch.com/webmasters/article.php/2168011.

# 8.
# Revenue, Ethics and Law

This chapter discusses certain issues that have
to be addressed both by news organisations and
by individuals responsible for the financial and
legal soundness of online news work, namely
journalists, advertising and management
personnel. These include ways of financing
websites through subscription and advertising,
and the ethical and legal issues involved in online
news publishing.

## Financing Online Journalism

Most internet users are accustomed to reading
news from websites that are online editions of
newspapers, magazines, or radio and television
channels. Though the cost of producing these
sites is usually borne by the parent media outlets,
they have to stand on their own feet in the long
run. For web-only publications, such as India's
*Tehelka.com* (until it launched its print edition
some time ago) or *rediff.com*, or the US-based
*Salon.com*, the struggle for survival starts from
the first day.

For both types of online media, it is important
to earn revenue to sustain themselves and to

grow. As with the older media, there are basically two ways of doing this – subscription and advertising.

## Revenue from Subscription

As we have noted earlier, the internet came into existence as a tool for sharing information among geographically dispersed researchers. When it was confined to the ARPAnet, this sharing was limited to scientists working in different US laboratories within the ambit of US defence projects. With networks like Usenet joining it, the internet soon became a network of the US university community as a whole (not yet a public network) and was infused with its communitarian ethos and hostility towards commercialism.

That ethos was carried over into the realm of media when online journalism appeared in the latter half of the 1990s. Websites of newspapers, magazines, radio stations and television channels offered free content and anyone could get all the news he wanted, gratis, from these sites. The cost of producing online editions was borne by the parent media which recovered a part of this cost from online advertisements.

But many news sites in the advanced industrial countries have begun to charge for content over the last few years. This is not because the parent companies are unable to bear the cost of producing online editions, which is small compared to the cost of print and broadcast. It is because these have been 'cannibalising' their own print editions, that is, eating into the readership of their parent print publications (see box).

However, charging for online content is a 'delicate balancing act', according to O. hAnluain[1], who quotes Alex Daley, head of UK's Association of Online Publishers (AOP), as saying that most publishers introduce a tiered system because consumers are unlikely to be willing to pay for all online content. Too many fees would drive away readers and this in turn would drive away advertising. This would have disastrous consequences, as advertising accounts for 70 to 80 per cent of all online broadsheet revenues in the UK.

## The Threat to Print in the West

"At stake is nothing less than the future of print journalism", writes Scherer.[1] "Several recent studies suggest that print readers are turning to the Web for news.

"Traffic on newspaper Web sites in seven of the ten largest U.S. markets grew far faster in the first half of 2002 than the total Internet User base ... At the same time, consumers with six years of Web experience are three times more likely than Internet newcomers to decrease their print newspaper reading ..." Another poll of people younger than 30, found that 31 per cent had reduced their print readership because the same material was online, and this number was expected to increase.

"Meanwhile," Scherer adds, "classified advertisers are continuing their flight to the Web, where costs are much lower. Between January 2001 and June 2002, U.S. newspaper revenue from help-wanted ads dropped by **40 percent** [emphasis added], a $5.4 billion shortfall ... Despite the current economic downturn, many analysts believe that much of that business, along with real estate and automobile listings, will never return to print papers given the rise of less expensive sites like Monster.com, Autotrader.com, and Realtor.com."

While the situation is worrying for the US print media, there may not be need for such concern in India as yet – the penetration of personal computers and the internet being low here, the online media are not in a position to take away large chunks of readership and advertising revenue from print.

However, it is possible that a similar trend will develop in India, too, in the coming years, at least among the more affluent sections of society that are taking to the internet in a big way. In fact, some Indian newspapers and magazines have already started charging for certain types of content, and in some cases, they deny even limited free access.

### Subscription Models

Friedman mentions the following models that have been tried by US, British and Japanese newspapers[3].

### The Albuquerque Journal Model

Byline news, sports and features created by newspaper staff are accessible only to print subscribers who register for access. Anyone else attempting to access these stories sees a message asking him to subscribe to the print or online edition.

Access to the following is free: classified and display advertisements, personal ads, obituaries, tourism information, 'News to Use', and the contact page. Seven-day subscribers to the printed newspaper have access to full online content as part of their print subscription. One can also opt for an online-only membership.

### The Business 2.0 Model

Non-subscribers can see the front-page 'promos' and can read the first pages of stories, but are prompted to subscribe if they try to go to the second page. There is no web-only subscription option. Online subscribers also get the print edition, and vice versa. Thus, in this case there is only one list of subscribers rather than two, unlike the *Albuquerque Journal*. If a subscriber does not want the print newspaper, it can be donated to such places as nursing homes and prisons.

### The Winnipeg Model

The *Winnipeg Free Press* allows only subscribers to see any news, headlines or news summaries. In India, the *India Today* magazine lies somewhere between the Business 2.0 and Winnipeg Free Press models, as it allows free access only to headlines accompanied by a sentence or two introducing the article. Access to articles themselves on its website is reserved for subscribers of its print edition, who have to log in with their subscription IDs (provided in the address label on the cover in which the printed magazine is mailed to them).

### The Borrell Premium Content Model

In the opinion of Borrell[*] most newspapers cannot successfully charge readers for accessing their main news content and should charge, instead, for value-added and premium content, such as archives, newsletters and personalized content delivered to the individual reader.

---

[*] Borrell Associates is a US consultancy firm specialising in the media business.

*The New York Times* follows this model, charging for stories from its archives, and for subscription to its News Tracker service which e-mails stories of interest to subscribers. It asks users of its website to register for certain types of content, such as crossword puzzles and archived articles more than seven days old, and this registration can only be done by providing one's credit card details.

In the UK, *The Guardian* charges for certain services, such as an ad-free version of its website and for its crossword puzzles. *The Financial Times* charges for parts of its site. In Japan, the *Asahi Shimbun* charges readers for news alerts.

### The Times of London Model

This is the practice of charging those readers who are located outside the paper's circulation area. *The Times* charges overseas users £8.99 per month or £89.99 per year to access the 'e-paper', that is, the online replica of the print edition, while most sections of *Times Online* (www.timesonline. co.uk), its web-specific edition, except for a few like the crossword puzzle (standard £9.99 per year and premium £24.99), are accessible to all and do not need any subscription.

In India, the *Hindustan Times* offers the e-paper service for $3 per month or $25 per year, throwing in audio versions of the news items along with the e-paper. Clearly, this is aimed mainly at overseas Indians. It also offers a fee-based archive service in the e-paper section. *The Times of India* offers access to its e-paper to registered users of its *Indiatimes* portal free of cost, but plans to charge Rs 50 per month for current editions of the e-paper and Rs 5,000 per month for its archive, in future.

## Revenue from Advertisements

As O. hAnluain has noted, 70 to 80 per cent of the revenues of online editions of broadsheets in the UK comes from advertising, not subscription. This is consistent with the trend worldwide, in the older media as well as the new.

Online advertising revenue is growing rapidly, especially in the developed industrial societies. Citing *Advertising Age, The Economist* wrote[4] on

27 April 2005, that during the year the combined advertising revenue of Google and Yahoo! was expected to rival the combined prime-time advertising revenues of the three big television networks, ABC, CBS and NBC, in the USA. This would represent a 'watershed moment' in the evolution of the internet as an advertising medium. "A 30-second prime-time TV ad was once considered the most effective – and the most expensive – form of advertising," *The Economist* added, "But that was before the internet got going." Online advertising revenue is growing in India, too, at a slower but still considerable pace.

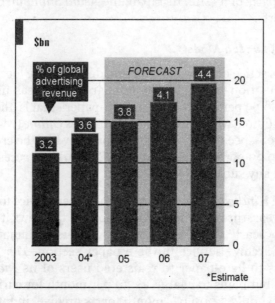

FIGURE **8.1** Global online advertising revenue

(Source: *The Economist*)

## Modes of Online Advertising

Growth in online advertising has come about because advertisers have begun to realise the intrinsic value of the net or web as an advertising medium. It arises from the fact that online marketing is a combination of several elements, as represented by Zeff[5] in Figure 8.2. As we can see in the figure, online marketing and advertising have the following four elements: traditional advertising, direct marketing, guerilla or grass roots marketing and e-commerce.

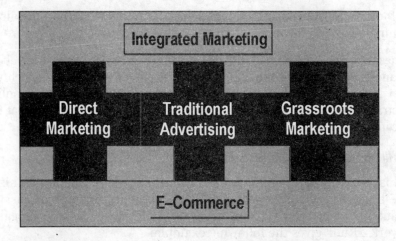

F IGURE **8.2** Online marketing and advertising

(Source: Robbin Zeff, *Internet Marketing and Advertising Primer*)

### Traditional Advertising

Its focus is on brand building, by reaching as many people as frequently as possible in order to build a lasting image. In the online environment, the brand-building function is performed by banners, buttons, sponsorship of web pages and sections, as well as interstitials – interruption-based online advertisements that interrupt what the user has been doing or viewing, somewhat like TV and radio commercials, by taking over a part or whole of the screen for some time.

Zeff points to the example of Yahoo! and Amazon.com to underscore the point that brand-building works very well online. To his example, we may add that of Google, which has become such a household name that it is often used as a verb ("I googled 'Satyajit Ray' to write my term paper on Indian cinema.") in the same way as 'xerox' is used as a verb to mean 'photocopy'.

### Direct Marketing

This has the capacity to target a desired audience, so that the right advertisement goes to the right person at the right time. The net is an effective vehicle for this, as it excels in targeting a desired audience. On the one hand, it possesses the broadcast media's ability to target audiences on the basis of content (programme for radio and television and page for the web) or context (time of programme for broadcast, area within the site for the web). On the other hand, it has the ability to support the direct mailing technique through email.

As these two can be combined with demographic and other information about the audience, including the habits and interests of individuals which the advertiser can acquire from what is provided by users themselves in online registration forms and through the use of cookies, it is easy to see that the net can be used as an extremely powerful vehicle for direct marketing.

### Guerilla or Grassroots Marketing

In this, the aim is to "creat(e) a buzz through word of mouth". This is done by getting involved with the target audience through discussion forums like chat rooms, email listservs, bulletin boards and blogging networks. Rudl[6] gives the following example:

> (I)f you sell mountain biking shoes, spend some time hanging out in mountain biking forums – that's where your target market's going to be. Or start your own blog in which you describe your latest mountain biking adventures, complete with attention-grabbing photos. You could even combine the two tactics and generate interest in your blog by mentioning it in forums and newsgroups.
>
> However, most newsgroups, blog networks and discussion forums do *not* allow people to blatantly advertise in them. If you want to generate traffic through these sites, the best way to do it is to offer friendly, useful advice to people who express a need for something, and then include a subtle link to your site at the end of all your messages. If people like what you say, they may decide to visit your site and check out your products or services.

### E-commerce

This involves transacting entire sales processes online without the customer having to leave his computer.

As Bruner[7] has noted, the year 2004 marked the first decade in the life of online advertising since the first web advertisement – a banner (Figure 8.3) – is thought to have appeared in *HotWired* (now known as *Wired News*), an online magazine on information technology and related culture in 1994.

However, online advertising does not consist only of banner advertisements. It presents several other options to the advertiser, such as buttons, interstitials like floating animated page takeovers, rich media advertisements, keyword targeted search engine advertising, sponsorship of web pages, and email. The banner advertisement itself has evolved from being a static object (text, image or a combination of these) to something that often contains text and images going through various types of movement, showing video clips, offering games for users to play, or allowing users to carry out transactions for purchasing something.

FIGURE **8.3** The banner advertisement believed to have been one of the first advertisements to appear on the web

(Source: *The Decade in Online Advertising: 1994–2004*, www.doubleclick.com)

## Online Advertising and Marketing Techniques

The following are some of the advertising and marketing techniques being used very successfully on the internet. Not all of these are widely used by news-oriented websites today, but the net being a hotbed of innovation, what is not seen today may be a common sight tomorrow. For instance, while most news sites do not engage in e-commerce, *The Times of India* group's *Indiatimes.com* portal does. See Glossary[8] for terms used in this field.

### Affiliate Marketing

This is the practice of a site selling the products of other sites – which are called its affiliates. In effect, this is about e-commerce. Amazon.com was the first large-scale affiliate programme, which started by selling the books of various publishers and has diversified into music and many other kinds of merchandise.

### Search Engine Marketing or Optimisation

Rudl says the free search engines, such as Google, Yahoo! and MSN, are still one of the most effective ways to advertise one's own site and thus one's products and services. There are several techniques for ensuring that a certain site gets a high ranking with these search engines. Among these are, submitting the site to the free search engines and online directories; optimising the site so that it is easily indexed by search engine spiders; paying close attention to one's keyword inclusion and placement (in the keyword meta-tag of the site); creating content-rich information pages to help direct traffic to the site (see chapter seven).

### Opt-in Email

This refers to email messages containing information or advertising that users request (opt) to receive. Some websites ask visitors to fill out forms stating subject or product categories about which they would like to receive email. The site then sells the visitors' names, email addresses and interests (with their permission, explicit or implicit) to a company that collects mailing lists of people with different interests. This company in turn sells its lists to advertisers. Every time it does so, the site which gave it the names and addresses, is paid a small sum for each name. Opt-in emails often start with a statement telling the recipient that he has earlier agreed to receive such mails.

### Viral Marketing

This term refers to any type of advertising that is self-perpetuating, and forces people to share it with others so that it spreads through a community like a virus. Hotmail is a classic example of online viral marketing. It was a free web-based email service that collected 12 million subscribers in its first year and a half. It did this by appending the following message at the end of every email: "Get your private, free email at http://www.hotmail.com". These are effective ways to market one's products and services through the internet, but advertisers and sites that accept ads need to remember that there are not many web users who actually like these, and there are in fact very strong sentiments against certain types of advertisements. Nielsen's[9] findings in a study conducted in 2004 confirm his findings from earlier studies (See Table 8.1).

Table 8.1 'The Most Hated Advertising Techniques'

| Design Element | Users Answering 'Very Negatively' or 'Negatively' |
|---|---|
| Pops-up in front of the user's window | 95% |
| Loads slowly | 94% |
| Tries to trick the user into clicking on it | 94% |
| Does not have a 'Close' button | 93% |
| Covers what the user is trying to see | 93% |
| Doesn't say what it is for | 92% |
| Moves content around | 92% |
| Occupies most of the page | 90% |
| Blinks on and off | 87% |
| Floats across the screen | 79% |
| Automatically plays sound | 79% |

(Source: Jacob Nielsen)

However, since advertising is essential for the media's survival in free market economies, the best a news site can do is to refuse advertisements that significantly degrade the quality of the readers' media experience, and the best an advertiser can do is to desist from offering such advertisements to news sites.

## Ethical Considerations

Just as the online journalist needs to understand the ways in which his work can be financed, he also needs to appreciate the ethical issues he is likely to face. Since ethical choices by nature depend on concrete situations, the journalist has to make these decisions on the facts of each individual case. The aim of this section is to sensitise readers to the issues that are commonly involved.

According to J. D. Lasica, Senior Editor, *Online Journalism Review*[†], the issues can be grouped under three broad categories: news gathering, news reporting, and news presentation.[10] As these often overlap, the taxonomy of Joann Byrd, professor of journalism ethics and member of the Pulitzer Prize Board, may be more helpful. Byrd identifies the concerns of online journalists as those related to six 'core values' of balance (balance/fairness/wholeness), accuracy (accuracy/authenticity), leadership, accessibility, credibility, and news judgment.[11]

### Balance and Accuracy

Speaking of issues related to news gathering, Lasica says the internet gives journalists "powerful tools of context and authentication", as they can use the net's hyperlink-based architecture to provide users with important background material, resources and archived articles that help the user follow the course of a news story over time. In chapter six, we have discussed how *The Guardian* does this in an excellent manner.

Equally important, and still underutilised in Lasica's view, is the ability to link to source material, transcripts, public records and other original

---

[†] Published online by the well-known Annenberg School of Communication, University of Southern California

documents to support the reporting in a story. "In this age of public mistrust of the media," Lasica writes, "such steps enhance a news organization's credibility. In my freshman year at college my journalism professor told us that the first rule of good journalism is: Show, don't tell. So: Don't tell readers to trust you. Show them the goods." As we noted in chapter four, Gary Webb had set a shining example of this kind of journalism as early as in 1996.

'Showing the goods', in the ways mentioned by Lasica above, ties in with the traditional issues of balance and accuracy. As Byrd has noted, the idea of balance now expands to include fairness and comprehensiveness, as the journalist has to ask himself the following questions:

- Under what circumstances is it right to link to advertisements, editorials or columns, sites of partisan organisations, hate groups, charitable organisations seeking contributions, and other news media?

- Since readers can leave a story before reading all sides of the account, by simply clicking on other links, what, if anything, should the journalist do to ensure these readers do not leave with a one-sided understanding of the news topic?

- Since it is technically possible to link all the photographs and textual elements collected from the news scene, under what circumstances is it right to provide these with the story through links?

In Byrd's opinion, the question of accuracy extends to include authenticity in the online context:

> Online media have room to get the facts right, and to cover the right facts. But authenticity also asks us to understand and convey background, context and nuance – in a medium that moves at the speed of light. Furthermore, reporters will come upon interesting remarks online and want to use them in stories. And if we divide news from advertisements on a page of newsprint, do we want some design devices for the computer screen?

In other words, a remark found on the net – say, on a listserv or in a chat room – may be interesting, but the journalist needs to ask himself whether he can be confident about its authenticity, that is, confident that it has been actually made, and by the person who supposedly made it. The other side of this coin is that a news site must make it clear which part of its content is authentic editorial matter and which is advertising matter, so that readers do not take commercial content as journalism.

## The 'Church–State' Divide

Lasica writes that the line of demarcation between editorial matter (church), on the one hand, and advertising and advertorial matter (state), on the other, is not yet as sharply defined on the internet as it is in the print media. *The New York Times* faced strong criticism in 1998 when it began to provide a link to the online bookstore barnesandnoble.com on the books pages of its online edition. Lasica feels that such links are useful to readers, but the paper should provide links to several commerce sites rather than just one. Even respected newspapers like *The Washington Post* have since incorporated e-commerce in their online editions.

"All these efforts bear close scrutiny to ensure that editorial decisions are not influenced by financial considerations, just as has long been the case in print newsrooms," Lasica remarks. In India, an interesting case in this respect is that of *The Times of India* group's *Indiatimes.com* site which has an elaborate e-commerce section through which registered users can purchase a huge variety of merchandise. This paper was also the subject of much discussion recently over its advertorials.

## Speed vs. Accuracy

One of the issues Byrd touches on – how to ensure accuracy and authenticity in a medium that "moves at the speed of light" – is in fact a major concern for online journalists. Since the internet is a medium that transcends differences of geographical space and time, and is 'on' 24 hours a day, seven days a week, online journalists find themselves struggling '24 × 7' to make sure that their respective sites are kept updated with the latest news and do not fall behind competing sites.

"In the current saturated media environment," writes Lasica, "the Internet heightens the intense competitive pressures to be first while a story is still developing and key facts remain unknown." But this, as one can imagine, puts a strain on accuracy and authenticity. The journalist, therefore, has to learn how to balance the demands of the continuous news cycle of the net with the demands of accuracy or authenticity.

"The challenge facing online journalists," Lasica writes, "is to balance the legitimate desires of the online audience for up-to-the-minute reports with the profession's traditions of fairness, completeness, balance and accuracy ... The guidepost must always remain: What best serves the interests of the reader and the public while remaining fair to those named in the story? Not: Can we beat our competitors even though we haven't nailed down this story?"

### Gathering News in Discussion Forums

Among other dilemmas faced by online journalists in the course of their news gathering activities, according to Lasica, are the following:

- Is it permissible for reporters to lurk in chat rooms without identifying themselves? (The same question also applies to other types of discussion forums, such as email listservs and bulletin boards.) Lasica says such behaviour is rarely permissible, and only when the subject is of 'significant public importance'.

- Is it permissible for reporters to quote from bulletin board postings, chat transcripts or, we should add, email listserv postings, without the user's permission? Lasica says that among netizens, such an action would be considered "bad form at best and unethical at worst", and might be violative of the terms and conditions of use set by some sites.

## Leadership

Interactivity, Byrd says, is an ideal mechanism for making people familiar with issues that are important to their lives, and with other people with whom they share certain problems as a community. But a section of the population does not have access to the internet, and interactive websites allow those who do, to personalise their news packages.

Thus, the population becomes fragmented in its knowledge of social reality. It falls to the media, including news sites, to give leadership in the task of holding communities together by devising a way to make sure that their members have some common knowledge despite distractions. "In an avalanche of information," writes Byrd, "glitter and noise attract attention. How can we rescue the planning commission report?"

## Accessibility

Interactivity, Byrd points out, implies accessibility. News sites have introduced chat rooms and other discussion forums in order to promote readers' engagement with a subject, with the newspaper and with one another. Here, Byrd is speaking of 'functional interactivity'.

But this may become problematic if such forums are not moderated by the sites' editors, that is, if any comment can appear on the forum without going through an editorial filter. For example, some comments may be defamatory or designed to incite particular communities against each other. On the other hand, Byrd notes, such filtering should not be too restrictive. Moreover, when readers are invited to respond to writers, photographers and editors, there may be a lack of civility in the exchange from either side, and the news site needs to decide how it will deal with such problems.

## Credibility

Byrd says that since space is not an expensive limiting factor online, unlike in the print media, reporting and the site's judgments can be made transparent with relative ease. "A linked sidebar explaining our news decisions and policies would announce we are accountable to our readers," she writes.

Readers will be able to make their own judgements if a site links its stories to the respective source material. However, it may be necessary for a source to be warned beforehand if the transcript of an interview with him is being posted online.

If this practice of linking source material like interview transcripts is followed, readers will become accustomed to knowing more about sources than is currently afforded by the traditional media, that is, accustomed to more transparency than that which is afforded by the traditional media. In this event, Byrd says, the media practice of quoting 'leaked' information and anonymous sources will lose whatever credibility it currently has.

## News Judgment

Byrd writes that good news judgment implies that journalists reflect on their coverage, possess intimate knowledge of the communities they serve and the issues important to them, offer "clear thinking and explanations", respect all sections of society and cover all dimensions of the community that constitutes its audience.

Since the 'news hole' online is not limited by space and time constraints, unlike in the print and broadcast media, coverage of the community served by an online news outlet need not be limited by such constraints. It is technically feasible for a news site to serve the community by posting large volumes of important information online, and keeping these posted for the readers' reference as and when needed.

Therefore, Byrd says, online journalism affords improved news judgment. However, understanding the community being served, thinking clearly and reflecting on coverage are not specific to any particular medium, and are the hallmarks of intelligent and wise journalism. "All in all," writes Byrd, "it's a sure bet that cyberspace will help (journalists) keep our promises."

## Cyberlaw

The internet has grown more or less spontaneously and at an explosive rate. Supreme Court Advocate Pavan Duggal notes that since the framers of older laws could not have visualised the properties unique to this medium, issues raised by online media defy satisfactory resolution within the framework of these laws. For instance, a genuine letter in the traditional sense, that is, one written on paper, has legal validity as a piece of evidence. But what if it was sent by email?

Because of this mismatch, the need has been felt for a body of laws specifically addressing the net. Such a corpus is taking shape all over the world, though at an uneven pace from country to country. The collective name of these laws and regulations is cyberlaw – law for cyberspace.

This is a vast field, to which justice cannot be done in these pages. As cyberspace cuts across national borders, we would have to deal with the legal systems of many countries, as well as international systems and conventions. The objective of this section is more realistic – setting out the main issues and considerations of cyberlaw as it is evolving today.

Samuelson[12] notes that policymakers have faced at least five challenges in this task:

- How to decide whether existing laws and policies can be applied or adapted to the regulation of online activities, or new laws or policies are needed;
- How to formulate a 'reasonable and proportional' response when new regulation is needed;

- How to design laws that are flexible enough to adapt to rapid changes in scenario;

- How to preserve fundamental human values in the face of economic or technological pressures that tend to undermine them; and

- How to coordinate with other nations in the framing of cyberlaw and policy in order to ensure that the legal environment is consistent across the globe.

Before turning our attention to the issues at the focus of cyberlegislation efforts, we need to note that a major legal consideration on the internet is that of multiple jurisdictions:

- Since the net cuts across national borders, cyberlaws have both national and supranational or global ramifications, with the two aspects clashing at times.

- When someone is in cyberspace, he is simultaneously[13] occupying two 'spaces' – cyberspace and real space – and is subject to the laws of both spaces, not of one or the other.

## Issues in Cyberlaw

The following are the main issues policymakers have had to address, and on which they sometimes have been required to frame new laws.

### *Governance and Regulation of the Internet*

The term governance refers to "the rules, processes and procedures, and specific actions that impact the way in which power is exercised on a specific area of concern ... (and) is ... a broader concept than government in that government essentially has 'governance' responsibilities limited to specific areas (constitution, judiciary, legislative, etc.)."[14]

Internet governance consists of three sets of issues, which can be visualised as three concentric circles. Each is 'governed' by a combination of governmental and non-governmental arrangements[15] : (1) ICT governance issues, which include (2) internet governance issues, which in turn include (3) administration and coordination of internet names and numbers.

Thus, the innermost circle (3) mainly corresponds to technical administration of the net, namely, ensuring its interoperability, functionality, stability, security and effectiveness over the long run. The two layers above this correspond to the policy domain. However, this separation of administration from policy is not absolute – due to the nature of software technology, approaches to policy problems as well as solutions often have both technological and policy components.

The main actors in the innermost circle, that is, technical management and administration of the net are: ICANN (Internet Corporation for Assigned Names and Numbers), IETF (Internet Engineering Task Force), ISOC (Internet Society), IAB (Internet Architecture Board), CERT (Computer Emergency Response Team) in the US and a growing number of other countries, RIRs (Regional Internet Registries), root server operators, W3C (World Wide Web Consortium), ITU (International Telecommunications Union), and top-layer ISPs, which provide the net's 'backbone' functions. ICANN has operated under contract with the US Department of Commerce, and some countries are concerned about this direct involvement of the US government, although more than half of the members of its Board of Directors are not from North America.

The layers above this core consist of public policy issues, which are as follows.

### Convergence

The domains of telecommunication, broadcasting and information technology are going through a process of convergence, which will be discussed in detail in chapter eleven. This process poses a challenge to policymakers, as older laws and regulatory mechanisms, designed with separate technologies in mind, are mostly inadequate in the new situation.

For instance, internet connectivity is currently available through television cable. Therefore, net telephony using voice over internet protocol or VoIP technology as well as streamed web radio and web TV are available through the TV cable along with normal cable TV signals. Which law should regulate which service? Clearly, the old laws regulating each of these individual services have become inadequate.

The European Union has been a pioneer in addressing convergence, having published a Green Paper on the subject as early as in 1997, as a 'forum for debate' between differing viewpoints.[16] The issue at the heart of the debate is deregulation (see box on p.169).

Realising the need for new legislation in the emerging convergence regime, the Government of India framed the Communications Convergence Bill, 2001. But its tabling in the Parliament had to be put off in 2002 in the face of protests from various quarters. Industry associations felt that too much power was being given to a single regulatory body, proposed to be called the 'Communications Commission of India'. The Parliamentary Standing Committee on Convergence also had serious reservations about the Bill, which has remained in cold storage ever since.

## Speech

The Global Internet Liberty Campaign has listed[17] the following ways in which governments have sought to restrict speech on the net:

### Through Laws Specific to the Net

Some governments have decreed criminal penalties for certain types of 'speech' on the net, such as child pornography.

---

### Extracts from the European Union Green Paper

"This Green Paper argues that the development of new services could be hindered by the existence of a range of barriers, including regulatory barriers, at different levels of the market. There are, however, differing views on the adequacy of existing regulatory frameworks to deal with the changing environment. One view is that the development of new products and services is being held back by regulatory uncertainty – that existing rules were defined for a national, analogue and mono-media environment, but that services increasingly cut across different traditional sectors and geographical boundaries, and that they may be provided over a variety of platforms. This calls into question the underlying rationale beneath regulatory approaches in the different sectors affected by convergence. Proponents of this view would argue that such regulatory uncertainty holds back investment and damages the prospects for the implementation of the Information Society.

An alternative view would hold that the specific characteristics of the existing separate sectors will limit the scope for service convergence. It further would contend that the role of the media industry as the bearer of social, cultural and ethical values within our society is independent of the technology relied upon to reach the consumer. This would mean that regulation of economic conditions and that of the provision of information services should be separated to ensure efficiency and quality."

### By Applying Existing Laws

Sometimes governments have used existing laws to restrict, on the internet, those types of 'speech' that would be unlawful if made in other ways, such as in the print media. Germany has used existing laws to act against a major ISP for providing access to material illegal under these laws. In India, a man in Kolkata was arrested a few years ago on the basis of existing laws when he put up material on a website that was apparently defamatory of former Chief Minister Jyoti Basu.

### Through Content-based License Terms

Several countries have put in place licensing systems that require net users and/or ISPs to agree to refrain from certain kinds of speech, or block access to these as a condition for getting a licence to use the net or to provide net access to subscribers. China has such rules for all net users, and Singapore's licensing conditions require ISPs to block access to foreign websites and newsgroups considered harmful to national morals.

### Through Compulsory Use of Filtering, Rating or Content Labeling Tools

There are techniques that can prevent people from exchanging information on certain predefined topics on the net, enable the development of country profiles to facilitate a universal rating system desired by some governments, block access to content on entire domains, block access to content on any domain or page containing a specific keyword or character string in the address, and over-ride self-rating labels provided by content creators and providers.

## Intellectual Property Rights

Intellectual property law has three main branches – law on patents, trademark and copyright. Patents provide an exclusive but limited right to the first person (or company) to invent something and exploit this invention. Patent laws usually vary from country to country and international agreements on patent laws are mainly designed to ensure that domestic patent holders are not given preferential treatment over those from other countries. Trademark law aims to protect the investment made by companies in earning 'goodwill' in their name or mark over time, and to protect consumers from confusion.

The issue of copyright is the most complex of the three, and the most frequently encountered in the online context. Copyright aims to provide economic incentives for the creativity employed by an author in producing a work, by giving him a monopoly over copying his creative work or the right to allowing others to do so. It includes the exclusive right to publish, produce or reproduce, to communicate a work to the public by telecommunications, etc.

Copyright applies to all original literary, dramatic, musical and artistic works inscribed in a fixed medium. These include books, other writings, music, sculptures, paintings, photographs, films, plays, television and radio programmes, computer programs, and sound recordings (such as records, cassettes, and tapes).

The internet has had a destabilising effect on intellectual property rights, especially copyright, as it has made it extremely easy to digitally copy and share all kinds of material among net users who are located in various countries and are often anonymous. P2P (peer to peer) networks like Napster came up in the west, exploiting this feature of the net to allow users to exchange copies of music files among themselves.

The US recording industry has been up in arms against this practice, claiming that such sharing is a violation of copyright, and Napster had to shut down for some time after losing court cases filed by the industry. It reopened subsequently, but with a 'legal' business model. However, other P2P networks like Morpheus, Grokster and KaZaa have continued to function, and have so far avoided being branded illegal. Meanwhile, the European Commission has led the way in copyright regulation and enforcement through its July 1995 Green Paper on Copyright and Related Rights in the Information Society.[18]

### E-commerce

Laws on e-commerce have two main components related to online transactions – issues of the legal validity of digital messages, and taxation issues. In taxation, the main issue is that of jurisdiction – which government should have the authority to tax a transaction that takes place across more than one jurisdiction.

The goal of e-commerce taxation policy is two-fold: to avoid both double-taxation and non-taxation; and to avoid differential treatment of transactions conducted offline (in real space) and online (in cyberspace).

A prominent initiative in this direction is that of OECD[19], the Organisation of Developed Industrial Countries, and this has been followed by the

European Union, which aims to tax e-commerce neutrally in relation to conventional trade within its border. The European Union model aims to apply Value Added Tax (VAT) at the place of consumption, subject to several adjustments. Electronic transmissions are taxed as services. Electronic services entering or leaving the European Union are taxed under the law of the country of their destination.

However, it is the more fundamental Model Law on Electronic Commerce, framed by the United Nations Commission on International Trade Law (UNCITRAL) and adopted by the UN General Assembly in January 1997[20] that makes e-commerce possible, as it grants legal validity to digitally transmitted messages and lays down rules for such things as digital signatures.

### India's Information Technology Act

Three years after the UN initiative, India framed the Information Technology Act, 2000,[21] "to provide legal recognition for transactions carried out by means of electronic data interchange and other means of electronic communication, commonly referred to as 'electronic commerce', which involve the use of alternatives to paper-based methods of communication and storage of information ..."

The aim was to facilitate electronic filing of documents with government agencies and also to amend the Indian Penal Code, the Indian Evidence Act, 1872, the Bankers' Books Evidence Act, 1891, the Reserve Bank of India Act, 1934, and the rules and regulations framed under these laws.

## Jurisdiction

This refers to the conflict of legal issues across national borders. For a long time, international law has had to grapple with the question: when does a citizen or company of one country come under the jurisdiction of another country's legal system? The internet has greatly exacerbated this problem, mainly because transactions can now take place across national borders with ease and the number of such transactions has therefore multiplied. The complexity of such transactions has also increased due to the borderless nature of the net.

For example, if someone in India attempts to buy something (say, digital music files or e-books or computer programs) over the net from a company based in Finland through a portal based in the USA, and a dispute arises in the course of this transaction, which country's courts have the right to adjudicate on this dispute? Similarly, can a trademark holder in France take a company using the same trademark in Germany to court for trademark infringement because the German company has put up a website that is available to French consumers? Which trademark law applies in this case – that of Germany or of France?

The GIPI website notes[22]:

> Jurisdiction issues, getting more and more attention as governments try to control online content and conduct originating beyond their borders. Examples include the French Yahoo! case, Saudi Arabia blocking 200,000 websites, claims by Italian and German courts of authority over sites abroad, the Chinese claiming rights to all Chinese language domain names, the EU proposing to have non-EU firms collect taxes for digitally delivered goods that come into the EU, and the US's efforts on Internet gambling and prescription drugs. These issues … (have) implications for privacy, freedom of expression and consumer protection.

The Hague Conference on Private International Law has been drafting an international convention in an effort to set international rules for determining the court in which foreign parties can be sued and when countries must recognize the judgments of foreign courts. 'Electronic Commerce and International Jurisdiction', Ottawa, 28 February to 1 March, Summary of discussions (http://www.hcch.net/upload/wop/jdgmpd12.pdf) and other documents on jurisdiction, such as the 'Convention on Choice of Court Agreements' (http://www.hcch.net/index_en.php?act=conventions.text&cid=98), are available on its website.

## Privacy

As we have noted in earlier chapters, the internet offers the means for easy and inexpensive search for and collection of data. In the past, the physical process of data collection discouraged large-scale collection of personal data.[23]

Now people's online activities can be tracked with the help of cookies and other technologies, without their knowledge. Sophisticated searchable databases are built with such data, which are often correlated with data collected from other sources, such as the individual's credit card transactions. The increasing ease of such data collection and its transfer presents a challenge to traditional privacy laws.

The laws and regulations relating to privacy vary from country to country, and the jurisdiction for each individual case may depend on the place in which the data is collected, used or transferred. Privacy is commonly seen as either a fundamental human right, or as a constitutional right – in which case it is sought to be balanced against other important national interests, thus reducing the degree of protection in comparison with the human rights approach.

### India

The Information Technology Act, 2000 makes a rather limited provision for privacy in Section 72, titled 'Penalty for Breach of Confidentiality and Privacy':

> Save as otherwise provided in this Act or any other law for the time being in force, any person who, in pursuance of any of the powers conferred under this Act, rules or regulations made thereunder, has secured access to any electronic record, book, register, correspondence, information, document or other material without the consent of the person concerned discloses such electronic record, book, register, correspondence, information, document or other material to any other person shall be punished with imprisonment for a term which may extend to two years, or with fine which may extend to one lakh rupees, or with both.

Duggal[24] points out that this section does not prohibit the invasion of an individual's privacy as such, nor does it prohibit spam (unsolicited emails). Duggal also notes that India does not have any specific law on privacy in general (as opposed to cyberspace).

### The European Union

However, as in other areas of cyberlaw, the European Union (EU) has made rigorous efforts to codify personal data protection in the online environment. In the EU's own words, Directive 95/46/CE (http://europa.eu.int/scadplus/leg/en/lvb/l14012.htm) is the 'reference text' on the protection of personal data at the European level.

This Directive (law) "sets up a regulatory framework which seeks to strike a balance between a high level of protection for the privacy of individuals and the free movement of personal data within the European Union." The Directive sets 'strict limits' on the collection and use of personal data and requires each EU member country to establish an independent national body responsible for the protection of such data.

## USA

In the USA, privacy is considered a constitutional right which is derived by inference from the Bill of Rights, since the Constitution does not contain a specific clause on privacy. There are also other forms of protection granted through federal laws covering certain specific categories of personal information, such as financial records, video rentals, cable television, educational records, motor vehicle registration and telephone records. The level of privacy depends on the type of personal information involved and on the context of its use, including, sometimes, on the question whether the user is a government agency or a private sector organisation.

## Cybercrime

An amazing variety of crimes are being committed on or through the internet every day. These include hate speech, stalking, fraud, hacking, theft, identify theft, pornography, bank fraud and bank theft.

Duggal and Vijayashankar have noted[25] that India's Information Technology Act, 2000,provides a fairly comprehensive framework for dealing with at least the common types of cybercrime. At least one case of cyber-stalking has been investigated by the Delhi Police and the culprit prosecuted.[26] The case involved a complaint lodged by a woman that another individual had been using her identity to chat on a certain website using obscene language. He had assumed her name, given her address and telephone number to other chatters and urged them to call her. As a result, she had received a large number of phone calls from various cities at odd hours and this had played havoc with her life.

However, the appearance of such crimes raises a large number of interesting questions[27] which can be answered by the courts only in the course of time. Experts like Dr Yaman Akdeniz of the School of Law, University of Leeds (UK) and Director of Cyber-Rights & Cyber-Liberties, have tried to address some of these issues.

The questions mentioned by the State University of New York, Buffalo are: Are these the same as, or similar to those experienced in the real world? Is there anything unique about these crimes except for the fact that their venue is cyberspace? Are these crimes likely to cause more harm or less when committed in cyberspace? Does the venue being cyberspace change the scale of the crimes' effect (say, in terms of the number of people and interests that can be affected)? Is harm to the persons different in nature when the crime is committed in cyberspace? Is harm to property different? How should law define harm against persons and society in cyberspace? Should policies be the same as or different from those of real space? How should activities be monitored, reported, policed, investigated and prosecuted, and by whom?

### Issues of Special Importance to the Media

In an interview to Madanmohan Rao, Duggal and Vijayashankar have addressed certain issues that have a high degree of relevance to the work of journalists and other professionals in the online environment. Some of the points made by them in an illuminating way and often from diametrically opposed perspectives, are given below. However, it is strongly recommended that the reader should read the full interview on the web.[‡]

According to the experts, in addition to the usual ethical issues, such as fairness, the online media should be aware of laws relating to intellectual property rights, especially copyright. Mere cut-and-paste and blatant copying of other people's content might invite problems. Websites need proper agreements with their contributors clarifying copyright issues. They also need a detailed linking policy setting out the legal aspects of their relationship with linked websites.

Strong disclaimers are needed on liability for third party content or data on the linked sites. Policies are needed to take care of the privacy rights of individuals, whose personal information becomes the subject matter of news. Online media need to pay attention to obscenity in content published on their sites, be aware of their accountability for message boards and other discussion forums, and for online advertisement messages. They need to protect themselves from liability for defamation, hacking and virus incidents. They should post detailed terms and conditions of use on their sites.

Jurisprudence on framing, deeplinking and spidering from news sites is developing. Duggal believes that the legality of framing is questionable, since it allows independently scrollable windows to be embedded within other web pages, giving the surfer the impression that he is viewing the contents of the site he has visited and not that of the framed site. This

---

[‡]  http://www.apnic.net/mailing-lists/s-asia-it/archive/2002/12/msg00042.html

creates confusion about the source of the framed website and the source of goods and services. This can be equated with deceptive association and presentation, and challenged in law. Also, framing can be considered an unlawful derivative work of the original content, involving copyright violation. The law on this issue is developing.

Similarly, deeplinking bypasses the home page of the linked site and links directly to its interior pages. The linked site loses control over the traffic flowing to itself. This has led to legal disputes. Duggal feels that specific permission needs to be taken for deeplinking. As for spidering (see Glossary), its legality is being debated.

In Vijayashankar's view, deeplinking is not a violation of any defendable right of a publisher:

> Just as we cannot expect a reader of the newspaper to always read the front page and see the front page solus ad first before turning on to the sports page or the stock market page, we cannot mandate the Netizens that they should always enter the publisher's Web site through the home page and add value to the advertisements therein. Any other site providing a deep link to an article is therefore not violating any right that is available to the publisher.

Moreover, technology permits any publisher to redirect any http request for an inside document through the home page. Therefore, a publisher who does not exercise this technical option does not have a right to object to the site which has enabled a deep link.

Vijayashankar believes that framing, if it does not block the masthead of the linked page and does not attempt to pass off the content as its own, is only a variation on hyperlinking and should be considered acceptable. Here, too, technology permits any web document owner to make it impossible for any document from within his site to be opened within another site's frame, hence not using such technologies should be considered "deemed permission" for "hyperlinking without hiding the source."

Spidering for information and representing it in such a way that the user is able to easily access it is nothing but a 'search engine' function, according to Vijayashankar. This is an essential service for the net community and no copyright violation should be ascribed to it. "Even in cases where a value added service is created out of such search and index services, it is not a violation of any rights of the original publisher since the link ultimately acknowledges the source and drives a customer to the publisher's site."

As for the Napster case and its effect on the entertainment and publishing media, Duggal supported the US court ruling against Napster, which held that the latter's users had infringed at least two exclusive rights of copyright holders – the right to reproduce and the right to distribute. The argument of fair use as an exception to the principle of copyright protection was rejected on the ground that the Napster users were engaged in commercial use, because when a file is sent to an anonymous person, it is not for personal use and that Napster's activities have directly resulted in reduction of CD sales. The ramification, Duggal felt, was that the publishing and entertainment industry would need to take charge of P2P technology and come up with 'appropriate' models.

Vijayashankar pointed out that copyright law exists for the protection of the rights of the original authors and within certain limitations that do not hurt the community. In the Napster case, the right of commercial intermediaries – not of the original authors – had been pitted against the larger interests of the community, and the latter had been made subservient to the former. Moreover, "(T)he findings of a survey conducted by Arbitron and Edison Media in July 2002 has held that the online music listeners have a tendency to buy more CDs than others and the RIAA argument that file sharing has adversely affected their sales is therefore untenable."

# References

[1]  O. hAnluain, Daithi, 'Free Content Becoming Thing of the Past for UK's Online Newspaper Sites', *Online Journalism Review*, 13 February 2004, accessed 21 November 2004 on http://www.ojr.org/ojr/business/1067472919.php.

[2]  Scherer, Michael, 'Newspapers Online: Why Information Will No Longer Be Free', *Columbia Journalism Review*, Jan/Feb 2003, vol. 41. no. 5, p.6, accessed 4 April 2004 on EBSCO database: http://search.epnet.com/direct.asp?an=8833031 &db=ufh.

[3]  Friedman, Donn, 'From Free to Fee in 10 Easy Steps', *Online Journalism Review*, 5 November 2003, accessed 18 March 2004 on http://www.ojr.org/ojr/business/ 1068080483.php.

[4]  'The Online Ad Attack', *The Economist*, 27 April 2005, accessed 19 July 2005 on http://www.economist.com/agenda/PrinterFriendly.cfm?Story_ID=3908700.

5 Zeff, Robbin, *Internet Advertising and Marketing Primer*, accessed 18 July 2005 on http://www.zeff.com/followup/zeff/index.htm.

6 Rudl, Corey, '10 No-Cost Ways to Generate Site Traffic', accessed 19 July 2005 on http://www.entrepreneur.com/article/0,4621,317700,00.html.

7 Bruner, Rick E., 'The Decade in Online Advertising: 1994-2004', *DoubleClick*, April 2005, accessed 18 July 2005 on http://www.doubleclick.com/us/ knowledge_central/documents/RESEARCH/dc_decaderinonline_0504.pdf.

8 *searchCIO.com Definitions - powered by whatis.com: advertising terminology on the Internet*, accessed 18 July 2005 on http://searchcio.techtarget.com/ sDefinition/0,,sid19_gci211535,00.html.

9 Nielsen, Jacob, 'The Most Hated Advertising Techniques', *Jakob Nielsen's Alertbox*, 6 December 2004, accessed 21 July 2005 on http://www.useit.com/alertbox/ 20041206.html.

10 Lasica, J. D., 'How the Net is Shaping Journalism Ethics', July 2001, accessed 21 July 2005 on http://www.jdlasica.com/articles/newsethics.html.

11 Byrd, Joann, 'Online Journalism Ethics: A New Frontier', The American Society of Newspaper Editors, published 22 March 1996, last updated 23 March 1997, accessed 21 July 2005 on http://www.asne.org/kiosk/editor/november/byrd.htm.

12 Samuelson, Pamela, 'Five Challenges for Regulating the Global Information Society', paper based on presentation given at a conference on Communications Regulation in the Global Information Society at the University of Warwick, June 1999, accessed 22 July 2005 on http://www.sims.berkeley.edu/~pam/papers/ 5challenges_feb22_v2(final).doc.

13 Magnant, Bob, 'Lessig's Code ...' (summary of Lawrence Lessig, *Code and Other Laws of Cyberspace*, Basic Books, 2000). Accessed 29 July 2005 on http:// www.code-is-law.org/magnant_sum.html.

14 Sadowsky, George et al, 'Internet Governance: A Discussion Document', background paper for the United Nations ICT Task Force, New York, March 2004, accessed 29 July 2005 on http://www.internetpolicy.net/governance/20040315paper.pdf.

15 'The Global Internet Policy Initiative', *What is "Internet Governance"?* accessed 30 July 2005 on http://www.internetpolicy.net/governance/.

16 Green Paper on the Convergence of the Telecommunications, Media and Information Technology Sectors, and the Implications for Regulation: Towards an Information Society Approach, European Commission, Brussels, 3 December 1997, accessed 30 July 2005 on http://europa.eu.int/ISPO/convergencegp/97623.html.

17 The Global Internet Liberty Campaign, '"Regardless of Frontiers": Protecting the Human Right to Freedom of Expression on the Global Internet', accessed 30 July 2005 on http://www.cdt.org/gilc/report.html.

[18] Green Paper on Copyright and Related Rights in the Information Society, European Commission, 27 July 1995, accessed 29 July 2005 on http://europa.eu.int/scadplus/leg/en/lvb/l24152.htm.

[19] 'Taxation of E-Commerce', *Global Internet Policy Initiative*, accessed 29 July 2005 on http://www.internetpolicy.net/taxation/.

[20] Agenda Item 148, United Nations General Assembly, 30 January 1997, accessed 29 July 2005 on http://daccessdds.un.org/doc/UNDOC/GEN/N97/763/57/PDF/N9776357.pdf?OpenElement.

[21] The Information Technology Act, 2000, *The Gazette of India*, 9 June 2000, accessed 29 July 2005 on http://www.mit.gov.in/itbill2000.pdf.

[22] The Global Internet Policy Initiative, 'Jurisdiction', accessed 30 July 2005 on http://www.internetpolicy.net/jurisdiction/.

[23] 'Information Technologies and Personal Data Privacy', *Computers, Cyberlaw, and Policy*, accessed 29 July 2005 on http://www.law.buffalo.edu/Academics/courses/629/materials/privacy.htm.

[24] Duggal, Pavan, 'Privacy in Cyberspace', accessed 26 November 2004 on http://cyberlaws.net/cyberindia/privacy1.htm.

[25] Duggal, Pavan and Na Vijayashankar, 'Cybertrends: Deep Linking, Copyright, Convergence and More', interviewed by Madanmohan Rao, originally published on *www.inomy.com*, December 2002, accessed 21 November 2004 on http://www.apnic.net/mailing-lists/s-asia-it/archive/2002/12/msg00042.html.

[26] Duggal, Pavan, 'India's First Cyberstalking Case: Some Cyberlaw Perspectives', accessed 26 November 2004 on http://cyberlaws.net/cyberindia/2CYBER27.htm.

[27] 'Cyber Crime', *Computers, Cyberlaw, and Policy*, accessed 29 July 2005 on http://www.law.buffalo.edu/Academics/courses/629/materials/cybercrime.htm.

# 9.
# Gatekeeping: The Changing Roles of Online Journalism

The previous chapters gave an account of the new forms of journalism that are coming into being due to the appearance of the internet and the web, along with related methods and practices. But the practitioner, to be effective, also needs to understand how these developments change the role of journalism as society's principal mode of storytelling and of the journalist as one who tells his audience what to think of itself and the rest of the world. The aim of this chapter is to address this question.

Singer[1] suggests four approaches to this issue – gatekeeping, diffusion of innovation, sociology of news work and an eclectic framework for studying journalism as a cohesive force in a fragmented society. Because of its focus, the last one can be viewed as belonging to the functionalist paradigm. We will deal with the first, and its extension, agenda-setting.

## The Journalist as a Gatekeeper

Gatekeeping theory appeared in communication studies almost six decades ago. The term was first introduced by social psychologist Kurt Lewin in his study of people's food habits. Lewin pointed out that decisions on what should reach the family table and what should not were made in certain areas of the food channel extending from the market or kitchen garden to the table. He termed these areas 'gates'. Lewin noted that the same was true for the movement of news items through communication channels.[2]

The gate sections were controlled either by rules, which he considered impartial, or by 'gatekeepers', that is, people in power. In 1949, D. M. White studied the last gate for wire service (news agency) items received at a US newspaper, namely the wire editor. She was responsible for selecting some of these stories for publication while discarding the rest. White found[3] that the news that reached readers was "highly subjective ... based on the 'gate keeper's' own set of experiences, attitudes and expectations".

Sociologist Warren Breed shifted the focus from the individual to the institutional level with his paper 'Social Control in the News Room: A Functional Analysis'[4] in 1955. His conclusion was that the news that reached readers was shaped by the publisher and the journalist's professional peer group because the journalist received his rewards not from readers but from his colleagues and superiors.

Subsequent empirical studies by a large number of researchers have identified a hierarchy of forces which shape media content. Figure 9.1 shows the way Shoemaker and Reese schematise this concept.[5] The

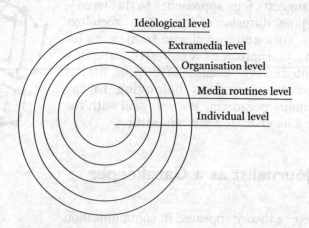

Ideological level

Extramedia level

Organisation level

Media routines level

Individual level

FIGURE **9.1** Influences on media content

(Source: Shoemaker and Reese)

individual journalist (gatekeeper) is located in the innermost of the concentric circles and acts as a conduit for influences from various levels to shape the content that finally reaches the audience. The forces range from the personal (individual) through institutional (media routines, organization, extramedia, etc.) to social (ideology).

## Disintermediation

Some writers have argued that this fundamental function of the media and of journalists – to decide what the audience is to know and what it is not to know – is nullified by the internet. We are witnessing a partial reversal of the mediation process which information had to always undergo through the traditional media until the advent of the net or web. This phenomenon is sometimes referred to as disintermediation.

When gatekeeping theory appeared in the USA in the late 1940s, the information environment was marked by scarcity as the public had to depend on newspapers and the radio for information. (Television had a minor role, if any, as it was still very young in the USA and non-existent in countries like India.) As a result, mainstream media organisations were in a position to control the flow of information to the public.

But the advent of the web, with billions of pages providing information on every conceivable subject and to anyone with access to the net, has created an information glut. Moreover, while citizens had been more or less passive receivers or consumers of information, they have become active seekers of information because of the nature of net or web technology.

Many consumers have also become information providers through such practices as blogging, moblogging (mobile blogging) and participatory journalism. They take advantage of easy-to-use and increasingly affordable technologies of information production, packaging and distribution, such as desktop and laptop computers with wired and wireless internet access, lightweight camcorders and mobile camera-phones (still and video). Bruns writes[6]: "(T)he gates are now located with the information providers (ultimately, with anyone who publishes a Website with potentially newsworthy information) as well as with the end user, who in navigating the Web constantly acts as their own gatekeeper – but no longer necessarily with the news media organisations."

# From Gatekeeping to Gatewatching

However, the abundance of information on the web also means the abundance of useless, misleading or false information. Writers like Singer have noted that users or consumers do want someone to direct them to reliable sources of information and perhaps to aggregate such information for them. Bruns notes that this activity can no longer take the form of gatekeeping in the style of the older media, as the concept of news itself has to change in the online environment:

> (S)uch views [traditional criteria for the acceptability of texts – TR] may be built on an overly narrow definition of news as 'hard news', that is, on a belief that there is a common core of news items which objectively are and should be of interest to everyone. By contrast, in online as well as offline media there exists an abundance of more or less specialised news categories from 'hard' and 'soft' news to political, economic, human interest, sports, and science news to even more tightly defined niche categories. Expanding the 'news gates' metaphor, then, not only is there a multitude of gates through which potentially newsworthy events and information emerge into the public arena, but there also exist any number of criteria for evaluating newsworthiness for specific audiences, *and* (especially online) there is a vast range of media outlets which are engaged in some form of 'news' reporting, policing their own gates.

Another reason for a change in the gate paradigm, cited by Bruns, is the fact that the physical capacity of the media to carry information, arising from their technical and commercial characteristics, has changed. One aspect of the gatekeeping function in the print and broadcast media is the fitting of available information into the 'news hole'. In print, the amount of information that can be conveyed to the reader is limited by the space left after accommodating advertisements, while time is the limiting factor in broadcast.

Since the low cost of digital memory makes it possible to store and carry virtually unlimited amounts of information, the online media have no such technical constraints on space or time (though limited audience attention is an issue that has to be addressed by communication professionals).

These two considerations, Bruns suggests, have changed the gatekeeping function to one of 'gatewatching'. In his opinion, the primary responsibility of online news operations is not to report objectively and impartially, or to tailor their work to a fixed amount of column inches or airtime, but to evaluate the reliability of available information. This becomes a critical task due to the abundance of potential news sources on the web. In the gatekeeping model, Bruns notes, the activity of preparing a story is focused on summarising information gathered from various news sources. The finished story is then posited as the primary source of information replacing the sources. Gatewatching marks a shift from this to a concern with leading the reader or user to the sources themselves as primary sources. In this case, the online journalist's own piece is positioned merely as a 'key node' connecting the reader to these primary sources of information, and its status changes to that of a secondary source.

Bruns notes that in the online environment, it is no longer possible to control the flow of information to users. Moreover, the communication model itself is different in that readers or users are no longer passive recipients of information. They are active seekers of information.

> (I)ndeed as we move away from a mass media 'information-push' news model to an individualized 'information-pull' approach, these gates no longer allow news to come to us, but enable us to access the news contained within. Therefore, as the term implies, gatewatchers keep a constant watch at the gates, and point out those gates to their readers which are most likely to open onto useful sources.

According to Bruns, several advantages follow from this shift from gatekeeping to gatewatching. Since readers are able to explore source material directly, stories can be more informative, the newsgathering process becomes more transparent, and the likelihood of readers being influenced by the journalist's personal bias is reduced. The speed of news publishing increases, since stories can be posted as soon as source information is found on the web, without necessarily waiting for reporters to file their stories. Moreover, news work becomes more inclusive as gatewatching can be performed by anyone with online research skills. The possession of journalistic skills is not essential for this purpose.

## 'Mythmaking' in the Age of Online Journalism

Since primary sources of information are now available to readers, and non-journalists can also perform such gatewatching as is necessary, one may be led to believe that journalists have become redundant. But this is not the case, as providing information does not exhaust the function of journalism.

No less important is the task of presenting a recognizable picture of the world to the audience, of tracing a pattern amid the chaos of facts and events, much as storytellers have done in oral cultures. It is not a coincidence, perhaps, that the commonly used term for a news report among journalists is 'story'.

This is the mythic function of journalism. Barthes used the term 'myth' to mean the way in which a culture conceptualises and understands the world through a chain of related concepts.[7] In *Mythologies*, an influential collection of essays, he writes that the journalist becomes the "producer of myths" when he "starts with a concept and seeks a form for it", leading to the concept being "naturalised", that is, made to appear as part of the natural order of things.[8] (In this sense, the concept of myth is closely related to that of ideology.)

One of the examples cited by Barthes is a bold newspaper headline: 'THE FALL IN PRICES: FIRST INDICATIONS. VEGETABLES: PRICE DROP BEGINS.' While the fall in vegetable prices was brought about by a seasonal increase in supply, Barthes points out, the headline 'naturalised' the concept of an efficient government that was able to keep prices under control.

Some writers, such as Lule, have noted a mythic function of journalism that corresponds to a more common usage of the term 'myth' as "a traditional story concerning the early history of a people or explaining a natural or social phenomenon, and typically involving supernatural beings or events" (*Concise Oxford English Dictionary*). Except for the simplest and most straightforward news reports, such as fires or sports scores, stories in the media, Lule observes, generally follow the 'archetype' of myths that can be found in every culture.[9]

Analysing *The New York Times*' coverage of floods caused by Hurricane Mitch in Central America in 1998, he shows that it follows the pattern of flood myths found in many cultures, including the Old Testament (the flood and Noah's ark), the Choctaw tribe of North America and the Incas.

These ancient myths have four features in common: (1) they are usually based on the premise that mankind had sinned or strayed from the path of righteousness, (2) they show that the flood does not discriminate between degrees of evil and causes complete devastation of entire ways of life, (3) they project human beings as being helpless against the power of the flood and people as being humbled as their struggles against it prove futile, and (4) they show that the flood purifies mankind, which is regenerated after it, and some good or fortunate individuals rebuild the world, chastened by the experience of the calamity.

The overall result of the *Times'* mythmaking is the affirmation of the US's superiority over other countries. He notes: "(M)yth has always affirmed the authority and superiority of the current social order. Myth legitimizes and justifies positions. Myth celebrates dominant beliefs and values. Myth degrades and demeans other beliefs. And myth has often fulfilled these roles through portrayals of disasters and calamities, such as the flood."

If journalism has this function of affirming the status quo, it is unlikely to readily adopt any innovation that tends to undermine the mythmaking, storytelling function. Allowing the reader to construct his own narrative or 'story' through hyperlinks that point outwards (to other sites) is such an innovation. This is why, even though writers like Bruns have suggested that a more reader-oriented gatewatching function can take the place of gatekeeping in the online environment, this is yet to take place in practice, at least in the mainstream media.

An interesting study by Dimitrova and others[10] comes to the finding that 15 newspapers rated as the best in the USA by the influential *Columbia Journalism Review* were "unwilling to give up their gatekeeping function by sending readers to outside websites". Even when they had sufficient time to find relevant material outside their own sites, most of the links they provided with their stories were to in-house material.

## Increased Gatekeeping

Hall notes that in the online environment, readers in fact have to contend not only with the traditional media gatekeepers (reporters and editors) but also with some who are outside media organizations. In North America and increasingly in other parts of the world, many libraries and colleges have begun to restrict internet access with the help of filtering software, such as SurfWatch, Cyber Patrol, Net Nanny and CyberSitter. [11] This is in response to the panic that has been caused by the presence of pornographic and hate sites on the net.

"Portals and service providers", Hall adds, "are also able to gain an editorial hold on consumers by offering unique, often sanitised views of the world." For instance, by providing links to information offered by other sites, portals and ISP sites like Yahoo!, Freeserve and AOL control access to those sources of information. The larger ISPs provide their own news packages, as well as pages of useful information on cities and communities, weather, shopping and entertainment. This, too, amounts to gatekeeping. Hall writes:

> Through cookies and other feedback, portal providers know their customers intimately. They control the first layer of links into the outside world and, increasingly, many consumers never click beyond that first layer. For those consumers the ISPs, or their editors, have taken over the role of gatekeeper once occupied by the news editors of our print and broadcast media. They are able to shape their customers' worlds by foregrounding certain sites, censoring others and adding a portfolio of pop-up information and advertisements very specifically tailored to individual consumers' tastes. Totalitarian states have always aspired to similar control.

## Setting the Agenda

Closely related to the gatekeeping function – indeed following from it – is the agenda-setting function. It refers to the way the media "wittingly or unwittingly structure public debate and awareness ... (and) focus public attention on a defined and limited set of issues, while ignoring others".[12]

This is the result of choices made by gatekeepers about the range of opinions, symbols, questions and other elements that are acceptable as elements to be included for the construction of a given story. Since readers are free to access sites representing every conceivable shade of opinion, irrespective of the choices made by gatekeepers or gatewatchers, the agenda-setting power of the media is somewhat diminished in the online environment.

The crucial factor in agenda-setting is the way in which different issues, opinions, symbols and questions are ranked in terms of legitimacy and priority. This relates to the construction of social reality for the audience and, therefore, as O'Sullivan et al point out, to the ideological power of the media. Any erosion of the agenda-setting ability then means an erosion of the ideological power of the media. Once again, we can see why many news sites try to keep readers confined to their own stories rather than helping them find additional sources of information by providing external links.

## Demand for Gatekeeping

Despite all that we have noted above, readers at large do not seem to be ready yet for an information order without gatekeepers. As Singer points out, the continued popularity of news sites – perhaps next only to that of search engines – attests to this fact. The same conclusion can be drawn from the popularity of knowbots which are small pieces of software that can be personalised in such a way as to continuously search the web for material matching the user's interests and sending these to the user. In this case, these programs act as gatekeepers.

## Continuity and Change in Journalism

What do these changes mean for the day-to-day work of journalists, and the journalism they produce? Bob Giles, Curator of Harvard University's Nieman Foundation for Journalism, has formulated the issues involved in the first question[13]. Mainstream news organizations, he says, "are struggling to apply old-fashioned news standards to the Web, but are discovering it is not easy to translate the virtues of accuracy, balance and clarity to a medium where the advantages of speed and timeliness prevail."

Giles points out that the technology of the internet has given journalism the tools for performing its traditional watchdog function in a more comprehensive way than before. The net allows reporters to probe deeper and more efficiently for information. The ability to search documents, find background material and historical context, and identify authoritative sources are important additions to the reporter's toolbox. Moreover, Giles says, the net "has introduced a fundamentally different culture built on interactivity, fewer rules, and fewer limits."

Speed and timeliness were once critical for newspapers. News agencies (called wire services in the USA) vied with one another to be the first to provide important stories, which would appear in newspapers. When television arrived on the media scene, its immediacy left the printed press far behind. Giles notes, "Now the Web has established its own advantages of speed and timeliness; and in doing so it has enabled newspapers to come full circle by posting breaking news and extending their brands through such innovations as online afternoon editions."

The advent of the web, says Giles, has led to a collision between the traditional standards of newspapers with other values such as freedom, irreverence, advocacy and attitude. Online journalists feel that the 'Olympian tones' of the print media are not appropriate for the online environment. They feel that the new medium conforms to the true spirit of the US First Amendment[*] in a way newspapers themselves did in an earlier era, when they were bold and combative. Giles quotes Ann Compton of ABCNews.com to describe the way she sees the key difference between her online staff and the ABC TV network's television journalists: "We write more brightly. We throw in more slang. There is a richness to the dot-com coverage that you really can't do on television." Similar comparisons, Giles notes, can be made between the web and daily newspapers.

An important question that needs to be answered, Giles feels, is whether such 'richness' is compatible with the highest standards of journalism: "Can the freewheeling, provocative, irreverent nature of the Web adapt to a culture whose traditions have been shaped by a more sober, structured medium?

In the opinion of journalists, the answer to the questions raised by Giles seems to be that there is both change and continuity. This is what emerged from the discussion that took place at a conference on Journalism and the Internet, co-sponsored by the Freedom Forum and the National Press Club of USA.[14] Llewelleyn King, a 40-year-old veteran of journalism, said that despite all the technological changes that had taken place, the basic task of journalism – "finding the news and presenting it and puncturing hypocrisy" – had remained unchanged. He felt that the internet as a

---

[*] "Congress shall make no law respecting an establishment of religion, or prohibiting the free exercise thereof; or abridging the freedom of speech, or of the press; or the right of the people peaceably to assemble, and to petition the Government for a redress of grievances." This amendment to the US Constitution, along with nine others, was ratified on 15 December 1791 and forms what is known as the Bill of Rights. (US National Archives: http://www.archives.gov/national_archives_experience/charters/bill_of_rights_transcript.html)

'productivity tool' had enabled reporters to ask 'better questions' and write more focused stories but had not produced a fundamentally new type of journalism.

Regarding journalistic standards and ethics, Rajiv Chandrasekaran of *The Washington Post* and John Markoff of *The New York Times* said the same rules of ethics and the same standards that governed traditional journalism ought to govern online news as well. But Steven Levy of *Newsweek* said there was a difference on the ground.

Since immediacy is one of the major characteristics of the internet as a news medium (online news can be, and is often, updated round the clock and there is therefore no such thing as 'news cycle') some news sites tend to sacrifice rigorous editing and fact-checking for the sake of immediacy. On the other hand, some 'ad hoc' (alternative) journalism sites actually employed stricter standards than the mainstream media because of their 'hostility' toward the way the latter operate.

Jai Singh, editor of the News.com site of CNET, a computer-news network, said his organisation placed a premium on adherence to high journalistic standards, because any slip on its part was likely to be seized upon by the traditional media and projected as a sign of the supposed inferiority of online journalism.

Pablo J. Boczkowski of MIT has sought to answer the second question I have mentioned, namely, how news has changed with the advent of online journalism. The changes he found after studying newsroom culture, technology and other factors in the online initiatives of *The New York Times, HoustonChronicle.com* (Virtual Voyager) and *New Jersey Online* (Community Connection) are multiple and complex. It should be noted that although all three of Boczkowski's case studies were conducted in the USA, his conclusions are relevant to any country, as the factors and processes identified by him are not specific to the USA but follow from the very nature of the net and the web.

Boczkowski notes[15] that the news is a culturally constructed category. Social histories of the press have thrown light on the institutional and technological factors shaping the news over two centuries, and ethnographic studies of news production have uncovered contingent factors that influence the reporting of current events. In Carey's words ('Reading the News', 1986), the news is not "some transparent glimpse at the world. News registers, on the one hand, the organizational constraints under which journalists labor [and] on the other hand, the literary forms and narrative devices journalists regularly use to manage the overwhelming flow of events."

Boczkowski discerns certain major changes in news production: its shaping by a more numerically and qualitatively diverse group of actors, which increases the importance of coordination among these groups. This changes the news from being an overwhelmingly journalist-centered, monologue type, and (in the US context) primarily local cultural product, to something that is "increasingly audience-centered, part of multiple conversations, and micro-local".

Boczkowski further notes that in the case of the online editions of traditional media, the dynamics of two newsrooms – the online one and its print or broadcast counterpart – and their interaction, may shape the news. Moreover, the advertising and marketing departments may influence the news via topic selection and budget allocation more tellingly than is usual in print newspapers. This could strengthen the trend towards 'market-driven journalism' (McManus, 1984) that has been growing in the US media since the 1980s.

Technical and design personnel also appear to influence the news through the use of multimedia, interactive tools, and the greater importance given to the visual interface as an integral part of the storytelling activity. Users, too, seem to shape the news – such things as what should be considered newsworthy and how it should be covered – by voicing their opinions in forums, chat rooms, and other sections within the news site and linking these pages to other sites, such as those of advocacy groups, through their personal blog sites. This increases the number and diversity of actors who shape the news in the online environment. This first transformation in the production processes, Boczkowski notes, leads to another, which involves the increased importance of coordination among the various groups that help shape the news.

Boczkowski notes that the greater user-centered nature of news in the online environment could deepen the 'civic' or 'public' journalism movement. He feels that the increased influence of the marketing and advertising departments, which are usually sensitive to the preferences and needs of consumers, may also add to a user-centeredness of news online.

Instead of being essentially a monologue with just a few readers' responses, if any (in the form of letters to the editor, etc.), Boczkowski sees online news as unidirectional statements "within a broader spectrum of ongoing conversations". The wider spectrum of voices elicited by online news leads to a higher degree of contestation, expressed directly through conflict of opinions or indirectly through a multiplicity of views. This conversation model, the writer notes, may be partly due to journalists' increased awareness of their audience's viewpoints and partly the public's increasing tendency to contribute content within news sites, as well as personal web logs.

## Effect on Older Media

When online news sites first appeared, they were usually conceived as mere appendages to existing print and broadcast media outlets. Editors and media managers were afraid that publishing an item on the website before publishing it in the parent print publication or airing it on the parent radio or TV channel would give rise to unhealthy competition within the organization and adversely affect readership of the older media outlet. As a result, the online editions carried news items only after these were printed or broadcast on the parent media.

This fear has dissipated with time. There have been several instances of stories breaking online and subsequently being picked up by print, radio and television. In other words, there have been instances of online journalism setting the agenda for print and broadcast journalism. In the following examples, online journalism not only set the agenda for the older media but also did this in respect of such major stories as to shake up the political establishments of the two largest democracies, India and the USA.

Chronologically, the US example – the Clinton-Lewinsky scandal – comes first. In early 1998, Michael Isikoff, a reporter with the *Newsweek* magazine, had heard tapes of telephone conversations between Monica Lewinsky, the former White House intern, and her friend Linda Tripp about Lewinsky's affair with President Clinton.[16] Isikoff filed a story on the basis of these conversations but *Newsweek* decided against publishing it, as the editors were not sure of the origin of the tapes and also because Kenneth Starr, who had been investigating scandals in the White House then, made a request to that effect.

This prompted an associate of Linda Tripp to give the story to Matt Drudge (mentioned in chapter four). He broke its main points on his *Drudgereport* site (www.drudgereport.com). Not only did this force *Newsweek* to publish a more complete account on its own website, but also prompted other media all over the world to give prominent coverage to the issue for months, often, in the case of the print media, on the front page. In a single month following the breaking of the story (after 10 August 1998), it attracted more than 13 million readers to the *Drudgereport* site.

The rest is history – President Clinton was investigated for his affair with Lewinsky and although he staved off impeachment, he had to admit to the affair and tender a public apology. Whether or not it was ethical on the part of the media to delve into the details of a President's sex life, the episode showed that online journalism had acquired tremendous agenda-setting power in the USA.

The second example pertains to an investigation into corruption in India's defence deals carried out in 2001 by *Tehelka.com*. The news website had no print edition at the time but was to launch a print weekly later, in July 2004. Code-named Operation West End, the sting operation used two Tehelka journalists armed with hidden video cameras and masquerading as defence contractors to record bribery and corruption in the political and defence procurement establishments.

The story was eagerly lapped up by the rest of the media and the 'Tehelka tapes', as they came to be called, were aired on television channels. The NDA government was shaken to its core and there was a spate of resignations, the most prominent being those of the Defence Minister George Fernandes, the Samata Party chief Jaya Jaitley and the BJP president Bangaru Laxman.

The real value of the exposé has been questioned by many, including Vir Sanghvi, the editor of the *Hindustan Times*.[17] But the story showed that in India, too, online journalism had become powerful enough to set the agenda for the older media. "Eat your heart out, Matt Drudge," wrote *Time* magazine on its website on 14 March 2001. "India's defense minister George Fernandes resigned Thursday, joining a growing number of leading politicians and senior army officers forced to stand down in a corruption scandal revealed by a tiny New Delhi dot-com."[18]

Thus, we see that online journalism can work in two directions. On the one hand, it creates conditions in which gatekeeping and agenda-setting cease to be the exclusive preserves of professional journalists and thereby creates conditions for a more inclusive and democratic type of journalism than the one offered by the print and broadcast media. On the other hand, it can set the agenda for these older media rather than act as a mere adjunct to them.

If and when these two trends come together – this can happen if the participatory media exemplified by *OhmyNews* become more prevalent, or if the mainstream media embrace democratic practices – the relationship between society and the media will undergo a qualitative change. The latter will become far more effective in serving the cause of democracy than it is today.

# References

1. Singer, Jane B., 'Online Journalists: Foundations for Research into their Changing Roles', *Journal of Computer Mediated Communication*, vol. 4, no. 1, September 1998, accessed 21 November 2004 on http://www.ascusc.org/jcmc/vol4/issue1/singer.html.

2. Lewin, Kurt, 'Group Decision and Social Change', *Readings in Social Psychology*, ed. Theodore M. and Eugene L. Hartley, (New York , Henry Holt and Co., 1947), p. 332.

3. White, David Manning, 'The "Gate Keeper": A Case Study in the Selection of News', *Journalism Quarterly*, 27, Fall 1950, pp. 383–390.

4. Breed, Warren, 'Social Control in the News Room', *Social Forces*, vol.33, no. 4, 1955, pp. 326–335, reproduced in Schramm, W., ed. *Mass Communications*, 2nd edition (Urbana, IL, University of Illinois Press, 1960), pp. 178–194.

5. Shoemaker, Pamela J., and Stephen D. Reese, *Mediating the Message: Theories on Influences on Mass Media Content*, 2nd Edition (New York, Longman, 1996), p.141.

6. Bruns, Axel, 'Gatewatching, Not Gatekeeping: Collaborative Online News', *Media International Australia* 107 (2003), pp 31–44, accessed 24 April 2005 on http://eprints.qut.edu.au/archive/00000189/01/Bruns_Gatewatching.PDF.

7. Fiske, John, *Introduction to Communication Studies*, 2nd Edition. (London and New York, Routledge, 1998), p.88.

[8] Barthes, Roland, *Mythologies*, tr. Annette Lavers. (London, Jonathan Cape, 1972), p.128.

[9] Lule, Jack, 'News, Myth and Social Order: The Myth of the Flood in *The New York Times*', AEJMC conference papers, accessed 12 May 2005 on http://list.msu.edu/cgi-bin/wa?A2=ind9909e&L=aejmc&F=&S=&P=1453.

[10] Dimitrova, Daniela V., et al, 'Hyperlinking as Gatekeeping: Online Newspaper Coverage of the Execution of an American Terrorist', *Journalism Studies*, vol. 4, no. 3, 2003, pp. 401–414, accessed 4 May 2005 on http://www.jlmc.iastate.edu/faculty-sites/danielad/hyperlinking.pdf.

[11] Hall, Jim, *Online Journalism: A Critical Primer*, (Virginia, London and Sterling, Pluto Press, 2001), pp.188–191.

[12] O'Sullivan, Tim et al, eds., *Key Concepts in Communication and Media Studies*, 2nd edition (London and New York, Routledge, 1994), p.8.

[13] Giles, Bob, 'Journalism in the Era of the Web: It's Feisty and Combative, But is it Compatible with Journalism's Highest Standards?' *Nieman Reports*, vol.54, no.4 (Winter 2000), The Nieman Foundation for Journalism at Harvard University, p.3 accessed 6 May 2004 on http://www.nieman.harvard.edu/reports/00-4NRwinter/NRwinter00.pdf.

[14] Arvidson, Cheryl, 'Is Online Journalism "Different"? A Wide Divergence of Views', *freedomforum.org*, 9 January 1998, accessed 21 November 2004 on http://www.freedomforum.org/templates/document.asp?documentID=11124.

[15] Boczkowski, Pablo J., *Digitizing the News: Innovation in Online Newspapers*, MIT Press, accessed 8 February 2004 on http://ojr.org/ojr/workplace/1075928349.php.

[16] Hall, Jim (2001), p.129.

[17] Sanghvi, Vir, 'Much Ado About Nothing?, *Seminar*, accessed 21 May 2005 on http://www.india-seminar.com/2002/509/509%20vir%20sanghvi.htm.

[18] Karon, Tony, 'India's Establishment Dot-Compromised', *Time Online Edition*, 14 March 2001, accessed 21 May 2005 on http://www.time.com/time/world/article/0,8599,102517,00.html.

# 10.
# Digital Determinism: Access and Barrier

In the previous chapters we discussed the internet's use as a medium of mass communication with immense potential for promoting democracy and also its use as a journalistic tool.

Since the number of net users has been swelling and technological novelties have been proliferating, negative developments like the dotcom crash are easily forgotten and many writers adopt an ecstatic tone while dealing with the net. This becomes self-serving when these pieces appear in online publications, which is often the case.

But the student of e-journalism, whether he is training to be a journalist or studying the subject as part of an academic course, needs to understand what the net actually can and cannot do. This chapter presents a brief discussion on this, with the emphasis on what the net *cannot* do and why.

## Determinism

The enthusiastic tone of journalists in discussion on the prospects of the online medium is not the result of numbers alone. Its origin lies in technological determinism. Technological determinism is "(a) theory of social change ... in which productive technique obeys a logic or trajectory of its own; and, in the process, acts as the principal determinant of institutions and social relationships."[1]

It is not as if writers adopt such a theory through conscious choice, though this may be the case for some individuals with expert knowledge. People usually have this type of attitude as part of their ideology, that is, the socially constituted system of meanings within which they automatically interpret facts and phenomena.

Determinism can take many forms and the type we most often see in relation to the net, particularly in popular genres like journalism, is technological utopianism. In this view, the net is the key to a perfect society, the specific nature of which depends upon the perspective of the writer. There is also a dystopian view of the net as a technology that has only, or overwhelmingly, negative consequences.

## Utopia

Utopian views can be understood through the words of John Perry Barlowe, the man who is said to have introduced the word 'cyberspace' in the English language.

He is a front-ranking campaigner for freeing the internet from government and corporate controls and co-founder of the San Francisco based-advocacy group Electronic Frontier Foundation. The following is an excerpt from his manifesto of February 1996, whose title, 'A Declaration of the Independence of Cyberspace', rings with a clear reference to the 13 American colonies' Declaration of Independence from Britain in 1776:

> Cyberspace consists of transactions, relationships, and thought itself, arrayed like a standing wave in the web of our communications. Ours is a world that is both everywhere and nowhere, but it is not where bodies live. We are creating a world that all may enter without privilege or prejudice accorded by race, economic power, military force, or station of birth.

> We are creating a world where anyone, anywhere may express his or her beliefs, no matter how singular, without fear of being coerced into silence or conformity. ...We believe that from ethics, enlightened self-interest, and the commonweal, our governance will emerge.[2]

Barlowe's approach is cultural, which is natural for someone who had been a songwriter for The Grateful Dead, a rock group that became an icon of the hippie counterculture.

As for technology and commerce, the most famous net utopian is Nicholas Negroponte, Wiesner Professor of Media Technology at MIT. He is also the founding chairman of the famed MIT Media Lab, chairman of Media Lab Europe, a founder of the perpetually net-enthusiastic magazine *Wired* and author of the 1995 *New York Times* bestseller, *Being Digital.*

As we will see later, Negroponte's optimism is not blind but tempered with an awareness of the net's pitfalls. His special significance is that he is a utopian in spite of this awareness. The following are excerpts from his epilogue to *Being Digital*[3]:

> I am optimistic by nature. However, every technology or gift of science has a dark side. Being digital is no exception ...
>
> The next decade will see cases of intellectual-property abuse and invasion of our privacy. We will experience digital vandalism, software piracy, and data thievery. Worst of all, we will witness the loss of many jobs to wholly automated systems ...
>
> But in the digital world, previously impossible solutions become viable ...
>
> Digital technology can be a natural force drawing people into greater world harmony ...
>
> But more than anything, my optimism comes from the empowering nature of being digital. The access, the mobility, and the ability to effect change are what will make the future so different from the present. The information superhighway may be mostly hype today, but it is an understatement about tomorrow. It will exist beyond people's wildest predictions ...
>
> My optimism is not fueled by an anticipated invention or discovery ... We are not waiting on any invention. It is here. It is now. It is almost genetic in its nature, in that each generation will become more digital than the preceding one ...

In a study of utopian and dystopian discourses, Howcroft and Fitzgerald[4] have shown that the first kind mainly concentrate on three areas – the conduct of business online, political democracy and interpersonal relationships.

## Commerce

While Barlowe's manifesto subsumes all three areas mentioned above, in fact the entire field of human existence, an example of utopianism specific to commerce is T. A. Stewart's prophecy, quoted by Howcroft and Fitzgerald:

> (E)lectronic markets will grow and begin operating over cheap, accessible public networks – the so-called electronic highway. Just as railroads opened up the West, the highway will open wide the electronic frontier. Whole industries will be destroyed and new ones born; productivity will leap and competitive advantage shift in the direction of small business.

For analysis of the highway as a metaphor see box.

### The Highway Metaphor

The phrases 'frontier' and 'the West' are references to the occupation of the western parts of the USA by pioneers (new settlers), who had spread out from the eastern coast. This colonization, often accompanied by violence against the indigenous American-Indians, has become an integral part of the American national lore.

The metaphor in 'electronic highway' – a clear reference to the phrase 'information superhighway' attributed to the great internet enthusiast, former US Vice-President Al Gore, as well as the earlier 'data highway' – has similar roots. Like the 'frontier', highways. for example, the old Route 66, running from Chicago to Los Angeles are also part of American lore.

As they are built to conquer space and time by taking people across large distances at high speed, American highways can be viewed as a manifestation of the colonising spirit in the automobile age. Therefore, though Stewart eulogises the net in the name of small businesses, at the heart of such eulogies lies free-market capitalism's urge for the freedom to conquer and colonise.

Patelis[5] explains the economic rationale implicit in this type of discourse. She notes that Bill Gates and others view unequal competition as an aberration of capitalism, one that will be replaced by a supposedly ideal state of perfect competition through the 'new economy' inaugurated by the internet.

It is a 'digital economy' based on abundance rather than scarcity; a market where supply equals demand and prices are set at the lowest optimum level; where oligopolies are avoided owing to low market-entry costs; where market dysfunctions are history and diversity is guaranteed. This market is a producer and consumer paradise. Its hallmark is dynamic competition.

It is claimed that an ideal market – in which demand is the driving force, hence the determinant for prices – will replace the existing seller's market, characterized by distortions arising from supply scarcity.

According to Gates, this change will take place because commerce on the net (e-commerce) enables product and service providers to see buyers' requirements much more efficiently than before and it also enables consumers to buy more efficiently than before. Moreover, as the net develops along the axes of broadband and global interactivity, capitalism's superiority over other systems will be magnified.

## Democracy

A typical illustration of net-utopian thinking on democracy can be found in a talk given by David Winston, a senior strategist of the US Republican Party who has served as a member of the US Congressional Web-based Education Commission. Speaking at a conference on 'Democracy and Digital Media' held at MIT in 1998,[6] Winston said:

> Today, we have the most fantastic means of communications in the history of the world literally at our fingertips, and more people are literate than ever before. Yet, we have a system of democracy where political conversation has become 10 second sound bites; where we hear media monologues instead of political dialogue; where politics has become the cult of personality instead of the power of ideas.

> The end result? People are rejecting current political conversation by simply saying, "This is not an important part of my world", returning politics more and more to the elite and that is dangerous to the future of democracy.

> But like I said earlier, I am an optimist, and I believe the era of digital communications is, in fact, the prescription for what ails our current political system. Digital technology is the best way to communicate ideas, and democracy is the best means of realizing those ideas. I believe this to be the most powerful combination for improving civilization in the future.

In the first two paragraphs, Winston refers to the superficial nature of television coverage of politics and the low popular interest in politics in the USA, resulting in low voter turnouts in recent decades. The Bush-Kerry contest of November 2004, marked by intense political interest, was an exception. Though Winston speaks of the USA here, the same sentiment is often heard expressed about television in other countries as well, including India.

In the third paragraph, he echoes a common claim made on behalf of the net, namely, that it can revitalise democracy. Barbrook refers to Newt Gingrich, a prominent Republican who has served as Speaker of the US House of Representatives, as holding the belief "that the Internet will create 'electronic town halls' where voters can directly participate within the political process."[7]

Dahlberg[8] has categorized all democracy claims into three groups.

1. Communitarian: Consists of those claims which stress the net's potential for enhancing a community spirit

2. Liberal individualistic: Speaks of the net as a powerful means for expressing individual interests

3. Habermasian: Views the net as a means of expanding what Jürgen Habermas has conceptualised as the 'public sphere' of 'rational-critical discourse' ideally free from any of the restrictions that can be imposed by the state and corporate power in other spheres. It is through this type of deliberation among citizens that public opinion is supposed to form in order to hold official decision makers to account. It is not difficult to see that the first two categories achieve their fulfilment through the third, in so far as the net's significance to democracy is concerned.

### Interpersonal Relationships

Some writers have dealt with what they view as the net's capacity to create a new type of selfhood and to liberate interpersonal relationships from the confines of physical locality, thus creating the possibility for new types of interpersonal relationships as well as new types of communities. The latter, called 'virtual communities', are geographically dispersed and formed on the basis of shared interests, not physical, geographical proximity. Chapter twelve addresses these issues in greater detail.

## Dystopia

Though utopian views are dominant in internet-related popular literature, including journalism, techno-dystopian views also exist. In this perspective, the internet "facilitate(s) a social order that is relentlessly harsh, destructive and miserable".[9] The following are some dystopian views.

1. The net is said to have produced alienation rather than a feeling of community, since many people have become so addicted to email and online chat that they do not feel the need to meet their next-door neighbours or office colleagues.

2. The net is also viewed as a technology of surveillance rather than a means of promoting democracy, as every website visited by an individual can be – and often is – tracked by government and corporate agencies hovering in the background of cyberspace, in order to create a precise and accurate psychological profile of the subject. Every purchase made with a credit card – whether a train or air ticket, groceries, clothes, or hotel bills – can be fed into the individual's database to enhance and develop this profile and track her movements in the physical world.

3. Langdon Winner's classic 1997 study[10] of a remote encoding centre of the US Postal Service, one of the 65 existing at the time, makes certain points about the conditions and the future of low-level jobs in the era of digital networks. He talks about workers' alienation from one another and the absence of job security.

   The centre, whose task was to read the addresses which postal computers had failed to decipher, employed 800 workers, only a quarter of whom were regular postal employees with proper benefits and pensions. The rest were temporary employees working four to six-hour shifts.

   Winner points out that even this level of employment was unlikely to be maintained for long, as pattern-recognition technology was constantly improving and computers soon would be able to read many of the addresses that were unreadable to them, hence required human readers, at the time of his study. Winner describes a digital dystopia of "numbing, stifling work, devoid of creativity, suppressing everything vital and interesting in the individual" (see box).

## Digital Dystopias in the USA and India

Winner's study describes the atmosphere in the encoding centre in grim terms: "The mood in the enormous work room is sober, bordering on grim. Although their activities depend on sophisticated communications equipment, there seems to be little communication among the clerks. Able to come and go as they please in prearranged, round-the-clock, flex-time schedules, they file into the building, stopping briefly at the coat room, clocking in and with plastic swipe cards, quietly taking a seat at a work station, logging into the computer. There is seldom any need to talk to another person all. In the brightly lit 'cafeteria' in an adjoining room, there are only food vending machines with several tables and hardback chairs for those taking their five-minutes-per-hour break. Nothing about the space invites social gatherings or conversation."

While computerisation of this type and scale is not yet common in India, analogies may be drawn between US Post's remote encoding centres and the call centres mushrooming in cities like Bangalore, Hyderabad and Kolkata.

These workers spend long hours staring at glowing computer screens while conversing in a carefully cultivated (mostly) American accent with customers located on the other side of the globe, where it is day while it is night outside the operator's office in India and vice versa.

The pay, though higher than on comparable levels of employment in many other sectors, is often insufficient to compensate for such strains, which sometimes result in cultural and identity-related disorientation.

## Access and Barrier

Whether one holds utopian or dystopian views, or more balanced ones, it should be recognised that the internet's effect on society largely depends on the degree of people's access to it. Only when an individual gains access to the net, not before, can it imbue her with communitarian sentiments or include her in the digital public sphere. Access to the net empowers individuals, organisations and nations, because it is a versatile means of communication and of accessing information of all kinds. Even success in warfare is increasingly dependent on a country's ability to deploy advanced information technologies in the battlefield. Unequal access to the net implies an exacerbation of inequalities in the distribution of power. The following factors act as barriers to internet access.

## Digital Divide

The Organisation for Economic Cooperation and Development (OECD) defines digital divide as "the gap between individuals, households, businesses and geographic areas at different socio-economic levels with regard both to their opportunities to access information and communication technologies (ICT*s) and to their use of the Internet for a wide variety of activities."[11]

It points out that the divide reflects various differences among and within countries. Internationally, it is manifested in differences in the ability of individuals and businesses located in OECD member-states (that is, developed countries) on the one hand, and non-OECD countries (the developing and underdeveloped countries) on the other, to take advantage of the net.

There are also gaps within the OECD itself and as Poster notes, within individual countries: "Even within the high-use nations, wealthy white males are disproportionate users."[12] Another fact, which the OECD document mentions as being of fundamental importance to the issue of digital divide is that access to basic telecom infrastructure precedes and is more widely available than access to the internet.

In other words, to be effective, strategies for bridging the digital divide must ensure the availability of telephone connections across geographic space and socio-economic strata before focusing on universal internet access.

At the end of July 2001, the ITU (International Telecommunication Union), an agency of the UNO, noted[13] that half the world's inhabitants had yet to make their first basic telephone call, and even fewer (naturally) had used the internet. "The majority of the more than 6 billion people who inhabit our planet," ITU pointed out, "have been completely shut out

---

* Also known as 'information, computing and telecommunication'

of the digital revolution and the promise it holds. As the pace of the technological revolution increases, so does the digital divide."

The report noted that the divide concerned all sectors – government, the private sector, multilateral organisations, financial institutions, non-governmental organisations and ordinary citizens. The international divide – a more appropriate term would be digital chasm, considering its magnitude – is illustrated with the help of Figures 10.1 and 10.2 and Table 10.1.

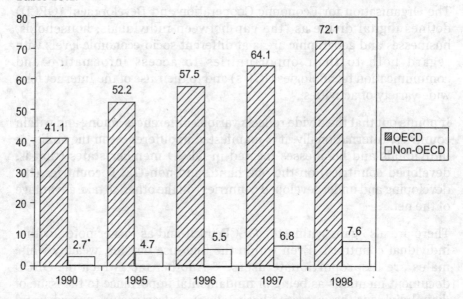

FIGURE **10.1** Fixed plus mobile telecommunication access paths per 100 inhabitants

(Source: OECD and ITU)[14]

## India's Position in the World

Table 10.1 brings out several crucial points. Despite the fact that India's telecommunication infrastructure has been upgraded and expanded in recent years and despite the country's strong position in the global software market, globally its place is very low in the availability of telephone connections, personal computers and internet use.

Countries like Malaysia, China and Romania have fared much better than India, not to speak of industrialised countries like Finland, Sweden, France, Germany, the UK and the USA.

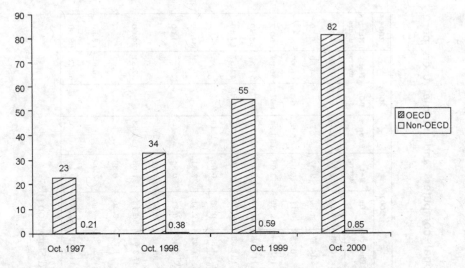

FIGURE **10.2** Internet hosts per 1000 inhabitants

(Source: Netsizer [www.netsizer.com])[15]

China's performance has been particularly spectacular in telephone penetration. At 0.59, it was slightly below India's 0.60 in terms of the number of telephones per 100 people in 1990. By 2002, however, its score had increased to 32.78 as against India's paltry 5.19.

Since mobile telephony has considerably expanded in the last two years, India's score probably has improved somewhat, but there is not much likelihood of a drastic change in the scenario. It is another matter that Sweden had 160.53 telephones for every 100 citizens in 2002 and the USA had 114.70. The corresponding figures for Ethiopia and Bangladesh were 0.62 and 1.32, respectively.

In terms of internet use, all the countries in the table other than Bangladesh, Ethiopia, Pakistan and Tanzania, were far ahead of India in 2001. The gap between India (0.68 per 100 population) and China (2.57 per 100 population) was substantial in this area, too, but much narrower than in telephone penetration. Romania scored 4.47 per cent in net use, Malaysia 27.31, Finland 43.03, Germany 36.36, the UK 32.96 and the USA 50.15.

Table 10.1 Number of telephone lines (including cellular), personal computers and internet users per 100 population

| Year Country | 1990 Phones | 1990 PCs | 1990 Net users | 1995 Phones | 1995 PCs | 1995 Net users | 2000 Phones | 2000 PCs | 2000 Net users | 2001 Phones | 2001 PCs | 2001 Net users | 2002 Phones | 2002 PCs | 2002 Net users | 2004 Net users |
|---|---|---|---|---|---|---|---|---|---|---|---|---|---|---|---|---|
| Bangladesh | 0.20 | | | 0.24 | | | 0.58 | 0.15 | 0.08 | 0.83 | 0.19 | 0.14 | 1.32 | 0.34 | 0.15 | 0.2 |
| China | 0.59 | 0.04 | | 3.60 | 0.23 | | 17.76 | 1.59 | 1.74 | 24.77 | 1.90 | 2.57 | 32.78 | | 4.60 | 6.80 |
| Ethiopia | 0.26 | | | 0.25 | | | 0.39 | 0.09 | 0.02 | 0.48 | 0.11 | 0.04 | 0.62 | 0.15 | 0.07 | |
| Finland | 58.57 | 10.00 | 0.40 | 74.35 | 23.18 | 13.71 | 127.06 | 39.61 | 37.23 | 135.14 | 42.35 | 43.03 | 139.24 | 44.17 | 50.89 | 50.7 |
| France | 50.02 | 7.05 | 0.05 | 58.26 | 14.69 | 1.64 | 107.04 | 30.43 | 14.37 | 117.88 | 32.86 | 26.38 | 121.59 | 34.71 | 31.38 | 38.70 |
| Germany | 44.46 | 8.99 | 0.14 | 55.89 | 17.84 | 1.83 | 119.66 | 33.61 | 30.15 | 131.65 | 38.22 | 37.36 | 136.71 | 43.49 | 42.37 | 57.10 |
| India | 0.60 | 0.03 | | 1.30 | 0.13 | 0.03 | 3.56 | 0.45 | 0.54 | 4.38 | 0.58 | 0.68 | 5.19 | | | 1.7 |
| Malaysia | 9.42 | 0.84 | | 21.57 | 3.03 | 0.15 | 41.23 | 9.45 | 17.19 | 51.21 | 12.61 | 27.31 | | | | 34.00 |
| Pakistan | 0.75 | 0.13 | | 1.70 | 0.35 | 0.07 | 2.41 | 0.42 | 0.21 | 2.89 | 0.41 | 0.34 | | | | 1.00 |
| Romania | 10.19 | 0.22 | | 13.13 | 0.22 | | 28.53 | 3.18 | 3.57 | 35.56 | 3.57 | 4.47 | | | | |
| Sweden | 73.45 | 10.48 | 0.58 | 90.76 | 24.89 | 5.09 | 146.28 | 50.67 | 45.58 | 152.94 | 56.12 | 51.63 | 160.53 | | 57.31 | 74.60 |
| Tanzania | 0.31 | | | 0.33 | | | 1.08 | 0.31 | 0.12 | 1.71 | 0.36 | 0.30 | | | | |
| UK | 46.01 | 10.77 | 0.09 | 59.97 | 20.13 | 1.88 | 131.31 | 33.78 | 26.44 | 135.78 | | 32.96 | | | 40.62 | 58.50 |
| USA | 56.85 | 21.79 | 0.80 | 73.15 | 32.62 | 9.45 | 105.35 | 57.21 | 44.06 | 111.79 | 62.50 | 50.15 | 114.70 | | 53.75 | 68.80 |

(Source: UNO and ITU (1990–2002); Nielsen, ITU, etc., quoted in Internet World Stats, 2004)[16]

In 2004, India's internet penetration reached an estimated 1.7 per cent as against China's 6.8 per cent, Malaysia's 34 per cent, France's 38.7 per cent, Germany's 57.1 per cent, the UK's 58.5 per cent and the USA's 68.8 per cent. According to the Telecom Regulatory Authority of India, ITU's Digital Access Index, which measures access to ICT[†] (information, computing and telecommunication) services, places India at the 119th position among 178 countries.[17]

## Partitioning the Internet through Broadband

A matter that may be of greater concern is a fundamental shift being consciously brought about in the very nature of the internet. Tseng and Eischen write[18] :

> We are in the process of partitioning (the internet's) infrastructure, both physical and logical, into information conduits of different speeds and sizes. *Access to these conduits depends on who and where you are* [emphasis mine]. These emerging Internet infrastructure technologies – Broadband Access Networks, Caching and Content Delivery Networks, Quality of Service and Policy Protocols – are shaped by geographical, economic and social factors in their development, deployment and use.

An OECD publication notes that broadband is adding a new dimension to the digital divide within that section of the population which does have internet connections.[19] Those who have access to rich, interactive audio and video services through high-speed broadband connections at home, are at an advantage over those who have low-bandwidth services. High bandwidth is becoming essential not only for the development of business, industry, shopping and trade, but also for services that are important from the point of view of human development, such as distance learning, telemedicine, and telecommuting.

This has an amplifying effect on the rural-urban divide, since net access in rural and remote areas, when available, is narrow-band and slow. In the case of India, where villages are largely outside net coverage, slow connectivity is the usual scenario in many of the towns where it is available, even in some of the larger ones. There has been talk of developing satellite-based and terrestrial wireless access for rural areas,[20] but this is yet to materialize on any useful scale.

---

[†] Also known as 'information and communication technologies'

## Language on the Net

The internet embodies a contradiction. As Bowen notes, "(Its) ability to connect a wide range of cultures would seem to bode well for diversity of all sorts. But ... the influences of political and economic power have made (it) a virtual English-language empire."[21]

In 2001, Israeli and US researchers found that while only about 44 per cent of net users were native speakers of English, about 70 per cent of net content was in English. Globally, native Spanish speakers outnumbered native English speakers and the number of native Chinese speakers more than equals that of both groups.

It is natural that English should enjoy a dominant position online since the net originated in English-speaking USA. According to a survey conducted by the marketing communication consultants Global Reach and quoted by *Wired* magazine, less than 10 per cent of net users were native speakers of languages other than English in 1995.

Within four years, that is, by 1999, their share had climbed to 50 per cent.[22] By the end of September 2004, this had climbed further to 64.8 per cent – according to Global Reach, out of the 801.4 million people who were using the internet globally at the end of September 2004, only 295.4 million or 35.2 per cent were English-speakers and the remaining 544.5 million or 64.8 per cent were non-English speakers.[23] This would seem to indicate that the predominance of English on the net is fast eroding. But that is not the case.

Table 10.2 Languages of Internet Users and Web Content

| Language | Native speakers as percentage of total user population | Web pages as percentage of total number |
|---|---|---|
| English | 35.2 | 68.4 |
| Chinese | 13.7 | 3.9 |
| Spanish | 9.0 | 2.4 |
| Japanese | 8.4 | 5.9 |
| German | 6.9 | 5.8 |
| French | 4.2 | 3.0 |
| Korean | 3.8 | 1.3 |
| Portuguese | 3.1 | 1.4 |
| Italian | 1.7 | 1.6 |
| Russian | | 1.9 |
| Other | | 4.6 |

(Source: Global Reach)

Though non-English speakers are going online in increasing numbers, overtaking English-speakers by a wide margin, the content of the net has remained predominantly English. Bowen writes that the popularity of English spurs more people to learn it, which increases incentives for content providers to cater to an English-speaking audience and this in turn increases its popularity.

## Surveillance, Censorship and Control

Journalism, as it is understood in democratic societies, cannot exist without the freedom of speech and expression. This applies to the internet as well. But the reality is that the internet today is far from being the haven of free speech, which libertarians believe is its rightful state.

Governments have put in place comprehensive systems of surveillance, censorship and control to fight pornography and various types of hate speech, such as xenophobia, racism and religious communalism (as in India), which together comprise less than three per cent of online activity according to experts. [24] Restrictions are also being placed in the name of terrorism, especially after the attack on New York City's World Trade Center on 11 September 2001.

While the above types of restriction are being imposed by most governments, including many democratic ones, authoritarian regimes have deployed these to prevent political opponents from getting their message across to the people. Corporate bodies resort to censorship and control to protect their commercial interests.

While one cannot turn a blind eye to child pornography, hate speech or terrorism, it is also true that the freedom of speech and expression is crucial to the key issue of politics in the modern world, namely, the creation of democracy where it does not exist and its continuous reproduction where it does. In the absence of such freedoms, the media cannot facilitate the free, rational-critical debate that is necessary for the existence of democracy.

Moreover, if we consider Amartya Sen's thesis that the economic well-being of a society substantially depends on openness, democracy and the existence of free media, we can see that the question of censorship and control is critical to development and poverty eradication. This is recognised by many groups advocating freedom of the media, such as

Privacy International and the GreenNet Educational Trust in a 2003 report.[25]

This report also notes that new laws on net surveillance have been used to expand surveillance in other areas of social life. In notes that "Cyberspace is not a separate place or domain; it is a key component of our legal, political, economic and social lives. It is indeed a battleground for policies on censorship and surveillance, as much as it is a techno-political pawn to the forces that wish to limit freedom."[26]

Thus, the issue of surveillance, censorship and control on the internet has major implications for society as a whole and not merely in proportion to the percentage of citizens who have internet access, which is small in all but the few advanced countries.

### Surveillance

Parallels are sometimes drawn between today's world and George Orwell's novel, *1984*, in which every citizen is under Big Brother's watchful gaze all the time. There is also a substantial body of academic and semi-academic literature, inspired by the writings of Michel Foucault that views the present world as a realisation of Jeremy Bentham's 'panopticon' scheme in which every citizen is always under surveillance by the authorities. While the unequal development of technology in different countries precludes the uniform application of this model across the world, it is a fact that the world as a whole is moving towards a surveillance regime.

The nature and scope of this move has been assessed by organisations campaigning for human rights and free speech. The Privacy and Human Rights Report, an annual publication of the UK-based Privacy International (PI) and the US-based Electronic Privacy Information Centre (EPIC), puts the USA at the forefront of the move which involves the limiting of individual privacy and enhancing the capability of police and intelligence services to eavesdrop on personal conversations.[27]

The USA and other governments are following two strategies. One is to promote laws making it mandatory for all companies developing communication technologies, including digital telephone switches and cellular and satellite phones, to include surveillance capabilities as an integral part of these products. The other strategy is to place limits on the development and distribution of any hardware or software that offers an encryption facility, that is, allows the user to scramble her communications and files in such a way that no one but the intended recipient can unscramble these for reading, viewing or hearing.

Such moves have gathered momentum since the early 1990s, and international cooperation has played a major role in this. But the best-known project, the US-led surveillance network codenamed Echelon, originated as early as in 1971, when the Cold War was raging.

According to the American Civil Liberties Union (ACLU), Echelon is an "automated global interception and relay system operated by the intelligence agencies in five nations: the United States, the United Kingdom, Canada, Australia and New Zealand."[28] The US National Security Agency (NSA) is the lead agency, and unlike many other surveillance systems, Echelon is mainly targeted at non-military targets, such as individuals, governments, organisations and businesses.

Echelon is said to be using large radio antennae located in the USA, Canada, UK, Italy, Turkey, New Zealand, Australia, and several other countries to intercept satellite transmissions, as well as surface transmissions. In addition, it uses satellites to intercept the 'spillover' from communications between cities, and beams this back to earth, to processing stations in the USA, UK, Australia and Germany.

A report prepared by the European Parliament's Department of Scientific and Technological Options Assessment called Echelon a "technology of political control".

The report also maintained that there was evidence of Russia operating a similar system. Other organizations, including ACLU, have mentioned massive and systematic surveillance systems operated by China and Israel. Echelon is not the only surveillance system in the USA – TIA (Total Information Awareness) and Carnivore are two other systems that have been in the news.

### Surveillance in India

The Government of India, too, has armed itself with laws that permit comprehensive surveillance. An instance of surveillance came to light in 2000 with the monitoring of the email messages being sent and received by Seema Kazi, an independent researcher and human rights activist, and the blocking of her account.[29] Such efforts seem to have increased after the terrorist attack on the Indian Parliament two months after the attack on the World Trade Center, on 13 December 2001.

Four internet exchange points (IXPs) were set up by the Central Government's Department of Information Technology in Delhi, Mumbai, Kolkata and Chennai during 2003 and 2004. These nodes, operated by the newly formed National Internet Exchange of India (NIXI), are meant to bring down the cost of internet connectivity in the country and improve the quality of internet services.[30]

By interconnecting ISPs in a region or country, IXPs "allow (ISPs) to exchange domestic Internet traffic locally, (and) thereby avoid routing the Internet traffic across multiple international hops to reach their destination within the country."[31]

While IXPs thus have obvious merits, we may recall that packet switching, one of the two basic design features built into the internet at its birth, had a different philosophy. In it, the path taken by a message to travel from sender to receiver was of no concern to anyone. In fact, the system ensured that no one – neither the sender, nor the receiver, nor any other person or agency – had any control over the path taken by individual 'packets' (the parts into which a message is broken up before being transmitted) to reach their common destination.

Therefore, a communication could be intercepted only at points where it existed as an integral whole, namely, at the source and the destination, but at no point in between. For agencies interested in large-scale interception, the ISPs are the obvious points of choice, since these are nodes through which every item of communication has to pass.

But most ISPs are in the private sector, and may not be uniformly quick to carry out orders to block websites or facilitate eavesdropping on email traffic. The IXPs, which can be said to function like ISPs for ISPs, seem to offer much greater opportunities for anyone wishing to misuse the system for intercepting the entire internet traffic of the country at four convenient points, which are under total government control.

Thus, NIXI seems to have the power to nix (negate) two of the most prized features of the internet, namely, the difficulties it presents to eavesdroppers and its ability to let communications work around obstacles. However, since the IXPs induce India's domestic internet traffic, which constitutes a third of its total internet traffic, to stay within the country rather than going through international hops, these result in 'major savings' on international bandwidth costs, says the technology magazine *Dataquest*, adding that "This (has) sent the industry into an upbeat mood."[32]

Whether these savings are being passed on to individual subscribers is not known. In any case, it is easy to see that as far as the internet is concerned, corporate interest may at times clash with the needs of an open internet that shields the user from the panoptic gaze of the state and corporate power.

## Censorship and Control

There are three ways of imposing censorship and control on the internet: legal, technological and practical. Legal strategies include such things as legislation by governments (as in India and many other countries); litigation by corporate bodies; and contracts, such as the terms and conditions that internet service providers often impose on their subscribers. Contracts and litigation can be utilized not only by the government and industry, but also by individuals (through defamation and libel suits, for instance).

### Legal Approaches

There are two main legal approaches to censorship, known as whitelist and blacklist. In the first, anything that is not explicitly permitted is forbidden, and in the second, anything that is not explicitly forbidden is permitted. Countries that have laws to block access to certain types of websites and other online material, such as India and Australia, belong to the blacklist category. Myanmar is an example of the whitelist approach.

In 2003, according to Privacy International and GreenNet, the Yangon regime permitted net access to only about 800 international sites and a few dozen sites hosted within the country. Moreover, it was illegal to own a modem or fax machine in Myanmar without a licence. But this approach is much rarer than the blacklist approach, which is prevalent in most countries, including Australia and India.

In Australia, laws cover pornography involving children, animals, or excessive violence and information about crime, violence and drug use. In India, the government derives the power of net censorship from the Information Technology Act, 2000. Two of the relevant Sections of the Act (No. 67 and 80) are quoted in the box on p. 216[33]:

## Extracts from the IT Act

### 67. Publishing of information which is obscene in electronic form.

Whoever publishes or transmits or causes to be published in the electronic form, any material which is lascivious or appeals to the prurient interest or if its effect is such as to tend to deprave and corrupt persons who are likely, having regard to all relevant circumstances, to read, see or hear the matter contained or embodied in it, shall be punished on first conviction with imprisonment of either description for a term which may extend to five years and with fine which may extend to one lakh rupees [Rs 100,000 or $2222.2] and in the event of a second or subsequent conviction with imprisonment of either description for a term which may extend to ten years and also with fine which may extend to two lakh rupees [Rs 200,000 or $4444.4].

### 80. Power of police officer and other officers to enter, search, etc.       (1)

Notwithstanding anything contained in the Code of Criminal Procedure, 1973, any police officer, not below the rank of a Deputy Superintendent of Police, or any other officer of the Central Government or a State Government authorised by the Central Government in this behalf may enter any public place and search and arrest without warrant any person found therein who is reasonably suspected or having committed or of committing or of being about to commit any offence under this Act.

*Explanation:* For the purposes of this sub-section, the expression 'public place' includes any public conveyance, any hotel, any shop or any other place intended for use by, or accessible to the public.

Siddharth Varadarajan points out[34] that the IT Act is vague in many respects. The first problem is that the issue of obscenity is treated differently by different agencies in the country. While the Supreme Court tends to interpret it in a liberal spirit, law-enforcement authorities and lower courts tend to entertain 'flimsy' complaints.

Furthermore, the Act does not adequately define what does and does not fall within the ambits of 'publishing' and 'transmitting' on the internet, nor whether action can be taken against sites that provide chatrooms, or against sites with search engines that display links to offending sites (as they often do) when used for searching with innocuous keywords or phrases. This vagueness, coupled with the sweeping powers of search and arrest granted to police and other officials, Varadarajan argues, have created a dangerous situation.

An official structure for implementing censorship on the net is already in place. The Indian Computer Emergency Response Team (CERT-In), set up under the auspices of the Department of Information Technology, Ministry of Communications and Information Technology, Government of India, occupies a nodal position in this structure. The team's main task is to respond to computer security problems, as its name suggests, but it also has a censorship function which it has already begun to discharge. The procedure is as follows[35] : Officers of the rank of Joint Secretary and above in certain specified agencies – including the Home Departments of the Central and State Governments, courts, the Central Bureau of Investigation, the Intelligence Branch, the police and the chairman of the National Human Rights Commission[36] – have been authorised to request the blocking of websites.

The danger represented by some provisions of the IT Act, as mentioned earlier in this chapter, escalated last year when the·Department of Information Technology issued an order extending the censorship net beyond the ambit of the IT Act to include such things as "hate content, slander or defamation of others".

Critics felt that this gave the government the authority to block sites that are politically damaging or inconvenient to the ruling party.[37] Moreover, no provision has been kept for giving a hearing to producers of the website facing such action. Already, the media have reported several cases of the authorities taking advantage of the IT Act and the above order in a drastic manner, but there may also have been others that have gone unreported.

### Technological Approaches

The use of technology may assume the following forms:

* Using software filters to block certain types of content to all users. Apart from India, government agencies in many countries, including

Argentina, Australia, Denmark, Saudi Arabia, South Korea and the USA, use this method.

- Using such filters to block all content to all but authorised users. This is mainly used by commercial sites that wish to charge subscribers in return for access to their resources.

- Using technical means to ensure that only entities holding large-scale content distribution rights (usually corporates) can use the net as a distribution medium.

According to Lawrence Lessig, Harvard University law professor and internet specialist, the third means, by which corporates and other large bodies are controlling the net is a serious threat to the open nature of the internet and is becoming a reality in the USA. Traditionally, Lessig explains,[38] the net's physical infrastructure (computers and telecommunication links) and content (web pages, documents on FTP locations, etc.) have been owned by individuals, corporates and other bodies, and governments. But its 'logic layer' consisting of its defining protocols has not been owned by anyone, and its architecture is such that no one's permission is required to introduce innovations to it. Moreover, the net has had the character of a 'digital commons', since, like parks and other such places, admission to it is open to everyone and the terms of admission, where present (such as entry fees of parks), are equal for everyone.[‡]

Lessig says that walls are coming up with the move from narrowband telephone lines to broadband cable lines. Cable companies in the US are deploying technologies that enable discrimination in the content and applications running on the network. The danger is multiplied by a move towards vertical integration, which is giving rise to a very small number of giant conglomerates that own everything, from the physical infrastructure to the logic layer to content. AOL, the largest ISP in the USA, has merged with Time Warner, which is the largest content owner through its print publications, television channels and films. Integration on this scale, Lessig says, makes it extremely difficult for other companies to compete in the same market.

---

[‡] We should note that one cannot adhere too strictly to the commons model, as there have been inequalities in the terms of entry, such as different costs of net access in different countries, from the very beginning. However, within a certain degree of approximation, it serves as a useful tool for conceptualising the net.

Though Lessig speaks of the USA (and Canada to some extent), it may not be unreasonable to fear for such developments in India, too, where the move towards cable has begun. Although conglomerates like AOL-Time Warner are yet to enter India and the country does not have indigenous corporate bodies on their scale, liberalisation may eventually bring in the global players.

In any case, strategies of integration similar to that of AOL-Time Warner are being followed by each of the three major players that dominate ICT. VSNL Tata Indicom, the largest Indian ISP jointly owned by the government and the Tata group, is working out arrangements with cable television operators for its broadband service. Reliance, the private sector giant, offers both telephony and internet services, and has been making arrangements to supply content through its network.[39] BSNL, a major player in public sector telephony, which also provides internet connectivity through its telephone lines, plans to provide cable television channels, film-on-demand and interactive TV in Kolkata and other places through broadband.[40] MTNL, a sister concern of BSNL in the public sector which operates in Delhi and Bombay, has similar plans.[41]

Early in 2004, the IT magazine *Dataquest* said India's internet subscriber population stood at 4.15 million, of whom 190,000 were using broadband services, mainly through the DSL (digital subscriber lines) and cable technologies. VSNL had become the leading broadband provider after taking over the company Dishnet DSL for Rs 270 crore (Rs 2700 million, or $60 million). Apart from VSNL, BSNL, MTNL and Reliance, Bharti, too, was concentrating on broadband. The company had set up its own submarine cable gateway at Chennai, and signed up over 50,000 DSL customers. There are two important strategies of control deployed to favour large-scale content distributors:

ASYMMETRY    One way of ensuring that the network favours large-scale content distributors over consumers is the introduction of asymmetry or asynchrony in the network  as in ADSL (asymmetric or asynchronous digital subscriber link). In this system, the upstream and downstream data transfer speeds, that is, the rates at which the user can send and receive data, respectively, are unequal. The downstream speed, for example, when downloading files, is several times the upstream speed and may be higher by a factor of 10 or more.

This is a deliberate design feature aimed at ensuring that the consumer can easily download large files provided for a fee by content distribution companies, such as music, films and video. Since the upstream speed is a fraction of the downstream speed, the same consumer finds it very difficult to send files of comparable size, and this prevents her from publishing or distributing content effectively.

Thus, an important attribute of the net – its ability to facilitate the creation of a participatory, democratic society by allowing every user to become a journalist or publisher – is defeated.

WALLED GARDEN   Another technological strategy of control is the 'walled garden' – the practice of dividing the network into favoured and disadvantaged zones, so that access to certain sites is made easy (fast) and access to certain other sites is made difficult (slow).[42] This not only marks a departure from the original design philosophy of the net, but also approaches censorship.

A typical application would be an ISP giving favoured status to the website of a magazine when this ISP and the magazine belong to the same conglomerate, and giving low status to the site of another magazine, which belongs to a different corporate group and is a competitor of the first. This effect is achieved with the help of 'intelligent' routers. (The router is a device located at gateways, with the task of determining the best possible paths for data packets and sending them along networks.) It has been noted that there is a growing tendency among ISPs in the West to put corporate traffic in the favoured category, thus putting individual subscribers at a disadvantage.

Tseng and Eischen note that technologies like content caching and Quality of Service (QoS) protocols allow large corporate customers to bypass the public internet infrastructure, partitioning the net into publicly and privately accessible data conduits. Since access is based on payment, they say, these private 'throughways' can be viewed as the new toll roads of the net.[43] We can see that the effect of this is similar to that of asymmetry or asynchrony.

It may seem that the trends we have been discussing, which as a whole are termed convergence and broadband (to be discussed in the next chapter), are a question of control rather than censorship. However, governments and corporate bodies seek to control the internet in order to exercise censorship for political or commercial reasons. Therefore, these trends in fact indicate a move towards a comprehensive censorship regime, and not simply a regulative system.

**Practical Methods**

When the legal and technical means of exercising censorship and control are not effective or feasible for some reason, certain practical means are employed. One of these involves the use of those features of existing technology which make content either unavailable to the potential audience or too expensive. A simple but effective technique used in many countries is to peg the cost of net access so high that only the rich and powerful can afford it.

Another straightforward method is to maintain government monopoly over the ISP business. This is the case in countries like Bahrain, Myanmar and Tunisia[44], and was also the case in India when VSNL, then a purely government organization, was the only ISP allowed to operate in the country.

## Strategies against Censorship, Control and Surveillance

However bleak the scenario may look in the above discussion, we should note that attempts to censor and control the net are being continuously challenged by its opponents through several means.

### Hacking

Technological means of fighting controls are sometimes called hacking, especially when these involve activities like breaking passwords or bypassing the code key protection of copyrighted digital files.

Hacking is often illegal and sometimes unethical, depending on the circumstances. Hence, hackers have to tread a fine line. Their task is complicated by the fact that law and ethics may not always be coterminous, and they should, ideally, analyze both the legality and the ethics of their actions on a case-by-case basis.

### Mirroring

Another effective method of fighting censorship is mirroring. When a government forces a site to be removed from the web, supporters of the site, often in other countries, put its content back on the web through other servers. Thus, Privacy International and GreenNet point out, such censorship often proves counterproductive, resulting in a proliferation of copies of the site that was intended to be blocked. Another simple but effective method is to circulate proscribed material by email.

### Anonymising

A less common but proven method of fighting not only censorship and control but also surveillance on the net is the use of anonymiser sites. Normally, when a user accesses a website, he leaves a digital trail that can be traced back to him. If he wishes to visit a site without leaving such a trail, or a site that is blocked, he may visit an anonymiser site and enter the desired address in the field provided there for the purpose. The anonymiser program then visits the desired site on his behalf without disclosing his identity through the usual digital trail or triggering the blocks put in place by banning agencies. Some of these sites also offer anonymous email services, which have already proved useful in difficult situations, such as in Kosovo, where opponents of the Serb regime have used it during the conflict for communicating with the outside world, as well as for accessing websites and discussion groups.[45]

While these sites themselves can be blocked, Privacy International and GreenNet point out that they can continue to offer their services by changing their web addresses, and users can still locate them at their new addresses through relatively simple web searches. To prevent this, the Chinese government has used its Golden Shield project to occasionally ban the major search engines and keep a close watch on Chinese language portals, both of which can be used by people wishing to locate anonymiser sites.

## Exercises

1. Study the way a major Indian newspaper and TV channel cover the internet. Compare this with (a) other Indian newspapers and TV channels, and (b) major international news websites, with reference to the expression of utopian and dystopian views.

2. Use a search engine like Teoma, Google or Yahoo! to find out what the central and state governments, and NGOs are doing in India to bridge the digital divide.

3. Use a search engine like Teoma, Google or Yahoo! to find cases of surveillance, censorship and control of the internet in India and discuss these with reference to the Constitution's democratic principles.

4. Use a search engine to find an anonymiser site, and surf the web through it.

# References

[1] *Oxford Dictionary of Sociology* (New York, Oxford University Press, 1998), p. 664.

[2] Barlowe, John Perry, 'A Declaration of the Independence of Cyberspace', quoted by the New York Public Library, accessed 13 November 2004 on http:// utopia.nypl.org/I_meta_2.html. Full transcript available, as of 14 November 2004 on http://www.eff.org/~barlow/Declaration-Final.html.

[3] Negroponte, Nicholas, 'Epilogue: An Age of Optimism', *Being Digital* (New York, Alfred A. Knopf, 1995), accessed 18 November 2004 on http://archives.obs-us.com/ obs/english/books/nn/ch19epi.htm.

[4] Howcroft, Debra and Brian Fitzgerald, 'From Utopia to Dystopia: The Twin Faces of the Internet', Proceedings of the International Federation for Information Processing Working Conference on 'Information Systems: Current Issues and Future Changes', Helsinki, 10–13 December 1998, pp. 49–69.

[5] Patelis, Korinna, 'The Political Economy of the Internet', *Media Organisations in Society*, ed. J. Curran (London, Arnold, 2000).

[6] Winston, David, 'Digital Democracy and the New Age of Reason,' conference on 'Democracy and Digital Media', Massachusetts Institute of Technology, 8–9 May 1998, accessed 18 March 2004 on http://web.mit.edu/m-i-t/articles/ index_winston.html.

[7] Barbrook, Richard, 'Electronic Democracy: Politics in Cyberspace', *nettime l - archive*, 4 October 1996 , accessed 14 October 2004 on http://www.nettime.org/ Lists-Archives/nettime-l-9610/msg00012.html.

[8] Dahlberg, Lincoln, 'The Internet and Democratic Discourse: Exploring the Prospects of Online Deliberative Forums Extending the Public Sphere', *Information, Communication & Society,* December 2001, vol. 4, no. 4, pp. 615–633. Database: Communication & Mass Media Complete, accessed 29 March 2004 on http:// search.epnet.com/direct.asp?an=5820550&db=ufh.

[9] Kling, R., quoted in Howcroft and Fitzgerald, 1998, p. 53.

10  Winner, Langdon, 'Technology Today: Utopia Or Dystopia?' *Social Research*, Fall 1997, vol. 64, no. 3, pp. 989–1018. Accessed 22 March 2004 on http://breeze.ifas.ufl.edu/readings/L.(a).PDF.

11  'Understanding the Digital Divide', Organisation for Economic Co-operation and Development (OECD), Paris, 2001, p. 5, accessed 20 March 2004 on http://www.oecd.org/dataoecd/38/57/1888451.pdf.

12  Poster, Mark, 'Postmodern Virtualities', *The Second Media Age*, accessed 18 March 2004 on http://www.hnet.uci.edu/mposter/writings/internet.html.

13  Overview of Digital Divide, International Telecommunication Union, 31 July 2001, accessed 21 November 2004 on http://www.itu.int/ITU-D/digitaldivide/.

14  'Understanding the Digital Divide', OECD, p.7.

15  Ibid., p.8.

16  Except for 2004, the data for which has been taken from *Internet World Stats,* accessed 22 November 2004 on http://www.internetworldstats.com/ all the data has been sourced from Millennium Indicators, United Nations and International Telecommunication Union, accessed 20 March 2004 on http://millenniumindicators.un.org/unsd/mi/mi_goals.asp.

17  Consultation Paper on 'Accelerating Growth of Internet and Broadband Penetration', Telecom Regulatory Authority of India, p. 3.

18  Tseng, Emy and Kyle Eischen, 'The Geography of Cyberspace', *M/C: A Journal of Media and Culture,* 26 August 2003, accessed 16 March 2004 on http://www.media-culture.org.au/0308/03-geography.html.

19  Xavier, Patrick, 'Bridging the "Digital Divide": Issues and Policies in OECD Countries', OECD, p. 9.

20  Consultation Paper on 'Accelerating Growth of Internet and Broadband Penetration', the Telecom Regulatory Authority of India, pp.32–33.

21  Bowen, Ted Smalley, 'English Could Snowball on the Net', *Technology Research News,* 21 November 2001, accessed 21 September 2003 on http://www.trnmag.com/Stories/2001/112101/English_could_snowball_on_Net_112101.html.

22  Sprenger, Polly, 'The Multilingual Net', *Wired News, SDNP Africa* listserv, accessed 21 September 2003 on http://www.sdnp.undp.org/rc/forums/mgr/sdnpaf/msg00647.html.

23  'Global Internet Statistics (By Language)', *Global Reach,* 30 September 2004, accessed 11 November 2004 on http://www.glreach.com/globstats/.

24  'Internet Under Surveillance 2004', *Reporters Without Frontiers,* accessed 27 November 2004 on http://www.rsf.fr/rubrique.php3?id_rubrique=433.

25 'Silenced', An International Report on Censorship and Control of the Internet, Privacy International and the GreenNet Educational Trust, September 2003, p.7, accessed 24 November 2004 on http://pi.gn.apc.org/survey/censorship/Silenced.pdf.

26 Ibid., p.11.

27 Ibid., p 132.

28 The American Civil Liberties Union (ACLU), 'Answers to Frequently Asked Questions about Echelon', accessed 28 November 2004 on http://archive.aclu.org/echelonwatch/faq.html.

29 Kazi, Seema, 'Covert Censorship', *The Hindu*, 11 November 2000, accessed 27 November 2004 on http://www.hindu.com/thehindu/2000/11/11/stories/05111305.htm.

30 Annual Report, 2003–2004, Department of Information Technology, Ministry of Communications and Information Technology, Government of India, New Delhi, pp. 62–63.

31 Ibid.

32 'Internet: Joining the Broadband Bash', *Dataquest*, accessed 26 November 2004 on http://www.dqindia.com/dqtop20/2004/ArtIndseg.asp?artid=59641.

33 The Information Technology Act, 2000 (No. 21 of 2000), Ministry of Law, Justice and Company Affairs (Legislative Department), *The Gazette of India*, New Delhi, 9 June 2000, accessed 25 November 2004 on http://www.mit.gov.in/itbill2000.pdf.

34 Varadarajan, Siddharth, 'Policing the Net: The Dangers of India's New IT Act', *Sarai Reader 2001: The Public Domain*, pp. 133–135, accessed 24 November 2004 on http://www.sarai.net/journal/pdf/133-135%20(bill).pdf.

35 Ninan, Sevanti, 'Resisting censorship', *The Hindu*, 12 October 2003, accessed 26 November 2004 on http://www.hindu.com/thehindu/mag/2003/10/12/stories/2003101200180300.htm.

36 Minwalla, Shabnam, 'Net Policing Comes to India', *The Times of India*, 1 August 2003, accessed 26 November 2004 on http://timesofindia.indiatimes.com/cms.dll/html/uncomp/articleshow?msid=105778.

37 Ibid.

38 Lessig, Lawrence, 'Controlling the Net: How Vested Interests Are Enclosing the CyberCommons and Undermining Internet Freedom', interview in the *Multinational Monitor*, March 2002, vol. 23, no. 3, accessed 25 November 2004 on http://multinationalmonitor.org/mm2002/02march/march02interviewlessig.html.

[39] 'BSNL, Reliance Broadband Threaten Cable Trade', *indiantelevision.com,* 18 April 2003, accessed 26 November 2004 on http://www.indiantelevision.com/headlines/y2k3/apr/apr137.htm.

[40] 'BSNL may Allow Isps in Broadband, Cable TV Bids', *The Economic Times,* 13 September 2002, accessed 27 November on http://www.bsnl.in/MediaTalk.asp?intNewsId=1913&strNewsMore=more. and 'BSNL to Offer Cable TV on Broadband in Kolkata', *rediff.com,* 6 June 2003 on http://inhome.rediff.com/money/2003/jun/06bsnl.htm?zcc=ar.

[41] 'MTNL to Launch Cable TV Services in Delhi', *The Times of India,* accessed 27 November 2004 on http://www.bsnl.in/intranetnews.asp?url=/bsnl/asp/content%20mgmt/html%20content/telecom/telecom3969.html.

[42] Stalder, Felix, 'The Culture of Broadband', *Openflows,* accessed 3 December 2004 on http://felix.openflows.org/html/broadband.html.

[43] Tseng, Emy and Kyle Eischen, 'The Geography of Cyberspace', *M/C: A Journal of Media and Culture,* 26 August 2003.

[44] *'Silenced',* Privacy International and the GreenNet Educational Trust, p.13.

[45] Hall, Jim, *Online Journalism: A Critical Primer,* (London and Sterling, Virginia, Pluto Press, 2001), p. 102.

# 11.
# Convergence and Broadband

The current move towards convergence and broadband was mentioned in the last chapter, while discussing the issue of access and barrier with respect to the internet. These technological trends, which are resulting in the destruction or significant curtailment of the net's open nature, will be discussed in greater detail in this chapter.

But before doing so, we should note that broadband and convergence are two aspects of a single phenomenon. The convergence of broadcast, telecommunications and information technologies is not technically feasible in the absence of transmission channels of large information-carrying capacity, that is, broadband. On the other hand, broadband links may not be economically viable if they are not used to deliver multiple high-value services typical of convergence.

## Convergence

Convergence informs all aspects of social life, spanning business, economy, politics, and culture in addition to technology. The following definition provided by the online encyclopedia

*Webopedia* is of interest to us: "The coming together of two or more disparate disciplines or technologies. For example, the so-called fax revolution was produced by a convergence of telecommunications technology, optical scanning technology, and printing technology."

Another online encyclopedia offers a more common definition: "a term for the combining of personal computers, telecommunication, and television into a user experience that is accessible to everyone." The 'converged' technology has come to be known as ICT, information and communication technologies or, according to the *Concise Oxford English Dictionary*, "information and computing technology".

The most obvious manifestation of convergence is globalisation. In economic terms, the term stands for the integration of national economies through the lowering of trade barriers, full currency convertibility, the creation of common currencies like the Euro, etc. In politics, it means the increasing legislative powers of global and multilateral agencies, such as the UNO and the European Union. In the cultural sphere, globalisation signifies the spread of local cultures and subcultures across the globe, and the resulting production of hybrid forms (as Henry Jenkins, Director of the Comparative Media Studies Program at MIT[1] points out, such things as 'world music' and Hollywood films influenced by Asian cinema).

Rich Gordon, a news industry veteran, who has served important newspapers in the US like *The Miami Herald,* discusses convergence with reference to two broad areas of the media – technology, and the social realm.[2] In the social realm we will look at convergence in ownership, tactical convergence and convergence in the organisational structure and practices. Jenkins' conception of organic convergence is also discussed in the chapter.

## Technological Convergence

This can be further divided into the technologies of creating, distributing and consuming content. Since the technologies of distribution and consumption are actually complementary parts of the same technology (for instance, television broadcasting and television reception, or the internet and personal computers), we really have two technologies – content creation and content distribution or consumption.

## Content Creation

Total convergence at the end of content creation is not possible either with information or with entertainment. Even though content is generated in digital form, the formats used are often mutually incompatible. For instance, it is not easy to convert a newspaper piece formatted and stored with QuarkXPress (a program used for making page layouts) into a web page. Similarly, a web page created for computers has to be converted into another format before it can be read on an internet-connected cell phone.

## Content Distribution and Consumption

The technologies of distribution and consumption are better integrated, thanks to the internet. From a text-only system, the net has developed into one that carries all kinds of traffic – text, graphics, voice, audio and video. The mobile phone is another example of convergence at the distribution or consumption pole. It can send and receive email messages, surf the web, take still photographs and video footage, and send these files to other people.

## The Future of Technological Convergence

According to Gordon, the following factors are responsible for increasing technological convergence in content creation and distribution and consumption.

- Increasing use of digital content management systems like Extensible Markup Language (XML), which facilitate smooth delivery of common content to different platforms

- The spread of wireless internet access, either through mobile telephone systems or through local wireless networks (say, wireless local area networks), which connect to the net

- Growing sophistication of TV sets, which will need to access the net, receive and store digital content, and allow viewers to interact with content as they do on personal computers. Net access is already available through TV cables in India as we have noted, and digital broadcasting has begun in some developed countries.

- A new generation of portable devices that approximate the characteristics of paper. Gordon says these may be derived from portable devices that are currently in use such as laptop computers, PDAs (personal digital assistants) and mobile phones, or from technologies like 'electronic ink' and 'e-paper', which are at the development stage.

However, some writers have a different view of technological convergence in the media. According to Jenkins, "There will *never* be one black box controlling all media [emphasis as in original]." Others have noted that convergence has not proved popular in many fields. For instance, people have continued to use kitchen appliances that perform individual functions rather than adopting those which can carry out a number of tasks.

A recent survey of digital TV owners conducted by a consultancy firm in association with the BBC in the USA, UK, France and Japan confirms these views.[3] It shows that there is a growing tendency to use multiple devices for consuming multimedia content, rather than a single device (TV or PC).

The arrival of multi-channel interactive digital TV is reinforcing the television set's place as the primary entertainment hub in consumers' minds. Those who own such sets, generally see the PC as the main gateway to the internet for using email and instant messaging services, accessing information and e-commerce sites (mainly shopping and purchasing tickets), and for a growing range of multimedia entertainment and multi-functionality, for example, streaming audio and video services, downloads, music, and online gaming. The PC's use is increasing because of the advent of broadband, with particularly high growth in entertainment content delivered through the net (see box).

## Convergence in the Social Realm

### Convergence of Ownership

This is taking place through mergers among media organisations. The most famous of these in recent times was one that took place in 2000 between AOL (America Online), the largest ISP in the USA, and Time Warner, the giant media house. Mergers that took place among other large conglomerates are those between the US-based groups Viacom and Disney, France-based Vivendi Universal and Germany-based Bertelsmann AG. All these are distinguished by large cross-media ownership, with each owning companies across the media spectrum, namely print (newspapers, magazines and books), radio, television, recorded music, music videos, films, and the internet.

## The Future according to Bill Gates

Microsoft chief Bill Gates provides some glimpses of the shape of things to come.[4] According to Gates, the linear concepts of TV channels and schedules in which programmes follow one another in a predetermined order are changing. The use of DVRs (digital video recorders) and the availability of a large number of cable and satellite channels are providing flexibility for the audience, and this will further increase with the introduction of software like the new MS operating system, Windows XP Media Center Edition 2005.

To appreciate the difference DVRs can make, we may note that the viewer can set these devices to automatically record television programmes of his choice, so that he may view these later according to his convenience, and while doing so, he can easily skip advertisements that do not interest him. The DVR also allows him to easily change the order of the recorded programmes.

"The ideal for many content people would be that they just put their content on the Internet and then they have a direct relationship with the viewer," Gates is quoted as saying. "That model for low-volume content is the future."

He adds that changing technology will change advertising as well, making it 'personalised' and sharply targeted at precisely those viewers whom the advertiser wants to reach.

In some Western markets, broadband service providers have begun to supply premium television channels to the ordinary TV sets currently owned by consumers. Kingston Interactive TV in the UK is the pioneer in this field. This company is offering a basic package costing £ 6.80 (about Rs 577) a month, which consists of 12 TV channels, video-on-demand, locally tailored BBC programmes, unlimited internet and email.[5]

On the other hand, smart TV sets with built-in hard drives are also beginning to be made for use with such broadband connections. Since these sets can be accessed through the internet, they can be used to search for material according to the user's interests, store them, augment them with computer-generated images if the user likes, and send them to others through the net.

In India, as we have noted in the last chapter, the government and two of the largest industrial houses, Tata and Reliance, have cross-media ownership in telephony, cable television and internet services. Limited cross-media holdings among media houses is also evident in print, television production and films. An example of this type of convergence in India is the joint venture set up by Rupert Murdoch's Star TV and ABP Limited, the newspaper group which owns two successful dailies, *The Telegraph* (English) and the *Ananda Bazar Patrika* (Bengali), and several magazines. The *Hindustan Times* group of publications had sought foreign investment for expanding its operations into radio, television, and entertainment, apart from print. *The Times of India* group, also owns in full or part the Radio Mirchi FM channel, the Times Music CD and cassette company, the Planet M chain of cassette and CD stores, and Times Multimedia.

## Tactical Convergence

According to Gordon, tactical partnerships between TV stations and newspapers in the US, mostly under different ownership, began to appear in the late 1990s. The main objective was to promote one another.

For instance, a television reporter's investigative report into bridge corrosion was given to the channel's partner-newspaper to be published first, and this resulted in a 25 per cent increase in audience ratings for that evening's TV news. Advertising also was being sold in a 'cross-platform' mode, that is, as a package for the newspaper and the TV channel together.

Sometimes, especially in cases where the same company owned the newspaper and the TV channel, print journalists were required to appear on TV to discuss stories they were covering. Newspaper reporters are required to provide updates to TV stations, TV camera crews are required to take still photographs for newspapers and newspaper photographers are required to carry lightweight digital video cameras in order to provide video clips to the TV stations. As a result, this type of convergence often means extra work and reduced employment opportunities for journalists.

## Convergence in Organisational Structure

Sometimes senior news personnel are recruited to coordinate between the newspaper's newsroom and the TV channel's newsroom in a tactical partnership. Gordon also gives examples of more conspicuous signs of convergence in organisational structures such as the setting up of a TV stage in the middle of the newsroom of the *Chicago Tribune* newspaper.

## Convergence in Storytelling

This refers to the simultaneous use of different media for presenting the same story, which takes us to the realm of multimedia. As different parts of an organisation or different organisations need to come together to produce content, incorporating text, audio and video, this implies some degree of convergence in organisational structures.

## Organic Convergence

Social or organic convergence is a phenomenon noted by Jenkins[6]. This refers to media consumer's "multitasking strategies for navigating the new information environment". An example is the teenager who may be watching sports on television while listening to music on his stereo system, all the while writing an essay for his class and exchanging emails with friends on his personal computer. Jenkins has American teenagers in mind, but this trend can also be seen in India.

We should note that this type of convergence is developing at the consumer's end, and at the level of perception. This is unlike the other types we have mentioned, which are occurring at the media producer's end, at the macro levels of technology, economics and organisational structure.

## Government Policies on Convergence

Now that the media and telecommunications sectors are coming together, along with the largely unregulated computing and internet sector, the need is felt for new mechanisms to regulate these spheres.

## Regulation in Europe and USA

The European Union's Green Paper of 1997,[7] was one of the first documents to address these issues. Humphreys observes[8] that the paper, which caused considerable controversy, noted a clear division in opinion between those who believed that convergence would lead to the complete collapse of traditional boundaries between telecommunication, information technology and media industries, and those who believed that the unique features of the individual sectors would help them retain their separate existence.

More recently, in June 2003, the US Federal Communications Commission (FCC) announced that it was significantly slackening controls over cross-media ownership and media monopoly, opening the door to media convergence in unprecedented ways. The policy change was strongly criticized by a section of ordinary Americans and many academics for showing the green light to increasing media monopoly. It was challenged in court and faced negative votes in the Senate.

### Regulation in India

India, too, has tried – unsuccessfully so far – to replace existing sector-specific regulatory laws for broadcast and telecommunications by a common convergence law. The Communication Convergence Bill, 2001, was drafted to replace the Indian Telegraph Act, 1885, the Indian Wireless Telegraph Act, 1931, the Telegraph Wires (Unlawful Possession) Act, 1950, the Telecom Regulatory Authority of India Act, 1987, and the Cable Television Networks (Regulation) Act, 1995. The Acts would be replaced with a single law to cover the entire converged ICT sector, and to set up a single body, the Communication Commission of India (CCI), to regulate the entire sector.

However, when the draft Bill was made public for discussion in 2002 and then tabled in the Lok Sabha, it came in for criticism from several quarters, including the concerned Standing Parliamentary Committee and industry bodies, for vesting too much power in the CCI among other things. The NDA government then decided not to press ahead with the Bill, which seems to have remained in deep freeze since then.

It should be noted that the issues that have invited criticism of the initiatives for regulation of convergence in India are different from those in the West. In the advanced capitalist markets of the European Union and the USA, the greatest worry is the increasing power of monopolistic media conglomerates and the consequent decrease in media diversity.

In India, on the other hand, concerns are centred around the government's attempt to exercise complete and arbitrary control over the converged sector of communication, including content. It has been noted[9] that the proposed Communication Commission of India would have been a fully government-controlled body, though nominally autonomous, and its mandate would have included the regulation not only of the 'carriage' of communication but also its 'content', that is, the Bill, if passed, would have legalised systematic censorship through the back door.

## Criticism of Convergence

In the previous chapter we noted that technological convergence and accompanying business convergence are transforming the internet from a domain of freedom and openness into a realm of corporate control. In the present chapter, we have mentioned the negative consequences of business and tactical convergence for journalists. Scholars like Don Corrigan argue that convergence is against the interests of the audience as well.[10]

Corrigan writes that the public loses an important service rendered by journalists when the demands of multimedia presentation prevent them from putting in the concentration needed to write thoughtful pieces on important subjects.

Moreover, if print journalists are required to contribute to TV channels, they have to make concessions to the latter's stress on appearance and their penchant for instant analyses. In the event of convergence, Corrigan feels, television culture is likely to dominate news in an organisation because of TV's glamour and technological edge over print. Also, since thinking reporters are likely to write controversial stories, media conglomerates may actually prefer this kind of superficiality to depth.

It should be noted that Corrigan refrains from specifically commenting on the culture of online news, obviously because the internet does not yet have a distinctive news culture – the net being a new medium, most online journalists are still drawn either from print or from broadcast. However, there is no doubt that as online journalism matures over the coming years, its own culture will take shape through the ongoing clash between the two older cultures of print and television.

## Broadband

As noted before, effective media convergence requires broadband connectivity. The common narrowband links available through ordinary telephone lines and dialup modems are inadequate for carrying the large volumes of data (binary bits) into which audio and video content translate when stored in digital form. It is virtually impossible to watch streamed web TV with such connections, and even downloading web pages becomes a slow process when the pages contain graphics, animation or flash objects. As most news sites contain photographs – some also have flash objects and a few have links to audio and video files – dialup access is an inefficient technology for consuming rich media content.

Since technology is constantly advancing, there are no fixed quantitative definitions of the terms narrowband and broadband. An ITU report points out that the latter is "like a moving target"[11]: internet access speeds considered 'fast' at present, will soon be considered 'slow'. Instead, the report defines broadband as a transmission capacity faster than 1.5 mbps (megabits per second), that is, 1500 kbps (kilobits per second), noting that a common practice is to designate speeds of 256 kbps and higher as broadband. In India, by comparison, the average information carrying capacity or 'throughput' of dialup connections is 10 kbps.[12]

Because of this absence of a fixed quantitative benchmark, broadband is sometimes defined according to the type of data transmission involved rather than speed, namely, as a single medium (wire pair or cable) carrying several channels simultaneously. An example is cable TV connections, which carry a large number of channels. The opposite of this is baseband transmission, which refers to the carrying of a single signal at a time, as in ordinary telephony.

The two most common technologies used to bring broadband access to subscribers are cable and DSL (digital subscriber line). The first, which utilises the coaxial lines of cable television service providers, is the more popular technology in North America. DSL technology, on the other hand, is the popular choice of Asia and Western Europe. This technology usually comes in asymmetric or asynchronous mode, as ADSL, which disempowers subscribers as content producers. A number of wireless net access technologies such as satellite links are also available in broadband mode, but their use is still much rarer than the wire-based technologies.

While the media are the focus of this book, they represent only one of the many possible uses of broadband. As the ITU report remarks, "The real gift of broadband is the greater scope it provides for developing applications listed by enabling new ones." Among the applications listed by the Confederation of Indian Industry are telemedicine, teleworking, e-governance, agriculture, distance education and public safety. BPO (business process outsourcing) is another financially lucrative application. Thus, although broadband is often used by corporate and government powers as a site of control and censorship (as we have noted in chapter ten), it does have beneficial effects on national economies.

## Broadband in India

Broadband is making rapid progress in this country. Many of the large ISPs – BSNL, VSNL and MTNL – have begun to offer this service. According to data published by TRAI[13], out of 4.93 million internet subscribers on 30 June 2005, a very small percentage – only 230,000 – had broadband access, but while the total internet subscriber base increased by 30.77 per cent over a period of one year (since end-June 2003), the corresponding rate of growth was 155.56 per cent for broadband. As Table 11.1 shows, the government expects broadband to account for half of all subscribers in this country at the end of 2010, by which time the total subscriber base is expected to reach 40 million.[14]

Table 11.1 Projeced internet and broadband growth

| Year Ending | Internet Subscribers | Broadband Subscribers |
|---|---|---|
| 2005 | 6 million | 3 million |
| 2007 | 18 million | 9 million |
| 2010 | 40 million | 20 million |

Since the quality of infrastructure is one of the factors that drive growth in content,[15] one may expect a rapid expansion of the broadband-based services mentioned earlier in this chapter. In the field of media, this may mean much greater use of multimedia as well as streamed content on TV and FM radio channels, or the emergence of new web-only channels that stream content but do not air it.

Such advances in content may trigger another growth cycle in the internet infrastructure and internet-related consumer hardware – personal computers, WAP (wireless application protocol, that is, internet-enabled) mobile phones, smart TV sets, et cetera – which in turn will lead to the further development of content, and this cyclic movement may repeat itself.[16]

# Exercises

1.  Can you find instances of convergence in the major Indian news media? If so, study and discuss the effects of such convergence on news values and ethics as reflected in their coverage of important issues and events.

2.  Visit a news organisation in which convergence of some type has been effected, and study the changes this has brought in various aspects of news work.

3.  Identify and discuss differences between news websites operating from the developed countries, in which broadband has spread in a big way, and those from the less developed countries, where it has not.

# References

[1]  Jenkins, Henry, 'Convergence? I diverge', *Technology Review*, June 2001, p. 93, accessed 30 November 2004 on http://web.mit.edu/21fms/www/faculty/henry3/converge.pdf.

[2]  Gordon, Rich, 'Workplace', *Digital Journalism: Emerging Media and the Changing Horizons of Journalism,* ed. Kevin Kawamoto (Rowman & Littlefield, 2003), accessed 18 March 2004 on http://www.ojr.org/ojr/business/1068686368.php.

[3]  'Consumers Take Digital Convergence in Stride', *Primedia*, 9 June 2003, accessed 30 November 2004 on http://millimeter.com/pressroom/video_consumers_digital_convergence/.

[4]  Marlowe, Chris, 'Gates: New Model for Broadcast TV', *Shoot,* 22 October 2004, vol. 45, no.37, p.7, accessed 1 December 2004 on database Business Source Premier, persistent link: http://search.epnet.com/login.aspx?direct=true&AuthType=cookie,ip,url,uid&db=buh&an=15055350.

[5]  Grassley, Tanya, 'Broadband; TV Culture Versus PC Culture', *Ericsson Telecom Report*, accessed 3 December 2004 on http://www.ericsson.com/telecomreport/article.asp?aid=19&tid=129&ma=1&msa=3.

[6]  Jenkins, Henry, 'Convergence? I diverge'.

[7]  'Convergence of the Telecommunications, Media and Information Technology Sectors, and the Implications for Regulation: Towards an Information Society Approach', Green Paper, European Commission, Brussels, 3 December 1997, accessed 3 December 2004 on http://europa.eu.int/ISPO/convergencegp/97623.html.

8  Humphreys, Peter, 'Regulating for Pluralism in the Era of Digital Convergence: the Issues of Media Concentration Control and the Future of Public-service Broadcasting', paper presented to the ECPR joint research sessions, Mannheim, March 1999, accessed 30 November 2004 on http://www.essex.ac.uk/ECPR/events/jointsessions/paperarchive/mannheim/w24/Humphreys.PDF.

9  Duggal, Pavan, 'Telecommunications Convergence Law in India – A Critique', *Murdoch University Electronic Journal of Law*, vol. 9, no. 1, March 2002, accessed 2 December 2004 on http://www.murdoch.edu.au/elaw/issues/v9n1/duggal91.html.

10 Corrigan, Don, 'Convergence Works for Media Owner but not News Consumer', *St. Louis Journalism Review*, vol. 34, no. 271, November 2004, pp. 14–15, Database:Communication & Mass Media Complete, accessed 1 December 2004, persistent link: http://search.epnet.com/login.aspx?direct=true&AuthType=cookie,ip,url,uid&db=ufh&an=14989468.

11 'Birth of Broadband', Executive Summary, ITU, 2003.

12 Consultation Paper on 'Accelerating Growth of Internet and Broadband Penetration', The Telecom Regulatory Authority of India, p.3.

13 The Indian Telecom Services Performance Indicators, April–June 2004, Telecom Regulatory Authority of India, p.4.

14 Broadband Policy 2004, Government of India, accessed 27 November 2004 on http://www.dotindia.com/broadbandpolicy2004.htm.

15 Consultation Paper on 'Accelerating Growth of Internet and Broadband Penetration', Telecom Regulatory Authority of India, p.8.

16 Ibid.

# 12.
# The Network Paradigm

While the previous chapters discussed the internet and online journalism at the macro level, this chapter will provide a brief account of the relationship between the net and its users at a deeper level – that of space and time. This will be addressed as part of the general area of culture and subjectivity.

The reference to 'relationship' actually is an approximation, because the net and its users are not separate entities. The computer network that constitutes the net's physical layer requires the insertion of users to become the internet as we know it, as distinct from a collection of inert machines. Equally, users become what they are, distinct from people in general, *because of* the net.

The real question then is not of 'relationship' but of something that is best expressed in the language of phenomenology as the net's 'being in and with' its users and vice versa. In this perspective, the media, including the internet, are part of the 'lifeworld' of the individual, whose existence cannot be meaningfully seen in isolation from this lifeworld.

# The Network Paradigm

Chapters ten and eleven dealt with certain socially significant facts about the net, which were treated as loosely connected but more or less discrete. In recent years, however, scholars treating society and the net holistically have produced a body of literature on the so-called 'network society' or 'networked society'.

Even as networks have become ubiquitous, Thacker notes[1], this paradigm has entered scientific thinking in several disciplines, including biology, technology, military studies and political studies. According to him, the two necessary and related conditions for the existence of networks are collectivity and connectivity.

Collectivity can be defined as an aggregate of individual units that stand in some relation, which is largely determined by the context, to each other. It presupposes spatial organisation, though not necessarily proximity, and can involve dispersal. Thus, the Indian diaspora can be seen as a collectivity. What holds a collectivity together is connectivity, which can be defined as "a way of relating individuated units within a wide array of possible topological configurations". Thus, people of Indian origin or believers of doomsday theories or fans of The Grateful Dead, living in Kenya, New Zealand and Canada can be said to form a collectivity only in the presence of connectivity. Thacker notes that connectivity can be high or low, wide or narrow, and centralized or decentralized. It presupposes, but is not synonymous with 'relation'. And while connectivity is a necessary condition for collectivity, the reverse is not true.

Perhaps the most influential sociological work in this rubric is Manuel Castells' three-volume series, *The Information Age: Economy, Society and Culture*. The title of the first volume (published in 1996) is, significantly, *The Rise of the Network Society*.

Thacker's definition of connectivity and collectivity helps us to see, with Castells, how the world today is organised like a network, an important underpinning of which is the internet, and more generally, ICT. In his opening address at a conference on Information Technologies and Social Development, organised by the United Nations Research Institute for Social Development (UNRISD), Castells described the 'information age' and the society he saw taking shape.[2]

He said a new form of socio-economic organisation had emerged in the last quarter of the twentieth century. It was fundamentally new, having been shaped by ICT (which has created new sources of productivity), new organizational forms, and the formation of a global economy. In the 1990s, the core sectors of this economy functioned "as a unit in real time, on a planetary scale". As capital markets were globally interlinked, the financial performance of savings and investment made anywhere, even in channels of local scope, depended on the global financial markets. People's lives ultimately depended on the globalised sector of the national economy, or on the direct connection of their economic units to global networks. The core of the world economy in the manufacturing, services, and finance sectors consisted of multinational corporations and their ancillary networks of small and medium businesses.

However, although the new global economy encompassed the entire planet, most people and regions were excluded as producers or consumers or both. The global system interconnected everything that was valuable "according to dominant values and interests", while disconnecting everything that was not valuable, or became devalued. The organisational basis for this, Castells noted, was networking – the creation of a set of nodes interconnected through relationships that were asymmetric but necessary for the network, that is, for the circulation of money, information, technology, images, goods, services, or people. "The most critical distinction in this organizational logic," Castells noted, "is to be or not to be – in the network. Be in the network, and you can share and, over time, increase your chances. Be out of the network, or become switched off, and your chances vanish, since everything that counts is organized around a worldwide web of interacting networks ..."

It should be noted, especially by those of us who live in India, that a major strength of Castells' argument is its ability to accommodate not only regions that lie within the network but also areas that are excluded from it – "in the American inner cities or in the French *banlieues*, as much as in the shanty towns of Africa or in the deprived rural areas of China or India".[3]

In other words, it is important for us to note that these 'excluded' areas do not escape the logic of the network simply because they lie outside it. This has profound consequences for societies such as ours. For this book, the special importance of Castells' theory arises from his privileging of ICT as the driving force behind society's transformation into a 'network society'.

# Culture, Subjectivity and the Net

While Castells' account can be viewed as sociological, Poster offers an important cultural perspective by exploring the relationship between the net and the cultural condition known as postmodernity. For him, the starting point is the Husserlian position that a human being becomes what (s)he is through the intersubjective process of making sense of the world in community with others, that is, through communication.

In Husserl's words:

> (I)n whatever way we may be conscious of the world as universal horizon, as coherent universe of existing objects, we, each 'I-the-man' and all of us together, belong to the world as living with one another in the world; and the world is our world, *valid for our consciousness as existing precisely through this 'living together'* [emphasis added].[4]

In his book, *The Second Media Age* (1995), Poster states that "a critical understanding of the new communications systems requires an evaluation of the type of subject it encourages, while a viable articulation of postmodernity must include an elaboration of its relation to new technologies of communication".[5]

The idea of 'postmodern culture', he notes, is often articulated as an alternative to existing society, one that does not inherit the latter's structural limitations or deep-seated imperfections. This substantially focuses on what is seen as a new individual identity or subject position that is coming into being by discarding the narrow scope of the rational and autonomous individual supposedly produced by modernity.

New communication systems are viewed as a potential means of bringing about a better life and a more equitable society, but this discussion does not foresee fundamental changes in the individual or society, focusing instead on the "technical increase in information exchange" and the manner in which this is expected to have a positive effect on individuals and institutions as they are today, essentially by opening up new avenues of investment, increasing productivity and creating new realms of leisure and consumption.

Poster draws an analogy between developments taking place in the advanced industrial societies in the mid-1990s, and the emergence of urban merchant culture within Western feudal society in the Middle Ages. In feudal culture, face-to-face encounters had a sanctity based on the code of honour of the aristocratic class, presupposing trust for one's word and hierarchical bonds of mutual dependence. Merchant culture, on the other hand, required people to interact in completely new ways: since the traders were often total strangers separated by large geographical distances, written documents were required as a guarantee for promises. Also needed was an attitude of 'arms length distance', even in face-to-face interactions, in order to provide a 'space' for the calculation of self-interest. Poster notes:

> A new identity was constructed, gradually and in a most circuitous path to be sure, among the merchants in which a coherent, stable sense of individuality was grounded in independent, cognitive abilities. In this way the cultural basis for the modern world was begun, one that would eventually rely upon print media to encourage and disseminate these urban forms of identity.

The movement from the modern to the postmodern takes place in what, according to Poster, is the 'second media age'. It involves the constitution of a fluid, decentred subject through the net's interactive feature, and the type of interaction that takes place in its virtual space.

We may note that the above account situates online interaction as the ideal visualised by Habermas for the public sphere, whose existence depends on the ability of people to engage freely in rational-critical debate without being weighed down by such social baggage as class, gender and ethnicity. In this sense, Poster's analysis can be considered congruent with the utopian view of the internet as a facilitator of democracy.

Poster himself acknowledged this fact in 2003, eight years after the above passage was published:

> ... (D)iverse figures such as Nicholas Negroponte of the MIT Media Lab, John Perry Barlow, co-founder of the Electronic Frontier Foundation, and Pierre Lévy, a student of Giles Deleuze in France and author of numerous books on new media ... depicted social betterment as a direct consequence of the introduction of information technology.

> They accounted far too little for the incursion into that technology by existing institutions such as the capitalist economy and the nation state. Perhaps some of my own work might be included in this category."[6] (*The Second Media Age*, 1995)

The 'incursion' to which Poster refers is the process of censorship and control, which we have discussed in the earlier chapters.

## Space, Time and Place

To better appreciate what online journalism means to its audience, we need to appreciate the way its medium, that is, the net, configures people's experience of space and time. Marshall Berman, Daniel Bell, and Frederic Jameson have noted that each cultural mode, such as the pre-modern, modern and postmodern, has its specific logic of time and space. Hence, understanding any of these requires an understanding of the specific ways in which time and space are experienced within it.

Poster's reference to "incursion ... by ... the nation state" brings us to the contested issue of territoriality, that is, of place, which is a function of space and time as socially experienced by the individual subject. From her standpoint, the place in which the individual is located has a specific geographic location defined by coordinates in space and a boundary that may be sharply delineated or fuzzy, and this location has continuity in time, that is, it does not shift geographically with the passage of time. (The place may shift if the subject moves, but at every moment, it has a stable material existence with respect to the subject.)

This is the basis of territoriality, in which the modern subject is rooted, and a major aspect of the post-modern subject constituted through online interaction with others is her supposed freedom from this rootedness in territoriality, of which nationality, "generally regarded as the strongest group identification in the modern period"[7], is an expression.

How does the internet disrupt territoriality? On the legal-political plane, it undermines the nation state's place-based authority by largely frustrating efforts to contain communication within national borders. Poster illustrates this with the example of the Teale-Homolka trial in a case of multiple murders including sexual assault and mutilation held in Canada in 1994.

The Canadian government's attempt to enforce an information blackout on the trial ended in failure because online discussion on the topic originating in the USA was available in Canada as well. "In order to combat communicative acts that are defined by one state as illegal," Poster points out, "nations are being compelled to coordinate their laws, putting their vaunted 'sovereignty' in question." An example from 2004 related to Indymedia (Independent Media Centre) provides a clear illustration of this trend (see box on p. 246).

## Indymedia's Borderless Travails

Acting on complaints from the Swiss and Italian authorities, the US Federal Bureau of Investigation (FBI) seized from the London office of a US-based internet hosting company, two servers that were being used to host 20 sites of Indymedia (Independent Media Centre). The Indymedia member-groups owning these sites were based in the USA, Brazil, the Czech Republic, Spain, Italy, Poland, Portugal, the UK, Uruguay, France and Belgium.

When the British government denied involvement even though the seizure had taken place in London, the British Indymedia commented on its website that "It is unclear ... how and why a server that is outside the US jurisdiction can be seized by US authorities."[8] This statement clearly pointed to a lingering attachment to the logic of modernity with its nation state and its stable subject rooted in territoriality. This, despite the fact that Indymedia itself illustrates the network paradigm clearly and on multiple levels.

In technology, it functions through the internet – a network of networks. In terms of organisation, internally, it is a network of independent media organizations. Externally, it has a loose network relationship with 'affinity groups' that mobilise in a dispersed manner through the extensive use of network-based technologies such as email lists, bulletin boards and mobile telephony. Thacker and others have noted that the anti-WTO protests held in Seattle in 1999 and the anti-war protests in New York and many other cities during the second Iraq war in 2003 were organised in this way.

So far, we have discussed the net's disruptive effect on place and territoriality on the legal-political level. It is important to recognise that it works in this manner on a deeper level as well, causing a rupture in the connection between place and space, which we take for granted in the condition of modernity.

The 'netizen' is not simply a citizen who uses the internet but the 'ego' that experiences the world (in the Husserlian sense mentioned earlier in this chapter) in 'virtual' community with others in 'cyberspace'. The existence of community and sociality in cyberspace makes it a 'place' of sorts, because it transcends geographic space, it is a place of 'pure' sociality, without spatial coordinates and boundaries. This marks a rupture in our *understanding* of 'place' just as it does in the *material connection* between place and space. And in this, Paul Virilio, sometimes described as the most important social theorist of technology in the internet age, sees the root of "a fundamental loss of orientation". "A duplication of sensible reality, into reality and virtuality," he writes, "is in the making. A stereo-reality of sorts threatens. A total loss of the bearings of the individual looms large. To exist, is to exist *in situ*, here and now, *hic et nunc*. This is precisely what is being threatened by cyberspace and instantaneous, globalized information flows."[9] The reference to 'information flows' brings us to the question of time, because a flow is both temporal and spatial – it implies a movement, taking place over time.

Virilio's work is helpful in understanding the way in which the internet reworks our experience of time. While the traditional concept of time is local, being rooted in space and place (a finite amount of time is needed for movement to take place from one place to another), Virilio's thesis is that global communication taking place at the 'absolute speed' of light, being immediate and instantaneous, takes away this locality and substitutes 'real time' in its place.

The internet, of course, perfectly fits this description: interacting online with someone located on the other side of the globe is no different from interacting with someone sitting in the next room. Virilio writes:

> Real time now prevails above both real space and the geosphere. The primacy of real time, of immediacy, over and above space and surface is a *fait accompli* and has inaugural value (ushers a new epoch). Something nicely conjured up in a (French) advertisement praising cellular phones with the words: 'Planet Earth has never been this small'. This is a very dramatic moment in our relation with the world and for our vision of the world.[10]

Here is a simple illustration of this effect from my own experience. In the spring of 2003, I attended a seminar session in Austria. Before going there, I had exchanged emails with a member of the seminar staff about lodging and other arrangements. While checking mail on my first day at the venue I found a message from this man, which had arrived in my inbox after I left Calcutta. I sent a response and he answered within minutes, signing off with "Looking forward to seeing you here" or words to that effect. I wrote back that I was already 'here', in the same building as he was. When we met, he told me he had laughed when he realised that I was in the same building and not in another continent as he had thought. Clearly, that moment of amazement marked the passage of his perspective from locality, from place-based time, to the real time of the internet, which transcends space. Virilio calls this the 'dictatorship of speed'.

"For the first time," he writes, "history is going to unfold within a one-time-system: global time." Until now, events have been perceived in local times and frames, in terms of regions and nations. This accounts for richness of history. But globalisation and 'virtualization', that is, the conduct of human affairs in cyberspace – imply that events will be perceived only in terms of global time. Thus, real time is supplanting real space. The minuscule time span of electronic signals (which travel at the speed of light) is reducing distance to irrelevance. As the global time of cyberspace comes to dominate the local time-frame of people's habitat, the global and the local are fusing together into a new experience that is sometimes called 'glocal'.

As the geographical difference between places is thus obliterated by electronic communication at the speed of light, Virilio says, the world sees the creation of a 'polar inertia'.[11] This takes hold not only of television addicts and other heavy media consumers, but also armies – in high-tech wars conducted mainly from the air, such as the conflict in Kosovo, the army "watches the battle from the barracks" and occupies the territory only after the war is over.

## Online News and Disrupted Territoriality

While these developments obviously have far-reaching consequences for humankind on multiple levels, their significance for online journalism cannot be overstated, as the net plays a crucial role in the process.

We have discussed the internet's effect on news in previous chapters, but it is worth repeating that the net places every 'wired' individual anywhere on earth, round the clock, in the middle of thousands of channels of information (news sites), many of which are highly interactive, some offer conflicting versions of events, and a sizeable section are frequently updated. Thus, the spatial coordinates of news events in relation to the audience are immensely reduced in salience, leaving the real time of the internet as the only coordinate of reality.

The picture of this reality from the point of view of the consumer of net news is forever shifting, sometimes self-contradictory and in danger of becoming sensorily excessive. Whether this will count as a danger or as an opportunity to enrich our understanding of the world will depend, as Tanzi argues,[12] on our ability to adapt to the new media technologies, on the "rapidity and ... the sharpness of the user's subjective judgement":

> This judgement is bound to become a dominant factor owing to the nature of the risks present in simultaneous and multi-directional communication. Users will have to know how to move, how to experiment, how to avoid cycles of hypnotic solicitations, so as not to be distracted by signals that are momentarily stronger or excessive, so as not to yield to pressure from whoever has been able to communicate on the same channel ...

> ... In the discontinuous reality of multimedia spaces, attention spaces are far more important than conceptual constructions, and the organization and selection of each element involves new skills in order to discern the different qualities, both symbolic and discursive, of data structures, which are formed thanks to the salience effect of their own components.

# References

[1] Thacker, Eugene, 'Networks, Swarms, Multitudes' Parts 1 and 2, *ctheory.net*, accessed 1 January 2005 on http://www.ctheory.net/text_file.asp?pick=422 and http://www.ctheory.net/text_file.asp?pick=423.

[2] Castells, Manuel, opening address at the UNRISD conference on Information Technologies and Social Development, 1 September 1998, accessed 28 December 2004 on http://www.unrisd.org/unrisd/website/newsview.nsf/(httpNews)/ D22ABFCFD0F2BB7D80256B75005196AB?OpenDocument.

[3] Castells, Manuel, *The Rise of the Network Society* (Blackwell Publishers, 2000), p. 33, accessed 28 December 2004 on http://www.amazon.com/gp/reader/ 1557866171/ref=sib_dp_bod_ex/102-8342789-9860941?%5Fencoding= UTF8&p=S01O.

[4] Husserl, Edmund, *The Crisis of European Sciences and Transcendental Phenomenology*, tr. David Carr (Evanston, IL, Northwestern University Press,1997), p. 108.

[5] Poster, Mark, 'Postmodern Virtualities' *The Second Media Age* (Blackwell Publishers, 1995), accessed 18 March 2004 on http://www.hnet.uci.edu/mposter/ writings/internet.html.

[6] Poster, Mark, 'What's Left: Materialist Responses to the Internet', *Electronic Book Review*, 13 September 2003, accessed 1 January 2005 on http://www.electronicbookreview.com/v3/servlet/ebr?command=view_essay&essay_id=posteraltx&glosses=on.

[7] Poster, Mark, 'Postmodern Virtualities'.

[8] 'US Authorities Seize IMC Servers in UK', *UK Indymedia*, accessed 25 November 2004 on http://www.indymedia.org.uk/en/2004/10/298741.html.

[9] Virilio, Paul, 'Speed and Information: Cyberspace Alarm!,' *ctheory.net*, article no. A030, 27 August 1995, accessed 3 January 2005 on www.ctheory.net/text_file?pick=72.

[10] Ibid.

[11] Armitage, John, 'Beyond Postmodernism? Paul Virilio's Hypermodern Cultural Theory', *ctheory.net,* article no. A090, 15 November 2000. Accessed 4 January 2004 on http://www.ctheory.net/text_file?pick=133.

[12] Tanzi, Dante, 'Time, Proximity and Meaning on the Net', *ctheory.net*, article no. A081, 8 March 2000, accessed 4 January 2004 on http://www.ctheory.net/text_file?pick=124.

# Glossary

Several excellent glossaries and encyclopedias of internet-related terms are to be found on the web. Among these are: *Webopedia* (http://webopedia.internet.com/), the *Glossary of Internet & Web Jargon* of the University of California in Berkeley (http://www.lib.berkeley.edu/TeachingLib/Guides/Internet/Glossary.html), and the *Jones Media and Information Technology Encyclopaedia* (http://www.jonesencyclo.com/). Definitions of some of the more common terms are presented here for ready reference.

BLOG or WEB LOG: A type of web page that serves as a publicly accessible personal diary or journal for an individual.

BOOLEAN LOGIC: Used in searches, including search engines, this is a way to combine search terms using operators such as 'and,' 'or,' 'and not' and sometimes 'near'. 'And' requires all the terms to appear in a record. 'Or' retrieves records with either term. 'And not' excludes terms. Parentheses may be used to sequence operations and group words.

BROWSE: To follow links in a page.

BROWSERS: Software programs that enable the user to view web documents. They 'translate' HTML-encoded files into the text, images, sounds, and other features the user sees. Examples are Microsoft's Internet Explorer (called IE), Mozilla Firefox, Neoplanet, Netscape, Mosaic, Macweb, and Netcruiser.

CACHE: This term refers to a space where web pages visited by the user are stored on the computer. A copy of documents retrieved by the user is stored in cache. When he uses the 'Go' or 'Back' links, or any other means to revisit a document, the browser first checks to see if it is in cache and retrieves it from there, because this is much faster than retrieving it from the server.

CACHED LINK: Search results from Google, Yahoo! and some other search engines usually contain a cached link that allows the user to view the version of a page that the search engine has stored in its database. The live page on the web may differ from this cached copy, because the cached copy was made when the search engine's 'spider' last visited the page and detected modified content. The cached link can be used to see when a page was last crawled and, in Google, where your terms are and why you got a page when all of your search terms are not in it.

COOKIE:  A message from a web server computer sent to and stored by the user's browser on his computer. When his computer consults the originating server computer, the cookie is sent back to the server, allowing the latter to respond to the user according to the cookie's contents. The main use for cookies is to provide customized web pages according to a profile of the user's interests. When a user logs onto a 'customise' type of invitation on a web page and enters his name and other information, this may result in a cookie on his computer, which will be accessed by that page to 'remember' the user and provide what he wants.

DOMAIN, TOP LEVEL DOMAIN (TLD): Hierarchical scheme for indicating logical and sometimes geographical venue of a web page from the network.

DOMAIN NAME, DOMAIN NAME SERVER (DNS) ENTRY: Both terms refer to the initial part of a URL, upto the first slash (/), where the domain and name of the host or server computer are listed (most often in reversed order, name first, then domain). The domain name gives you who 'published' a page, that is, put it up on the web. A domain name is translated in tables into a numeric IP address unique to the host computer sought. These tables are maintained on computers called domain name servers. Whenever a user asks the browser to find a URL, the browser must consult the table on the domain name server that particular computer is networked to consult. When this lookup fails for some reason, the 'lacks DNS entry' error message appears in the browser. In such cases, the user should try the URL again, when the domain name server is less busy.

DOWNLOAD: To copy something from a primary source to a more peripheral one, such as, saving something found on the web (currently located on its server) to a floppy disk or to a file on the user's local hard drive.

EXTENSION or FILE EXTENSION: Refers to one or several letters at the end of a filename in Windows, DOS and some other operating systems. Filename extensions usually follow a period sign (dot) and indicate the type of file. For example, dog.txt denotes a plain text file, cat.htm or cat.html denotes an HTML file. Some common image extensions are picture.jpg or picture.jpeg or picture.bmp or picture.gif.

FAVORITES: In the Internet Explorer browser, a means to get back to a URL, similar to Bookmarks in Mozilla Firefox and Netscape.

FRAMES: A format for web pages that divides the screen into segments, each with a scroll bar as if it were a 'window' within the window.

FTP: File Transfer Protocol. System of rapidly transferring entire files from one computer to another, intact for viewing or other purposes.

FUZZY AND: In ranking search results, documents with all terms (Boolean 'and') are ranked first, followed by documents containing any terms (Boolean 'or'). The fewer the terms, the further down a page comes in the results. At least one term should always be present for a page to appear in the results.

HOST: A computer that provides web documents to 'clients' or users.

HTML: Hypertext Markup Language. A standardized language of computer code, embedded in 'source' documents behind all web documents, containing the textual content, images, links to other documents (and/or other applications, such as sound or motion), and formatting instructions for display on the screen. Browsers are programmed to interpret HTML for display. HTML often imbeds within it other programming languages and applications, such as SGML, XML, Javascript, and CGI-script. One can see HTML in Internet Explorer by selecting the 'View' pop-down menu tab, then 'Source'.

IP ADDRESS or IP NUMBER: Internet Protocol address or number. A unique number consisting of four parts separated by dots (for example, 123.456.789.09). Every machine connected to the Internet has a unique IP address.

ISP: Internet Service Provider. A company that sells internet connections via modem (for example, VSNL, BSNL and Satyam).

JAVA: A network-oriented programming language invented by Sun Microsystems and specifically designed for writing programs that can be safely downloaded through the internet and immediately run without fear of viruses or other harm to the user's computer or files. Web pages implement such functions as animation and calculators, using small Java programs called applets.

JAVASCRIPT: A simple programming language developed by Netscape to enable greater interactivity in web pages. It shares some characteristics with Java but is independent of it. It interacts with HTML, enabling dynamic content and motion.

LINK 'ROT': Term used to describe problems caused by the constant change in URLs. Sometimes a web page or search engine offers a link, but the user gets an error message (for example, 'not available') or a page saying the site has moved to a new URL when he clicks on it. Search engine spiders cannot keep up with the changes. URLs may change because documents are moved to new computers, the file structure on the computer is reorganized, or sites are discontinued.

META-SEARCH ENGINE: Search engines that automatically submit the user's keyword search to several other search engines, and retrieve results from all their databases.

NESTING: A term used in Boolean searching to indicate the sequence in which operations are to be performed. Enclosing words in parentheses identifies a group or 'nest'. Groups can be within other groups. The operations will be performed from the innermost nest to the outmost, and then from left to right.

PACKET, PACKET JAM: When a user retrieves a document through the web, it is sent in 'packets' which fit in between other messages on the telecommunications lines, and are reassembled when they arrive at the user's end. This occurs using TCP/IP protocol. The packets may be sent via different paths on the networks. If any of these packets are delayed, the document cannot be reassembled and displayed. This is called a packet jam, which can often be resolved by pressing 'Stop' then 'Refresh' or 'Reload', thus requesting a new copy of the document.

PLUG-IN: An application built into a browser or added to a browser to enable it to interact with a special file type (such as video, audio, word document, etc.).

POPULARITY RANKING of SEARCH RESULTS: Some search engines rank the order in which search results appear, mainly on the basis of the number of other sites that link to each page (something like a popularity vote on the assumption that other pages link to the 'best' pages). Google follows this practice.

RELEVANCY RANKING of SEARCH RESULTS: The most common method for determining the order in which search results are displayed. Each search tool uses its own unique algorithm. Most use 'fuzzy and' combined with factors such as how often your terms occur in documents, whether they occur together as a phrase, and whether they are in the title or how near the top of the text.

SCRIPT: A type of programming language that can be used to fetch and display web pages. There are many kinds and uses of scripts. They can be used to create all or part of a page, and communicate with searchable databases. Forms (boxes) and many interactive links, which respond according to entries made by the user, require some kind of script language.

SERVER, WEB SERVER: A computer running that software, assigned an IP address, and connected to the internet so that it can provide documents via the web. It is also called host computer. Web servers can be viewed as the online equivalent of the publisher of a print document.

SERVER-SIDE: Something that operates on the 'server' computer (providing the web page), as opposed to the 'client' computer (which is with the user).

SHTML, usually seen as .shtml: A filename extension that identifies web pages containing SSI commands.

SPIDERS: Computer programs, sometimes called 'crawlers' or 'knowledge-bots' or 'knowbots', used by search engines to roam the web through the internet, visit sites and databases, and keep the search engine database up-to-date. They find new pages, update known pages, and delete obsolete ones. Their findings are integrated into the 'home' database. Although large search engines often operate several knowbots all the time, the web is so large that it can take six months for spiders to cover it. This results in the search engine's database being out-of-date to some extent.

SUBJECT DIRECTORY: A lexicon of subject terms hierarchically grouped. It may be browsed or searched by keywords. Subject directories are smaller than other searchable databases, because of the human involvement required to classify documents by subject.

TCP/IP: Transmission Control Protocol/Internet Protocol. The collection of protocols that defines the internet. Originally designed for the UNIX operating system, TCP/IP software is now available for every major kind of computer operating system. To be truly on the internet, a computer must have TCP/IP software.

TELNET: Internet service allowing one computer to log onto another, connecting it as if it were not remote.

URL: Uniform Resource Locator. The unique address of any web document, found in the address field of the browser.

XHTML: Extensible Hypertext Markup Language. It is a variant of HTML, actually a hybrid between HTML and XML, and is more universally acceptable in web pages and search engines than XML.

XML: Extensible Markup Language. It is a version of SGML (Standard General Markup Language) diluted for web page use, since SGML is not readily viewable in ordinary browsers and is difficult to apply to web pages. XML is useful, among other things, for pages emerging from databases and other applications where parts of the page are standardized and needs to reappear repeatedly.

## Advertising Terms

AD ROTATION: Ads are often rotated into ad spaces from a list. This is usually done automatically by software on the website in question, or at a central site administered by an ad broker or server 'serving' ads for a number of websites.

AD SPACE: This is a space on a web page that is reserved for ads. An ad space group is a group of spaces within a website that share the same characteristics so that an ad purchase can be made for the group of spaces.

AD VIEW: This is the same as the more common ad impression, and refers to a single ad that appears on a page when that page appears on the viewer's screen. Ad views or impressions are what most websites like to sell. A web page may offer space for a number of ad views. An ad view has visibility and branding value, even if the user does not click on the ad.

BANNER: This is an advertisement in the form of a graphic image that typically runs across a web page or is positioned in the margin or other space reserved for ads. Banner ads are usually Graphics Interchange Format (GIF) images. In addition to adhering to size, many websites limit the size of the file to a certain number of bytes so that the file will display quickly. Most ads are animated GIFs, since animation attracts a larger percentage of user clicks. The most common large banner ad is 468 pixels wide by 60 pixels high. Smaller sizes include 125 by 125 and 120 by 90.

BEYOND THE BANNER: This is the idea that there are more ways than the banner to communicate marketing messages. Among these methods are: sponsoring a website or a particular feature on it, advertising through email newsletters, co-branding with another company and its website, contest promotion, and generally speaking, devising new ways to engage and interact with the target audience. Beyond the banner can also include the interstitial and streaming video infomercial. The banner itself can be turned into a small rich media event, as already mentioned.

BOOKED SPACE: The number of ad views for an ad space that are currently sold out.

BRAND, BRAND NAME, and BRANDING: A brand is a product, service, or concept that is publicly distinguished from other products, services, or concepts so that it can be easily communicated and usually marketed. A brand name is the name of the distinctive product, service, or concept. Branding is the process of creating and disseminating the brand name. Branding can be applied to the entire corporate identity as well as to individual product and service names. In web and other media advertising, it is recognized that there is usually some kind of branding value whether or not an immediate, direct response can be measured from an ad or campaign.

CACHING: Caching pages in a cache server or on the user's computer is a way of speeding up the download process for the site concerned, but it also means some ad views will not be detected by the ad counting programs. This is, naturally, a source of concern for advertisers. However, there are several techniques for instructing the browser not to cache particular pages.

CLICK: A click is usually defined as having taken place when a visitor interacts with an advertisement by clicking on it, so that the intended destination page begins to load on the visitor's computer.

CLICK STREAM: This is a recorded path of the pages a visitor requested for in going through one or more sites. This information helps site owners understand how visitors are using their sites and which pages are being used the most by visitors It can help advertisers understand how users get to the client's pages, what pages they view, and how they go about ordering a product.

CLICKTHROUGH: This is counted by the sponsoring site as a result of an ad click. While the term refers to almost the same thing as a click, it implies that the user actually received the page. A clickthrough has several useful features: it indicates the ad's effectiveness and takes the visitor to the advertiser's website, where other messages can be provided. Sometimes a click directly opens a product order window rather than taking the visitor to another site. Some advertisers pay only for clickthroughs rather than for ad impressions.

CLICK RATE: This is the percentage of ad views that result in clickthroughs. The rate depends on several factors, such as the objectives of the campaign, how enticing the banner message is, how explicit the message is (a message that is complete within the banner may be less prone to be clicked), audience or message matching, how new the banner is, how often it is displayed to the same user, etc. Click rates for frequently repeated, branding banners usually vary from 0.15 to 1 per cent. Ads with provocative, mysterious, or other compelling content can induce click rates ranging from one to five per cent and sometimes higher. The click rate for an ad tends to diminish with repeated exposure.

CO-BRANDING: It means two sites or sections of sites or features displaying their logos (and thus their brands) together, so that the viewer sees the site or feature as a joint enterprise. Co-branding is often, though not always, associated with cross-linking between the sites.

COOKIE: This is a file on a user's hard drive, used by sites to record data about the user. Some ad rotation software use cookies to see which ad the user has just seen so that a different ad will be rotated into the next page view.

COST-PER-ACTION: What an advertiser pays for each visitor that takes some specifically defined action in response to an ad beyond simply clicking on it. For example, a visitor might visit an advertiser's site and request to be subscribed to their newsletter.

CPM: Cost-per-thousand ad impressions. An industry standard measure for selling ads on websites. The 'M' here is taken from the Roman numeral for 'thousand'.

DEMOGRAPHICS: Data about the size and characteristics of a population or audience, for example, gender, age group, income group, purchasing history, personal preferences, etc.

FILTERING: Sometimes a piece of software is used by the ad server to analyse a web page request received from the user's browser, in order to determine which ad or ads should be sent with the requested page. This is called filtering. The server makes its decision on the basis of information it gleans from the request, on such things as the address of the latter's source or the level of the user's browser.

FOLD: This is borrowed from the print media, in which 'above the fold' refers to news items or ads appearing above the fold. In online ads, it refers to ads that can be viewed as soon as the page starts to load on the user's computer and he does not have to scroll down or sideways to see it.

IMPRESSION: This is the count of a delivered basic advertising unit from an ad distribution point. Most web advertising is sold by this measure and the cost is quoted in terms of the cost-per-thousand impressions (CPMs).

INTERSTITIAL: See Splash Page.

PAY-PER-CLICK: In pay-per-click advertising, the advertiser pays a certain amount for each clickthrough to the advertiser's site.

PAY-PER-LEAD: In pay-per-lead advertising, the advertiser pays for each sales lead generated. For example, an advertiser may pay for every visitor who clicks on a site and then fills out a form.

PAY-PER-SALE: This is not commonly used for ad buys, for paying sites that participate in affiliate programs, such as those of Amazon.com and Beyond.com.

RICH MEDIA: This refers to ads containing perceptual or interactive elements such as short video clips which are more elaborate than the usual banner ad.

RUN-OF-SITE: An ad designed to rotate on all nonfeatured ad spaces on a site. CPM rates for run-of-site ads are usually less than for rates for specially-placed ads or sponsorships.

SPLASH PAGE: A preliminary page that appears before the home page of a website and usually promotes a particular site feature or provides advertising. It is designed to move on to the home page after a short period of time. Also known as interstitial.

SPONSORSHIP: An arrangement with a website in such a way that it gives an advertiser visibility and advantage above that of run-of-site advertising. Combined with specific content, sponsorship can provide a more targeted audience than run-of-site ads.

UNIQUE VISITOR: Someone with a unique address who is accessing a website for the first time that day (or some other specified period). Thus, a visitor that returns within the same day is not counted twice. A unique visitors count indicates how many different people make up the audience during the specified time period, but not how much they used the site during the period.

VIEW: The term is used to refer to either an ad view or a page view, usually the first. There can be multiple ad views per page views. Advertisers need to remember that a small percentage of users choose not to display the images by turning the graphics off in their browsers.

VISIT: This refers to a user with a unique address entering a site at some page for the first time that day (or for the first time in a lesser time period). The number of visits approximates the number of different people who visit a site.

# Index

*Notes*

# Notes